Yii 1.1 Application Development Cookbook

Over 80 recipes to help you master using the
Yii PHP framework

Alexander Makarov

BIRMINGHAM - MUMBAI

Yii 1.1 Application Development Cookbook

First published: August 2011

Production Reference: 1170811

Published by Packt Publishing Ltd.
Livery Place
35 Livery Street
Birmingham B3 2PB, UK.

ISBN 978-1-849515-48-1

www.packtpub.com

Cover Image by Jasmine Doremus (jasdoremus@gmail.com)

Credits

Author
Alexander Makarov

Reviewers
Anatoliy Dimitrov
Antonio Ramirez Cobos
SAKURAI, atsushi
Kyle Ferreira

Acquisition Editor
Usha Iyer

Development Editor
Hyacintha D'Souza

Technical Editors
Azharuddin Sheikh
Conrad Sardinha

Copy Editor
Neha Shetty

Project Coordinator
Michelle Quadros

Proofreader
Steve Maguire

Indexers
Hemangini Bari
Tejal Daruwale

Graphics
Nilesh Mohite

Production Coordinator
Aparna Bhagat

Cover Work
Aparna Bhagat

Foreword

When Alex told me he was about to write a Yii cookbook about a year ago, I was wondering how original it would be, considering the fact that there was already an online user-contributed cookbook (also known as Yii wiki). It turned out Alex produced a book that is not only full of wisdom about how to use Yii effectively, but also presented in such a systematic way that it can be taken as an essential companion book to the definitive guide to Yii. In fact, Alex has successfully intrigued the interest of every member in the Yii developer team when he asked for reviews and comments on his newly finished book chapters.

As the founder and the lead developer of the Yii framework, I feel this book is a must-read for every Yii programmer. While this book does not describe directly the rules set by Yii, it shows how to program with Yii from a practical perspective. People who are driven by tight project schedules will find this book very handy, as it gives ready-to-use solutions to many problems they may face in their projects. People who are already familiar with Yii will also find this book very informative as most problem solutions given in the book can be considered as officially recommended because they have undergone thorough a review by every Yii developer team member. Alex, through this book and his active participation in the Yii project, proved himself to be a great programmer, as well as a good writer.

Qiang Xue

Lead Developer of the Yii framework

About the Author

Alexander Makarov graduated from Voronezh State University in 2007 with a master degree in computer science. During his study, he started working on homegrown PHP frameworks and projects trying various design patterns and techniques.

During the last year of his study, he spent a year working for Siemens mainly doing Java coding and complex SQL reports and also did many small and medium freelance projects in his free time.

In 2007, he joined an outsourcing company, Murano Software, and had a lot of experience with web development in general, J2EE, PHP, and client-side technologies working on projects such as `wrike.com` and `docufide.com`. As in previous years he did some notable freelance jobs, including social network for Russia Today built with Yii in 2009 and heavy loaded NNM.ru portal in 2008.

Between 2008 and 2010, he helped the Russian CodeIgniter community to grow and started actively to contribute to open source projects.

In 2009, Alexander joined Yii camp and started growing the Russian Yii community, translated documentation into Russian and, since May 2010, has become a passionate Yii framework core developer.

He has published several articles in Smashing Magazine and a lot more in his Russian blog `http://rmcreative.ru/`, and has presented numerous talks on Yii and web development in general at various conferences.

Alexander currently resides in Voronezh, Russia, with his beloved wife and daughter. Besides the web, he enjoys movies, rock music, travelling, photography, and languages.

I would like to thank Qiang Xue, Maurizio Domba, Sebastián Thierer, Alexander Kochetov, Antonio Ramirez Cobos, and all people who reviewed the RAW book. Your suggestions and critics helped to improve this book a lot.

I would like to thank Qiang Xue and Wei Zhuo for creating Yii.

I would also like to thank Packt Publishing for inviting me to write this book and helping me to actually get it done. I would like to thank all the past and current Yii core team members for keeping Yii in a good shape and making it better and better. You guys rock!

About the Reviewers

Anatoliy Dimitrov has an O'Reilly certificate in PHP/MySQL programming and he is a great supporter of Yii. Besides that, he is experienced in website security, server hardening, and secure services configuration.

He has held senior technical positions for some of the largest hosting companies, payment processors, and many freelance projects.

I would like to thank Rali, the love of my life, for everything and especially allowing me to stay late in the evenings working.

Antonio Ramirez Cobos (aka tonydspaniard), self-educated programmer, jumped into the world of coding while studying hardware and client support at TAFE, Melbourne.

He has more than 12 years of experience and has been working in the field using Javascript, C++, Java, ASP.net (with C#), Visual Basic (COM, COM+), Dynamic DLL, until he met PHP and the wonders of open source. Since then, he has not left that language and specializes in building web applications.

A Yii lover, he maintains his blog at www.ramirezcobos.com, which has been lately used to propagate the wonders of such frameworks. He is also a regular user of Yii's forum.

SAKURAI, atsushi is a microprocessor expert, as well as a PHP programmer for over 10 years. As a manager of a design team of microprocessors, he has been working to build the support website for their microprocessors. Recently, his efficiency for developing web application is drastically increasing, thanks to Yii. His main contribution to the Yii community includes the translation of the documentations into Japanese.

www.PacktPub.com

Support files, eBooks, discount offers, and more

You might want to visit www.PacktPub.com for support files and downloads related to your book.

Did you know that Packt offers eBook versions of every book published, with PDF and ePub files available? You can upgrade to the eBook version at www.PacktPub.com and as a print book customer, you are entitled to a discount on the eBook copy. Get in touch with us at service@packtpub.com for more details.

At www.PacktPub.com, you can also read a collection of free technical articles, sign up for a range of free newsletters and receive exclusive discounts and offers on Packt books and eBooks.

http://PacktLib.PacktPub.com

Do you need instant solutions to your IT questions? PacktLib is Packt's online digital book library. Here, you can access, read, and search across Packt's entire library of books.

Why Subscribe?

- ▶ Fully searchable across every book published by Packt
- ▶ Copy and paste, print and bookmark content
- ▶ On demand and accessible via web browser

Free Access for Packt account holders

If you have an account with Packt at www.PacktPub.com, you can use this to access PacktLib today and view nine entirely free books. Simply use your login credentials for immediate access.

Table of Contents

Preface

Yii is a very flexible and high-performance application development framework written in PHP. It helps building web applications from small ones to large-scale enterprise applications. The framework name stands for Yes It Is. This is often the accurate and most concise response to inquires from those new to Yii:

Is it fast? ... Is it secure? ... Is it professional? ... Is it right for my next project? ... The answer is Yes, it is!

This cookbook contains 13 independent chapters full of recipes that will show you how to use Yii efficiently. You will learn about the hidden framework gems, using core features, creating your own reusable code base, using test-driven development, and many more topics that will bring your knowledge to a new level!

What this book covers

Chapter 1, Under the Hood provides information about the most interesting Yii features hidden under the hood: events, import, autoloading, exceptions, component, and widget configuration, and more.

Chapter 2, Router, Controller, and Views is about handy things concerning the Yii URL router, controllers, and views: URL rules, external actions and controllers, view clips, decorators, and more.

Chapter 3, AJAX and jQuery focuses on the Yii's client side that is built with jQuery—the most widely used JavaScript library out there. It is very powerful and easy to learn and use. This chapter focuses on Yii-specific tricks rather than jQuery itself.

Chapter 4, Working with Forms. Yii makes working with forms a breeze and documentation on it is almost complete. Still, there are some areas that need clarification and examples. Some of the topics covered in this chapter are creating own validators and input widgets, uploading files, using, and customizing CAPTCHA.

Chapter 5, Testing Your Application covers both unit testing, functional testing, and generating code coverage reports. Recipes follow a test driven development approach. You will write tests for several small applications and then will implement functionality.

Chapter 6, Database, Active Record, and Model Tricks is about working with databases efficiently, when to use models and when not to, how to work with multiple databases, how to automatically pre-process Active Record fields, and how to use powerful database criteria.

Chapter 7, Using Zii Components covers data providers, grids, and lists: How to configure sorting and search, how to use grids with multiple related models, how to create your own column types, and more.

Chapter 8, Extending Yii shows not only how to implement your own Yii extension but also how to make your extension reusable and useful for the community. In addition, we will focus on many things you should do to make your extension as efficient as possible.

Chapter 9, Error Handling, Debugging, and Logging reviews logging, analyzing the exception stack trace, and own error handler implementation.

Chapter 10, Security provides information about keeping your application secure according to the general web application security principle "filter input escape output". We will cover topics such as creating your own controller filters, preventing XSS, CSRF, and SQL injections, escaping output, and using role-based access control.

Chapter 11, Performance Tuning shows how to configure Yii to gain extra performance. You will learn a few best practices of developing an application that will run smoothly until you have very high loads.

Chapter 12, Using External Code focuses on using the third party code with Yii. We will use Zend Framework, Kohana, and PEAR but you will be able to use any code after learning how it works.

Chapter 13, Deployment covers various tips that are especially useful on application deployment, when developing an application in a team, or when you just want to make your development environment more comfortable.

What you need for this book

In order to run the examples in this book, the following software will be required:

► **Web server**:

- ❑ 2.x version of Apache web server is preferred
- ❑ Other versions and web servers will work too, but configuration details are not provided

▶ **Database server**: MySQL is recommended

    ❏   MySQL 4+ with InnoDB support, MySQL 5 or higher recommended

▶ **PHP**: PHP 5.3 is recommended

    ❏   PHP 5.2 or PHP 5.3, PHP 5.3 recommended

▶ **Yii**:

    ❏   latest 1.1.x

Additionally, the following tools are not strictly required but are used for specific recipes:

▶ PHPUnit

▶ XDebug

▶ Selenium RC

▶ PEAR

▶ Smarty

▶ memcached

Who this book is for

If you are a developer with a good knowledge of PHP5, are familiar with the basics of Yii, have checked its definitive guide, and have tried to develop applications using Yii, then this book is for you. Knowledge of the object-oriented approach and MVC pattern will be a great advantage as Yii uses these extensively.

Conventions

In this book, you will find a number of styles of text that distinguish between different kinds of information. Here are some examples of these styles, and an explanation of their meaning.

Code words in text are shown as follows: "We can include view partials through the use of the `include` directive."

A block of code is set as follows:

```
defined('YII_DEBUG') or define('YII_DEBUG', false);
defined('YII_TRACE_LEVEL') or define('YII_TRACE_LEVEL', 0);

$yii=dirname(__FILE__).'/../framework/yii.php';
$config=dirname(__FILE__).'/../app/config/production.php';

require($yii);

Yii::createWebApplication($config)->run();
```

When we wish to draw your attention to a particular part of a code block, the relevant lines or items are set in bold:

```
defined('YII_DEBUG') or define('YII_DEBUG', false);
defined('YII_TRACE_LEVEL') or define('YII_TRACE_LEVEL', 0);

$yii=dirname(__FILE__).'/../framework/yii.php';
$config=dirname(__FILE__).'/../app/config/production.php';

require($yii);

Yii::createWebApplication($config)->run();
```

Any command-line input or output is written as follows:

cd path/to/protected/tests

phpunit unit/BBCodeTest.php

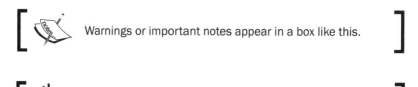

Warnings or important notes appear in a box like this.

Tips and tricks appear like this.

Reader feedback

Feedback from our readers is always welcome. Let us know what you think about this book—what you liked or may have disliked. Reader feedback is important for us to develop titles that you really get the most out of.

To send book author feedback about the book, simply fill a form at http://yiicookbook.org/feedback.

If there is a book that you need and would like to see PACKT publish, please send a note in the **SUGGEST A TITLE** form on www.packtpub.com or e-mail suggest@packtpub.com.

If there is a topic that you have expertise in and you are interested in either writing or contributing to a book, see author guide on www.packtpub.com/authors.

Customer support

Now that you are the proud owner of a Packt book, we have a number of things to help you to get the most from your purchase.

Downloading the example code

To get the example code files for this book visit `http://yiicookbook.org/code`.

You can download the example code files for all Packt books you have purchased from your account at `http://www.PacktPub.com`. If you purchased this book elsewhere, you can visit `http://www.PacktPub.com/support` and register to have the files e-mailed directly to you.

Errata

Although we have taken every care to ensure the accuracy of our content, mistakes do happen. If you find a mistake in the book—maybe a mistake in the text or the code—we would be grateful if you would report this. By doing so, you can save other readers from frustration and help us improve subsequent versions of this book. If you find any errata, please report them by visiting `http://yiicookbook.org/feedback` and entering the details of your errata. Once your errata are verified, your submission will be accepted and the errata will be uploaded on the book website at `http://yiicookbook.org/errata`.

Piracy

Piracy of copyright material on the Internet is an ongoing problem across all media. At Packt, we take the protection of our copyright and licenses very seriously. If you come across any illegal copies of our works, in any form, on the Internet, please provide us with the location address or website name immediately so that we can pursue a remedy.

Please contact us at `copyright@packtpub.com` with a link to the suspected pirated material.

We appreciate your help in protecting our authors, and our ability to bring you valuable content.

Questions

You can contact the book's author using `http://yiicookbook.org/feedback` if you are having a problem with any aspect of the book, and he will do his best to address it.

1
Under the Hood

In this chapter, we will cover:

- ▶ Using getters and setters
- ▶ Using Yii events
- ▶ Using import and autoloading
- ▶ Using exceptions
- ▶ Configuring components
- ▶ Configuring widget defaults
- ▶ Using Yii core collections
- ▶ Working with request

Introduction

In this chapter, we will cover the most interesting Yii features that are hidden "under the hood". These are mostly described in the framework API, but since they are not mentioned in the official guide (`http://www.yiiframework.com/doc/guide/`) or mentioned very briefly, only experienced Yii developers usually use these. Yet, features described here are relatively simple and using them makes development with Yii much more fun and productive.

Using getters and setters

Yii has many features that came from other languages, such as Java or C#. One of them is defining properties with getters and setters for any of the class extended from `CComponent` (that is, virtually any Yii class).

From this recipe, you will learn how to define your own properties using getters and setters, how to make your properties read-only, and how to hide custom processing behind native PHP assignments.

How to do it...

1. As PHP does not have properties at the language level, we can only use getters and setters in the following way:

```php
class MyClass
{
    // hiding $property
    private $property;

    // getter
    public function getProperty()
    {
        return $this->property;
    }

    // setter
    public function setProperty($value)
    {
        $this->property = $value;
    }
}

$object = new MyClass();

// setting value
$object->setProperty('value');

// getting value
echo $object->getProperty();
```

2. This syntax is very common in the Java world but it is a bit long to use in PHP. Still, we want to use the same functionality C# properties gives us: calling getters and setters like class members. With Yii, we can do it in the following way:

```php
// extending CComponent is necessary
class MyClass extends CComponent
{
    private $property;

    public function getProperty()
    {
        return $this->property;
    }
}
```

```php
    public function setProperty($value)
    {
        $this->property = $value;
    }
}

$object = new MyClass();
$object->property = 'value'; // same as $object->
  setProperty('value');
echo $object->property; // same as $object->getProperty();
```

3. Using this feature, you can make properties read-only or write-only while keeping the simple PHP syntax as follows:

```php
class MyClass extends CComponent
{
    private $read = 'read only property';
    private $write = 'write only property';

    public function getRead()
    {
        return $this->read;
    }

    public function setWrite($value)
    {
        $this->write = $value;
    }
}

$object = new MyClass();

// gives us an error since we are trying to write to read-only
   property
$object->read = 'value';

// echoes 'read only property'
echo $object->read;

// gives us an error since we are trying to read to write-only
   property
echo $object->write;

// writes 'value' to private $write
$object->write = 'value';
```

4. Yii uses this technique extensively because almost everything is a component. For example, when you are calling `Yii::app()->user->id` to get the currently logged in user ID, what's really called is `Yii::app()->getUser()->getId()`.

How it works...

To use getters and setters like properties, `CComponent` uses the PHP magic methods: `__get`, `__set`, `__isset`, and `__unset` (`http://php.net/manual/en/language.oop5.magic.php`). The following example shows what Yii **1.1** `CComponent::__get` looks like:

```
public function __get($name)
{
    $getter='get'.$name;
    if(method_exists($this,$getter))
        return $this->$getter();
...
```

This magic PHP method intercepts all calls to missing real properties, so when we are calling `$myClass->property`, it receives `property` as `$name` parameter. If a method named `getProperty` exists, then PHP uses its return value as a `property` value.

There's more...

For further information, refer to the following URL:

`http://www.php.net/manual/en/language.oop5.overloading.php#language.oop5.overloading.members`

See also

▶ The recipe named *Using Yii events* in this chapter
▶ The recipe named *Configuring components* in this chapter

Using Yii events

Most Yii classes are extended from `CComponent` which allows us to achieve great application flexibility by using events. An event is a message indicating that the application did something. We can register several event handlers that will react to certain event types. A handler can get parameters from an event it works with and react accordingly. Using events allows achieving great application flexibility.

In this recipe, you will learn how to declare and use both predefined and custom events in your application.

How to do it...

To declare an event in your CComponent child class, you should add a method with a name starting with **on**. For example, if you add the onRegister method, you will get a corresponding event declared.

 A method used to declare an event becomes the default event handler.

Typically, events are used like this:

- ▶ Declare an event by adding a corresponding method
- ▶ Attach one or multiple event handlers
- ▶ The component raises an event by using the CComponent::raiseEvent method
- ▶ All subscribed handlers are called automatically

Let's look at how we can attach an event handler to an event. To achieve it, we can use the CComponent::attachEventHandler method. It accepts the following two parameters:

- ▶ $name: Event name
- ▶ $handler: Event handler; a standard PHP callback should be used

In PHP, we have several ways to define a callback as follows:

- ▶ Use a global function and just pass its name as a string, such as 'my_function'.
- ▶ Use a static class method. You should pass an array: array('ClassName', 'staticMethodName').
- ▶ Use an object method: array($object, 'objectMethod').
- ▶ Create and pass anonymous function using create_function as follows:

```
$component->attachEventHandler('onClick',
    create_function('$event', 'echo "Click!";'));
```

- ▶ Since PHP 5.3, you can use anonymous functions without create_function:

```
$component->attachEventHandler('onClick', function($event){

    echo "Click!";
});
```

 When you use CComponent::attachEventHandler, event handler is added to the end of the handlers list.

- ▶ To keep your code shorter, you can use component properties to manage event handlers as follows:

```
$component->onClick=$handler;
// or:
$component->onClick->add($handler);
```

- ▶ To manage event handlers more precisely, you can get handlers list (CList) using CComponent::getEventHandlers and work with it. For example, you can attach an event handler the same way as with attachEventHandler using the following code:

```
$component->getEventHandlers('onClick')->add($handler);
```

- ▶ To add an event handler to the beginning of handlers list, use:

```
$component->getEventHandlers('onClick')->insertAt(0, $handler);
```

- ▶ To delete a particular handler you can use CComponent::detachEventHandler as follows:

```
$component->detachEventHandler('onClick', $handler);
```

- ▶ Alternatively, get a list of handlers as shown earlier and delete handlers from it.

> CComponent::hasEvent checks if event specified is defined in the component.
>
> CComponent::hasEventHandler checks if there are handlers attached to the event specified.

As we now know how to define and use handlers, let's review some real life examples as follows:

- ▶ It is common practice to compress your application output using gzip to save client bandwidth and speed up page loading time. If you have an access to fine-tune your server, then you can instruct it to do so, but in some environments such as shared hosting, you can't.

- ▶ Fortunately, PHP can gzip the application output using output buffering and ob_gzhandler. In order to do so, we should start buffering the output when the application starts and releases the gzipped output, when it finishes.

- ▶ Yii's application component has two events that will come in handy in this case: CApplication::onBeginRequest and CApplication::onEndRequest. Let's use them. Put the following in index.php after configuring an application but before running it:

```
...
require_once($yii);
$app = Yii::createWebApplication($config);
```

```
// attaching a handler to application start
Yii::app()->onBeginRequest = function($event)
{
    // starting output buffering with gzip handler
    return ob_start("ob_gzhandler");
};
// attaching a handler to application end
Yii::app()->onEndRequest = function($event)
{
    // releasing output buffer
    return ob_end_flush();
};
$app->run();
```

 There are many handy events defined inside Yii core classes. You can get them all by searching for "function on" text in the framework folder using your favorite IDE.

Now, let's look at another example. In Yii, you can translate strings to different languages using Yii::t. As we all love perfect projects all language translations should be up to date. If they are not, we would like to receive an e-mail about it.

Events come in handy again here. In particular, the CMessageSource::onMissingTranslation event that is called when the translation for a string passed to Yii::t is missing.

This time we will use the application configuration file protected/config/main.php to attach an event handler as follows:

```
...
'components' => array(
    ...
    // messages component class is CPhpMessageSource by default
    'messages' => array(
        // using static class method as event handler
        'onMissingTranslation' => array('MyEventHandler',
'handleMissingTranslation'),
    ),
    ...
)
...
```

Now, we should implement our handler. Create `protected/components/MyEventHandler.php` as follows:

```
class MyEventHandler
{
    static function handleMissingTranslation($event)
    {
        // event class for this event is CMissingTranslationEvent
        // so we can get some info about the message
        $text = implode("\n", array(
            'Language: '.$event->language,
            'Category:'.$event->category,
            'Message:'.$event->message
        ));
        // sending email
        mail('admin@example.com', 'Missing translation', $text);
    }
}
```

Let's look at the last example. We have a blog application and we need to send an e-mail when there is a new comment (`Comment`) to the blog post (`Post`).

Comment is a standard AR model generated with Gii. Post is the same Gii-generated model except some customized methods. We will need a custom event `NewCommentEvent` to store both `Post` and `Comment` models and a handler class `Notifier` that will do the work.

1. Let's start with `protected/components/NewCommentEvent.php`:

   ```
   class NewCommentEvent extends CModelEvent {
       public $comment;
       public $post;
   }
   ```

   It is pretty simple. We have just added two properties.

2. Now, let's move on to `protected/models/Post.php`. All standard AR methods are omitted to emphasize on what was added:

   ```
   class Post extends CActiveRecord {
       // custom method for adding a comment
       // to current post
       function addComment(Comment $comment){
           $comment->post_id = $this->id;

           // creating event class instance
           $event = new NewCommentEvent($this);
           $event->post = $this;
           $event->comment = $comment;
   ```

```
        // triggering event
        $this->onNewComment($event);
        return $event->isValid;
    }

    // defining onNewComment event
    public function onNewComment($event) {
        // Event is actually triggered here. This way we can use
        // onNewComment method instead of raiseEvent.
        $this->raiseEvent('onNewComment', $event);
    }
}
```

3. Now, it is time to implement a notifier. Create `protected/components/Notifier.php` as follows:

```
class Notifier {
    function comment($event){
        $text = "There was new comment from
          {$event->comment->author} on post {$event->post->title}";
        mail('admin@example.com', 'New comment', $text);
    }
}
```

4. Now, it is time to get these together in `protected/controllers/PostController.php`:

```
class PostController extends CController
{
    function actionAddComment()
    {
        $post = Post::model()->findByPk(10);
        $notifier = new Notifier();

        // attaching event handler
        $post->onNewComment = array($notifier, 'comment');

        // in the real application data should come from $_POST
            $comment = new Comment();
            $comment->author = 'Sam Dark';
            $comment->text = 'Yii events are amazing!';

        // adding comment
            $post->addComment($comment);
    }
}
```

5. After the comment has been added, admin will receive an e-mail about it.

It is not always necessary to attach an event handler. Let's look at how we can handle an event that is already declared inside an existing component by overriding a base class method. For example, we have a form model `UserForm` used to collect some information about our application user and we need to get the complete name from the first and the last name entered by the user.

Fortunately, in `CModel`, which is a base class for all Yii models including form models, `CModel::afterValidate` method is defined. This method is being called after a successful form validation. Let's use it in our `protected/models/UserForm.php` model:

```php
class UserForm extends CFormModel
{
    public $firstName;
    public $lastName;
    public $fullName;

    public function rules()
    {
        return array(
            // First name and last name are required
            array('firstName, lastName', 'required'),
        );
    }

    // $event argument here is CEvent instance that
    // was created passed when an event method was called.
    // This time it was happened inside of
    // CModel::afterValidate().
    function afterValidate()
    {
        // If this method was called then
        // the model is already filled
        // with data and data is valid
        // so we can use it safely:
        $this->fullName = $this->firstName.' '.$this->lastName;

        // It's important to call parent class method
        // so all other event handlers are called
        return parent::afterValidate();
    }
}
```

We need to call parent method inside of `afterValidate` because parent implementation calls `onAfterValidate` that actually raises events:

```
protected function afterValidate()
{
    $this->onAfterValidate(new CEvent($this));
}
```

> An event method name should always be defined as `function eventHandler($event) {...}`, where $event is a `CEvent` instance. The `CEvent` class contains just two properties named `sender` and `handled`. First property contains an object that called the current event while the second can be used to prevent calling all others not yet executed handlers by setting it to `false`.

The approach described above can be used to customize your Active Record models and implement your own model behaviors.

Further reading

For further information, refer to the following URLs:

- http://www.yiiframework.com/doc/api/CComponent/#raiseEvent-detail
- http://www.yiiframework.com/doc/api/CComponent/#attachEventHandler-detail
- http://www.yiiframework.com/doc/api/CComponent/#getEventHandlers-detail
- http://www.yiiframework.com/doc/api/CComponent/#detachEventHandler-detail

See also

- The recipe named *Using getters and setters* in this chapter
- The recipe named *Configuring components* in this chapter

Using import and autoloading

When programming with PHP, one of the most annoying things is loading additional code with `include` and `require`. Fortunately, you can do it automatically using the `SPL` class loader (http://php.net/manual/en/function.spl-autoload.php).

Autoloading is one of the features which Yii relies on. Still, there are many questions about it on the forums. Let's get it clear and show how we can use it.

When we are using a class, for example, `CDbCriteria`, we are not including it explicitly so PHP initially cannot find it and is trying to rely on the autoloading feature; SPL autoloader to be precise. In most cases, Yii default autoloader (`YiiBase::autoload`) will be used.

For the sake of speed and simplicity, almost all core framework classes are loaded when needed without including or importing them explicitly. It's done through `YiiBase::$_coreClasses` map, so loading core classes is very fast. Zii classes, such as `CMenu`, extension classes or your own classes are not loaded automatically, so we need to import them first.

To import classes, we will use `Yii::import`:

- ▶ Import does not include a class immediately by default
- ▶ It does not include a class if it is not used
- ▶ It will not load a class twice, so it is safe to import the same class multiple times

How to do it...

1. Let's assume that we have a custom class named `LyricsFinder` that finds lyrics for a given song. We have put it under `protected/apis/lyrics/` and in our `protected/controllers/TestController.php`, we are trying to use it in the following way:

```
class TestController extends CController
{
    public function actionIndex($song)
    {
        $lyric = 'Nothing was found.';
        $finder = new LyricsFinder();

        if(!empty($song))
            $lyric = $finder->getText($song);

        echo $lyric;
    }
}
```

2. When executing it, we will get the following PHP error:

```
include(LyricsFinder.php) [<a href='function.include'>function.
include</a>]: failed to open stream: No such file or directory.
```

3. Yii helps us there a bit because at the error screen, we can see that autoloader fails because it doesn't know where to look for our class. Therefore, let's modify our code:

```
class TestController extends CController
{
    public function actionIndex($song)
    {
        $lyric = 'Nothing was found.';

        // importing a class
        Yii::import('application.apis.lyrics.LyricsFinder');

        $finder = new LyricsFinder();

        if(!empty($song))
            $lyric = $finder->getText($song);

        echo $lyric;
    }
}
```

Now our code works.

> The built-in Yii class loader requires that each class should be placed into a separate file named the same as the class itself.

How it works...

Let's look at `application.apis.lyrics.LyricsFinder`:

`application` is a standard alias that points to your `application` protected folder and is translated into a filesystem path. The following table shows some more standard aliases:

Alias	Path
application	path_to_webroot/protected
system	path_to_webroot/framework
zii	path_to_webroot/framework/zii
webroot	path_to_webroot
ext	path_to_webroot/protected/extensions

You can define your own aliases using the `Yii::setPathOfAlias` method. Typically, it can be done as the first lines of `protected/config/main.php`, so all other config parts will be able to use these new aliases.

`apis.lyrics` are translated to `apis/lyrics` and are appended to a path retrieved from the `application` alias, and `LyricsFinder` is the class name we want to import.

If `LyricsFinder` requires some additional classes located in its directory, then we can use `Yii::import('application.apis.lyrics.*')` to import the whole directory. Note that `*` does not include subfolders, so if you need `lyrics/includes`, you should add another import statement `Yii::import('application.apis.lyrics.includes.*')`.

For performance reasons, it is better to use explicit paths with a class name instead of `*` if you are importing a single class.

There's more...

If you want your classes to be imported automatically like the Yii core classes, then you can configure global imports in your `main.php` configuration file:

```
return array(
    // ...

    // global imports
    'import'=>array(
       'application.models.*',
        'application.components.*',
        'application.apis.lyrics.*',
        'application.apis.lyrics.includes.*',
        'application.apis.albums.AlbumFinder',
    ),
```

 Note that using `*`, with a huge amount of global imports could slow your application down as there will be too many directories to check.

 Downloading the example code

You can download the example code files for all Packt books you have purchased from your account at `http://www.PacktPub.com`. If you purchased this book elsewhere, you can visit `http://www.PacktPub.com/support` and register to have the files e-mailed directly to you.

Using exceptions

Exceptions are a core PHP feature, but they are seldom used fairly. Yii makes exceptions very useful.

There are two main areas where Yii exceptions come in handy, which are as follows:

1. Exceptions allow simplifying the process of detecting and fixing application errors and special situations, such as database connection failure or API failure.
2. Exceptions allow generating different HTTP responses in a very clean way.

Generally, an exception should be thrown when a component cannot handle a special situation, such as the one said earlier, and needs to leave it to higher-level components.

How to do it...

1. Let's assume that we have an `application/apis/lyrics/LyricsFinder.php` class that makes an HTTP request to an API using CURL and returns song lyrics based on its name. This is how we can use exceptions inside of it:

```php
// create some custom exceptions to be able to catch them
// specifically if needed

// general lyrics finder exception
class LyricsFinderException extends CException {}

// used when there is a connection problem
class LyricsFinderHTTPException extends LyricsFinderException{}


class LyricsFinder
{
    private $apiUrl = 'http://example.com/lyricsapi&songtitle=%s';

    function getText($songTitle)
    {
        $url = $this->getUrl($songTitle);
        $curl = curl_init();
        curl_setopt($curl, CURLOPT_URL, $url);
        curl_setopt($curl, CURLOPT_RETURNTRANSFER, 1);
        $result = curl_exec($curl);
```

```
        // if there is an HTTP error, we'll throw an exception
           if($result===false)
        {
           $errorText = curl_error($curl);
           curl_close($url);
           throw new LyricsFinderHTTPException($errorText);
        }

        curl_close($curl);
        return $result;
     }

     private function getRequestUrl($songTitle)
     {
        return sprintf($this->apiUrl, urlencode($songTitle));
     }
  }
```

2. As we don't know how a specific application needs to handle its API connection, we will leave it to the application itself by throwing a custom `LyricsFinderHTTPException`. This is how we can handle it in our `protected/controllers/TestController.php`:

```
class TestController extends CController
{
  public function actionIndex($song)
  {
    $lyric = 'Nothing was found.';

    // importing api class
    Yii::import('application.apis.lyrics.LyricsFinder');

    $finder = new LyricsFinder();

    if(!empty($song))
    {
       // We don't want to show user an error.
       // Instead we want to apologize and
       // invite him to try again later.
       try {
          $lyric = $finder->getText($song);
       }
       // we are looking for specific exception here
       catch (LyricsFinderHTTPException $e)
       {
```

```
            echo 'Sorry, we cannot process your request. Try again
                later.';
        }
    }

    echo $lyric;
    }
}
```

3. Another usage of Yii exceptions is the generation of different HTTP responses by throwing CHttpException. For example, an action that displays a blog post represented by a Post model, loaded by its ID will look like this:

```
class PostController extends CController
{
  function actionView()
  {
    if(!isset($_GET['id']))
      // If there is no post ID supplied, request is definitely
         wrong.
      // According to HTTP specification its code is 400.
      throw new ChttpException(400);

      // Finding a post by its ID
      $post = Post::model()->findByPk($_GET['id']);

    if(!$post)
        // If there is no post with ID specified we'll generate
        // HTTP response with code 404 Not Found.
        throw new CHttpException(404);

        //  If everything is OK, render a post
        $this->render('post', array('model' => $post));
    }
  }
}
```

How it works...

Yii converts all *non-fatal* application errors to CException automatically.

Additionally, the default exception handler raises either the onError or an onException event. The default event handler writes a log message with error level set to error. Additionally, if your application's YII_DEBUG constant is set to true, unhandled exception or error will be displayed at a handy error screen. This screen includes a call stack trace, a code area where the exception was raised, and the file and line where you can look for the code to fix.

There's more...

For further information, refer to the following URLs:

- ▶ `http://php.net/manual/en/language.exceptions.php`
- ▶ `http://www.yiiframework.com/doc/api/CException/`
- ▶ `http://www.yiiframework.com/doc/api/CHttpException/`

Configuring components

Yii is a very customizable framework. Moreover, as in every customizable code, there should be a convenient way to setup different application parts. So in Yii, this is provided through a configuration file named `main.php` located at `protected/config/`.

How to do it...

If you have worked with Yii before, then you have probably configured a database connection:

```
return array(
    ...
    'components'=>array(
        'db'=>array(
            'class'=>'system.db.CDbConnection',
            'connectionString'=>'mysql:host=localhost;dbname=database_
name',
            'username'=>'root',
            'password'=>'',
            'charset'=>'utf8',
        ),
        ...
    ),
    ...
);
```

This way of configuring component is used when you want to use a component across all application parts. With the preceding configuration, you can access a component by its name, such as `Yii::app()->db`.

How it works...

When you are using the `Yii::app()->db` component for the first time directly or through active record model, Yii creates a component and initializes its public properties with the corresponding values provided in `db` array under the `components` section of the `main.php` application configuration file. In the preceding code, `'connectionString'` the value will be assigned to `CDbConnection::connectionString`, `'username'` will be assigned to `CDbConnection::username`, and so on.

If you want to find out what `'charset'` stands for or want to know what else you can configure in the `db` component, then you need to know its class. In case of db component, the class is `CDbConnection`. You can refer to its API page at `http://www.yiiframework.com/doc/api/CDbConnection/` and look for its public properties you can set from config.

In the preceding code, the `'class'` property is a bit special because it is used to specify component class name. It does not exist in the `CDbConnection` class. Therefore, it can be used to override a class as follows:

```
return array(
    ...
    'components'=>array(
        'db'=>array(
            'class'=>'application.components.MyDbConnection',
            ...
        ),
        ...
    ),
    ...
);
```

This way, you can override each application component and it is very useful whenever a standard component does not fit your application.

There's more...

Now, let's find out which standard Yii application components you can configure. There are two application types bundled with Yii which are as follows:

1. Web application (`CWebApplication`)
2. Console application (`CConsoleApplication`)

Both are extended from `CApplication`, so both console and web applications are sharing its components.

You can get the component names from API pages (`http://www.yiiframework.com/doc/api/`) and the source code of the `registerCoreComponents` application method, but let's list them here so the list can be used as a reference.

Both console and web application components are listed in the following table:

Component name	Default/suggested component class	Description
coreMessages	CPhpMessageSource	This component provides the source for translating Yii framework messages.
db	CDbConnection	This component provides a database connection.
messages	CPhpMessageSource	This component provides the source for translating application messages.
errorHandler	CErrorHandler	This component handles PHP errors and uncaught exceptions.
securityManager	CSecurityManager	This component provides security-related services, such as hashing, encryption, and so on.
statePersister	CStatePersister	This component provides global state persistence methods.
format	CFormatter	This component provides a set of commonly used data formatting methods.
cache	CFileCache	This component provides a caching feature.

Additional components available only for web application are listed in the following table:

Component name	Default component class	Description
session	CHttpSession	This component provides the session-related functionalities.
request	CHttpRequest	This component encapsulates the $_SERVER variable and resolves its inconsistency among different web servers.
		It also manages the cookies sent from and to the user.
urlManager	CUrlManager	URL router; used both to generate and resolve application URLs.

Component name	Default component class	Description
assetManager	CAssetManager	This component manages the publishing of private asset files.
user	CWebUser	This component represents the user session information.
themeManager	CThemeManager	This component manages themes.
authManager	CPhpAuthManager	This component manages role-based access control (RBAC).
clientScript	CClientScript	This component manages client scripts (JavaScript and CSS).
widgetFactory	CWidgetFactory	This component creates widgets and supports widget skinning.

You can add your own application components (classes extended from CComponent) by simply adding new configuration items and pointing their class properties to your custom classes.

See also

▶ The recipe named *Configuring widget defaults* in this chapter

Configuring widget defaults

In Yii, code pieces commonly used in views are placed into widgets. For example, a widget can render a tag cloud or provide a custom form input type. Core widgets are highly configurable and are used in views as follows:

```
<?$this->widget('CLinkPager', array(
'pages' => $pages,
'pageSize' => 15,
))?>
```

In the preceding code, we are using $this->widget that calls a CLinkPager widget with an array of parameters to display a pagination. pages and pageSize are both assigned to the corresponding public properties of CLinkPager before it is being rendered.

Note that we have changed the count of items per page to 15 in our example. If we want our pagination to display 15 items per page on all pages of our application, then we will need to provide a pageSize parameter with value 15 for all CLinkPager widget calls. Is there a better way? Definitely, yes.

How to do it...

A Yii web application provides a bunch of components. One of them is a widget factory that since Yii 1.1.3 can be used to set widget defaults.

1. Let's use it to set `pageSize` application-wide. We will need to edit the application configuration file `main.php` as follows:

```
return array(
    …
    'components'=>array(
        'widgetFactory'=>array(
            'widgets'=>array(
                'CLinkPager'=>array(
                    'pageSize'=>15,
                ),
                …
            ),
        ),
        …
    ),
);
```

2. Now, the default value for `CLinkPager`'s `pageSize` will be 15, so if we omit this parameter for all the application `CLinkPager`s then it will be 15, application-wide.

3. Moreover, we still can override the `pageSize` value for a specific widget:

```
<?$this->widget('CLinkPager', array(
'pages' => $pages,
'pageSize' => 5,
))?>
```

This works much like the CSS cascade. You are setting the default overall style in an external file, but are still able to override this through inline styles for individual widgets.

See also

▶ The recipe named *Configuring components* in this chapter

Using Yii core collections

Yii has a set of collection classes used mainly for internal purposes which are not described in the Definitive Guide, but are still very useful for applications:

▶ Lists: `CList`, `CTypedList`

▶ Maps: `CMap`, `CAttributeCollection`

▶ Queue: `CQueue`

▶ Stack: `CStack`

How to do it...

All collections implement SPL `IteratorAggregate`, `Traversable`, and `Countable`. Lists and maps also implement SPL `ArrayAccess`. It allows using collections like a standard PHP construct. The following is a snippet from the `CList` API:

▶ The following is the snippet from `CList` API:

```
// append at the end
$list[]=$item;

// $index must be between 0 and $list->Count
$list[$index]=$item;

// remove the item at $index
unset($list[$index]);

// if the list has an item at $index
if(isset($list[$index]))

// traverse each item in the list
foreach($list as $index=>$item)

// returns the number of items in the list
$n=count($list);
```

▶ `CList` is an integer-indexed collection. Compared to the native PHP array, it adds stricter checks, can be used in OO fashion, and allows to make a collection read-only:

```
$list = new CList();
$list->add('python');
$list->add('php');
$list->add('java')

if($list->contains('php'))
    $list->remove('java');

$anotherList = new CList(array('python', 'ruby'));
$list->mergeWith($anotherList);

$list->setReadOnly(true);

print_r($list->toArray());
```

▶ There is another list collection named `CTypedList` that ensures that the list contains only items of a certain type:

```
$typedList = new CTypedList('Post');
$typedList->add(new Post());
$typedList->add(new Comment());
```

As we are trying to add a comment to a posts list, the preceding code will give you the following exception:

```
CTypedList<Post> can only hold objects of Post class.
```

▶ `CMap` allows using every value, integer or not, as a key. Just like in `CList`, it can also be used in the native PHP style, has almost the same set of OO-methods, and allows making a collection read only:

```
$map = new CMap();
$map->add('php', array('facebook', 'wikipedia', 'wordpress',
'drupal'));
$map->add('ruby', array('basecamp', 'twitter'));
print_r($map->getKeys());
```

▶ There is also one handy static method named `CMap::mergeArray` that can be used to recursively merge two associative arrays while replacing scalar values:

```
$apps1 = array(
    'apps' => array(
        'task tracking',
        'bug tracking',
    ),
    'is_new' => false
);

$apps2 = array(
    'apps' => array(
        'blog',
        'task tracking',
    ),
    'todo' => array(
        'buy milk',
    ),
    'is_new' => true
);

$apps = CMap::mergeArray($apps1, $apps2);
CVarDumper::dump($apps, 10, true);
```

The result of the preceding code is as follows:

```
array
(
    'apps' => array
    (
        '0' => 'task tracking'
        '1' => 'bug tracking'
        '2' => 'blog'
        '3' => 'task tracking'
    )
    'is_new' => true
    'todo' => array
    (
        '0' => 'buy milk'
    )
)
```

- CAttributeCollection includes all CMap functionality and can work with data just like properties:

```
$col = new CAttributeCollection();

// $col->add('name','Alexander');
$col->name='Alexander';

// echo $col->itemAt('name');
echo $col->name;
```

- CQueue and CStack implement a queue and a stack respectively. A stack works as LIFO: last in, first out, and the queue is FIFO: first in, first out. Same as list and map collections these can be used in native PHP style and have OO style methods:

```
$queue = new CQueue();

// add some tasks
$queue->enqueue(new Task('buy milk'));
$queue->enqueue(new Task('feed a cat'));
$queue->enqueue(new Task('write yii cookbook'));

// complete a task (remove from queue and return it)
echo 'Done with '.$queue->dequeue();
echo count($queue).' items left.';
// return next item without removing it
echo 'Next one is '.$queue->peek();
```

```
foreach($queue as $task)
    print_r($task);

$garage = new CStack();

// getting some cars into the garage
$garage->push(new Car('Ferrari'));
$garage->push(new Car('Porsche'));
$garage->push(new Car('Kamaz'));

// Ferrari and Porsche can't get out
// since there is…
echo $garage->peek(); // Kamaz!

// we need to get Kamaz out first
$garage->pop();

$porsche = $garage->pop();
$porsche->drive();
```

Working with request

You can work with request data directly using PHP superglobals such as $_SERVER, $_GET, or $_POST but the better way is to use Yii powerful CHttpRequest class that resolves inconsistencies among different web servers, manages cookies, provides some additional security, and has a nice set of OO methods.

How to do it...

You can access the request component in your web application by using Yii::app()->getRequest(). So, let's review the most useful methods and their usage, methods that return different parts of the current URL. In the following table, returned parts are marked with a bold font.

getUrl	http://cookbook.local/**test/index?var=val**
getHostInfo	**http://cookbook.local**/test/index?var=val
getPathInfo	http://cookbook.local/**test/index**?var=val
getRequestUri	http://cookbook.local/**test/index?var=val**
getQueryString	http://cookbook.local/test/index?**var=val**

The methods that allow us to ensure request type are `getIsPostRequest`, `getIsAjaxRequest`, and `getRequestType`.

 ▶ For example, we can use `getIsAjaxRequest` to serve different content based on request type:

```
class TestController extends CController
{
    public function actionIndex()
    {
        if(Yii::app()->request->isAjaxRequest)s
            $this->renderPartial('test');
        else
            $this->render('test');
    }
}
```

  In the preceding code, we are rendering a view without layout if the request is made through AJAX.

 ▶ While PHP provides superglobals for both POST and GET, Yii way allows us to omit some additional checks:

```
class TestController extends CController
{
    public function actionIndex()
    {
        $request = Yii::app()->request;

        $param = $request->getParam('id', 1);
        // equals to
        $param = isset($_REQUEST['id']) ? $_REQUEST['id'] : 1;

        $param = $request->getQuery('id');
        // equals to
        $param = isset($_GET['id']) ? $_GET['id'] : null;

        $param = $request->getPost('id', 1);
        // equals to
        $param = isset($_POST['id']) ? $_POST['id'] : 1;
    }
}
```

▶ get PreferredLanguage tries to determine the user's preferred language. It can't be completely accurate, but it is good to use it as a fallback in case the user has not specified a preferred language manually.

```
class TestController extends CController
{
   public function actionIndex()
   {
       $request = Yii::app()->request;
       $lang = $request->preferredLanguage;

       // trying to get language setting from DB
       $criteria = new CDbCriteria();
       $criteria->compare('user_id', $request->getQuery('userid'));
       $criteria->compare('key', 'language');
       $setting = Settings::model()->find($criteria);
       if($setting)
           $lang = $setting->value;

       Yii::app()->setLanguage($lang);

       echo Yii::t('app', 'Language is: ').$lang;
   }
}
```

▶ sendFile allows to initiate file download as follows:

```
class TestController extends CController
{
   public function actionIndex()
   {
   $request = Yii::app()->getRequest();
       $request->sendFile('test.txt', 'File content goes here.');
   }
}
```

This action will trigger a file download and send all necessary headers, including content type (mimetype) and content length. Mimetype, if not set manually as a third parameter, will be guessed based on the filename's extension.

▶ The last thing we are going to show in this chapter is the get Cookies method. It returns a CCookieCollection class instance that allows us to work with cookies. As CCookieCollection extends CMap, we can use some native PHP methods as follows:

```
class TestController extends CController
{
   public function actionIndex()
```

```
        {
            $request = Yii::app()->request;
            // getting a cookie
            $cookie = $request->cookies['test'];
            if($cookie)
                // printing cookie value
                echo $cookie->value;
            else {
                // creating new cookie
                $cookie=new CHttpCookie('test','I am a cookie!');
                $request->cookies['test'] = $cookie;
            }
        }
    }
```

There's more...

If you are working with a lot of cookie values and want to shorten the code provided, then you can use a helper as follows:

```
class Cookie
{
  public static function get($name)
  {
        $cookie=Yii::app()->request->cookies[$name];
        if(!$cookie)
            return null;

        return $cookie->value;
  }

  public static function set($name, $value, $expiration=0)
  {
        $cookie=new CHttpCookie($name,$value);
        $cookie->expire = $expiration;
        Yii::app()->request->cookies[$name]=$cookie;
  }
}
```

After you drop this code into `protected/components/Cookie.php`, you will be able to perform the following:

```php
class TestController extends CController
{
    public function actionIndex()
    {
        $cookie = Cookie::get('test');
        if($cookie)
            echo $cookie;
        else
            Cookie::set('test','I am a cookie!!');
    }
}
```

2
Router, Controller, and Views

In this chapter, we will cover:

- ▶ Configuring URL rules
- ▶ Generating URLs by path
- ▶ Using regular expressions in URL rules
- ▶ Creating URL rules for static pages
- ▶ Providing your own URL rules at runtime
- ▶ Using base controller
- ▶ Using external actions
- ▶ Displaying static pages with `CViewAction`
- ▶ Using flash messages
- ▶ Using controller context in a view
- ▶ Reusing views with partials
- ▶ Using clips
- ▶ Using decorators
- ▶ Defining multiple layouts
- ▶ Paginating and sorting data

Introduction

This chapter will help you to learn some handy things about Yii URL router, controllers, and views. You will be able to make your controllers and views more flexible.

Configuring URL rules

Yii URL router is quite powerful and does two main tasks: it resolves URLs into internal routes and creates URLs from these routes. Router rules description is scattered over the official Yii guide and API docs. Let's try to understand how to configure application rules by example.

Getting ready

1. Create a fresh Yii application using `yiic webapp` as described in the official guide (`http://www.yiiframework.com/doc/guide/`) and find your `protected/config/main.php`. It should contain the following:

```
// application components
'components'=>array(
    ...
    // uncomment the following to enable URLs in path-format
    /*
    'urlManager'=>array(
        'urlFormat'=>'path',
        'rules'=>array(
            '<controller:\w+>/<id:\d+>'=>'<controller>/view',
            '<controller:\w+>/<action:\w+>/<id:\
                    d+>'=>'<controller>/<action>',
            '<controller:\w+>/<action:\w+>'=>'<controller>/<action>',
        ),
    ),
```

2. Delete everything from rules as we are going to start from scratch.

3. In your `protected/controllers`, create `WebsiteController.php` with the following code inside:

```
class WebsiteController extends CController
{
    public function actionIndex()
    {
        echo "index";
    }
}
```

```
public function actionPage($alias)
{
    echo "Page is $alias.";
}
}
```

This is the application controller we are going to customize URLs for.

4. Configure your application server to use clean URLs. If you are using Apache with `mod_rewrite` and `AllowOverride` turned on, then you should add the following lines to the `.htaccess` file under your `webroot` folder:

```
Options +FollowSymLinks
IndexIgnore */*
RewriteEngine on

# if a directory or a file exists, use it directly
RewriteCond %{REQUEST_FILENAME} !-f
RewriteCond %{REQUEST_FILENAME} !-d

# otherwise forward it to index.php
RewriteRule . index.php
```

How to do it...

Our website should display the index page at `/home` and all other pages at `/page/<alias_here>`. Additionally, `/about` should lead to a page with alias `about`.

1. Add the following to your rules in `protected/config/main.php`:

```
'home' => 'website/index',
'<alias:about>' => 'website/page',
'page/<alias>' => 'website/page',
```

2. After saving your changes, you should be able to browse the following URLs:
   - ❑ `/home`
   - ❑ `/about`
   - ❑ `/page/about`
   - ❑ `/page/test`

The following screenshot shows part of a page that opens when /about URL is used:

How it works...

Let's review what was done and why it works. We'll start with the right part of the first rule:

```
'home' => 'website/index',
```

What is website/index exactly?

In the Yii application, each controller and its actions have corresponding internal routes. A format for an internal route is moduleID/controllerID/actionID. For example, the actionPage method of WebsiteController corresponds to the website/page route. So, in order to get the controller ID, you should take its name without the Controller postfix and make its first letter lowercased. To get an action ID, you should take action method name without the action prefix and, again, make its first letter lowercased.

Now, what is home?

To understand it in a better way, we need to know, at least perfunctorily, what's happening when we access our application using different URLs.

When we are using /home, URL router checks our rules one by one starting from the top trying to match URL entered with the rule. If the match is found, then the router is getting controller and its action from an internal route assigned to the rule and is executing it. So, /home is the URL pattern that defines which URLs will be processed by the rule it belongs to.

> The fewer rules you have, the fewer checks are needed if URL does not match. Less URLs means more performance.

There's more...

You can create parameterized rules using a special syntax. Let's review the third rule:

```
'page/<alias>' => 'website/page',
```

Here, we are defining an alias parameter that should be specified in URL after /page/. It can be virtually anything and it will be passed as $alias parameter to WebsiteController::actionPage($alias).

You can define a pattern for such a parameter. We did it for the second rule:

```
'<alias:about>' => 'website/page',
```

Alias here should match `about` or else, the rule will not be applied.

Further reading

For further information, refer to the following URLs:

► http://www.yiiframework.com/doc/guide/en/basics.controller

► http://www.yiiframework.com/doc/guide/en/topics.url

► http://www.yiiframework.com/doc/api/1.1/CUrlManager

See also

► The recipe named *Generating URLs by path* in this chapter

► The recipe named *Using regular expressions in URL rules* in this chapter

► The recipe named *Creating URL rules for static pages* in this chapter

► The recipe named *Providing your own URL rules at runtime* in this chapter

Generating URLs by path

Yii allows you not only to route your URLs to different controller actions but also to generate a URL by specifying a proper internal route and its parameters. This is really useful because you can focus on internal routes while developing your application and care about real URLs only before going live.

 Never specify URLs directly and use the Yii URL toolset. It will allow you to change URLs without rewriting a lot of application code.

Getting ready

1. Create a fresh Yii application using `yiic webapp` as described in the official guide and find your `protected/config/main.php`. Replace rules array as follows:

```
// application components
'components'=>array(
    ...
    // uncomment the following to enable URLs in path-format
    /*
```

```
'urlManager'=>array(
    'urlFormat'=>'path',
    'rules'=>array(
    '<alias:about>' => 'website/page',
    'page/about/<alias:authors>' => 'website/page',
    'page/<alias>' => 'website/page',
),
```

2. In your `protected/controllers`, create `WebsiteController` with the following code inside:

```
class WebsiteController extends CController
{
    public function actionIndex()
    {
        echo "index";
    }

    public function actionPage($alias)
    {
        echo "Page is $alias.";
    }
}
```

This is our application controller that we are going to generate custom URLs for.

3. Configure your application server to use clean URLs. If you are using Apache with `mod_rewrite` and `AllowOverride` turned on, then you should add the following lines to the `.htaccess` file under your `webroot` folder:

```
Options +FollowSymLinks
IndexIgnore */*
RewriteEngine on

# if a directory or a file exists, use it directly
RewriteCond %{REQUEST_FILENAME} !-f
RewriteCond %{REQUEST_FILENAME} !-d

# otherwise forward it to index.php
RewriteRule . index.php
```

How to do it...

We need to generate URLs pointing to `index` and `page` actions of `WebsiteController`. Depending on where we need it, there are different ways for doing it, but the basics are the same. Let's list some methods that generate URLs.

`CHtml::link()` and some other `CHtml` methods such as `form`, `refresh`, and `ajaxLink` all accept URLs and are typically used in views. These are using `CHtml::normalizeUrl` internally to resolve internal routes. Therefore, you should pass data in one of the following formats:

- URL string: In this case, URL passed will be used as is.
- array(internal route, param => value, param => value, …). In this case, URL will be generated.

What is internal route? Each controller and its actions have corresponding routes. A format for a route is `moduleID/controllerID/actionID`. For example, `actionPage` method of `WebsiteController` corresponds to `website/page` route. To get a controller ID, you should take its name without `Controller` postfix and make its first letter lowercased. To get an action ID, you should take action method name without `action` prefix and, again, make its first letter lowercased.

Parameters are `$_GET` variables that will be passed to an action with internal route specified. For example, if we want to create a URL to `WebsiteController::actionIndex` that passes `$_GET['name']` parameter to it, it can be done like this:

```
echo CHtml::link('Click me!', array('website/index',
   'name' => 'Qiang'));
```

URLs are also helpful when using controller. Inside the controller, you can use `createUrl` and `createAbsoluteUrl` to get both relative and absolute URLs:

```
class WebsiteController extends CController
{
   public function actionTest()
   {
      echo $this->createUrl('website/page', 'alias' => 'about');
      echo $this->createAbsoluteUrl('website/page',
         'alias' => 'test');
   }

   // the rest of the methods

}
```

As we have URL rules defined in the router configuration, we will get the following URLs:

- `/about`
- `http://example.com/about`

Relative URLs can be used inside your application while absolute ones should be used for pointing to locations outside of your website (like other websites) or for linking to resources meant to be accessed from outside (RSS feeds, e-mails, and so on).

When you cannot get controller instance, for example, when you implement a console application, you can use application's methods:

```
echo Yii::app()->createUrl('website/page', 'alias' => 'about');
echo Yii::app()->createAbsoluteUrl('website/page', 'alias' => 'test');
```

The difference is that when using controller-specific methods, you can omit both controller and module names. In this case, the current module name and the current controller name are used:

```
class MyController extends CController
{
  public function actionIndex()
  {
    // As we're inside of controller, createUrl will assume that URL
    // is for current controller
    echo $this->createUrl('index');
  }
}
```

How it works...

All URL building tools we have reviewed are internally using the `CWebApplication::createUrl` method that is calling `CUrlManager::createUrl`. It tries to apply routing rules one by one starting from the top. If no rules are matched, then the default URL form is generated.

There's more...

For further information, refer to the following URLs:

- http://www.yiiframework.com/doc/guide/en/basics.controller
- http://www.yiiframework.com/doc/guide/en/topics.url
- http://www.yiiframework.com/doc/api/CUrlManager
- http://www.yiiframework.com/doc/api/CHtml/#normalizeUrl-detail
- http://www.yiiframework.com/doc/api/CHtml/#link-detail
- http://www.yiiframework.com/doc/api/CController/#createUrl-detail
- http://www.yiiframework.com/doc/api/CWebApplication/#createUrl-detail

- ▶ The recipe named *Configuring URL rules* in this chapter
- ▶ The recipe named *Using regular expressions in URL rules* in this chapter
- ▶ The recipe named *Creating URL rules for static pages* in this chapter
- ▶ The recipe named *Providing your own URL rules at runtime* in this chapter

Using regular expressions in URL rules

One of the "hidden" features of Yii URL router is that you can use regular expressions that are pretty powerful when it comes to strings handling.

Getting ready

1. Create a fresh Yii application using `yiic webapp` as described in the official guide and find your `protected/config/main.php`. It should contain the following:

```
// application components
'components'=>array(
    …
    // uncomment the following to enable URLs in path-format
    /*
    'urlManager'=>array(
        'urlFormat'=>'path',
        'rules'=>array(
            '<controller:\w+>/<id:\d+>'=>'<controller>/view',
            '<controller:\w+>/<action:\w+>/<id:\
                d+>'=>'<controller>/<action>',
            '<controller:\w+>/<action:\w+>'=>'<controller>/<action>',
        ),
    ),
```

2. Delete everything from rules as we are going to start from scratch.

3. In your `protected/controllers`, create `PostController.php` with the following code inside:

```
class PostController extends CController
{
    public function actionView($alias)
    {
        echo "Showing post with alias $alias.";
    }
```

```php
        public function actionIndex($order = 'DESC')
        {
            echo "Showing posts ordered $order.";
        }

        public function actionHello($name)
        {
         echo "Hello, $name!";
        }
    }
```

This is our application controller we are going to access using our custom URLs.

4. Configure your application server to use clean URLs. If you are using Apache with `mod_rewrite` and `AllowOverride` turned on, then you should add the following lines to the `.htaccess` file under your `webroot` folder:

```
Options +FollowSymLinks
IndexIgnore */*
RewriteEngine on

# if a directory or a file exists, use it directly
RewriteCond %{REQUEST_FILENAME} !-f
RewriteCond %{REQUEST_FILENAME} !-d

# otherwise forward it to index.php
RewriteRule . index.php
```

How to do it...

We want our `PostController` actions to accept parameters according to some rules and give "404 not found" HTTP response for all parameters that do not match. In addition, post index should have an alias URL `archive`.

Let's use regular expressions to achieve it:

```
    'post/<alias:[-a-z]+>' => 'post/view',
    '(posts|archive)' => 'post/index',
    '(posts|archive)/<order:(DESC|ASC)>' => 'post/index',
    'sayhello/<name>' => 'post/hello',
```

Now, you can try the following URLs:

// success

http://example.com/post/test-post

// fail

http://example.com/post/another_post

// success

http://example.com/posts

// success

http://example.com/archive

// fail

http://example.com/archive/test

// success

http://example.com/posts/ASC

// success

The following screenshot shows that the URL `http://example.com/post/test-post` has run successfully:

The following screenshot shows that the URL `http://example.com/archive/test` did not run successfully and encountered an error:

How it works...

You can use regular expressions in both parameter definition and the rest of the rule. Let's read our rules one by one.

```
'post/<alias:[-a-z]+>' => 'post/view',
```

Alias parameter should contain one or more English letter or a dash. No other symbols are allowed.

```
'(posts|archive)' => 'post/index',
```

Both `posts` and `archive` are leading to `post/index`.

```
'(posts|archive)/<order:(DESC|ASC)>' => 'post/index',
```

Both `posts` and `archive` are leading to `post/index`. Order parameter can only accept two values: `DESC` and `ASC`.

```
'sayhello/<name>' => 'post/hello',
```

You should specify the `name` part but there are no restrictions on what characters are allowed.

Note that regardless of the rule used, the developer should never assume that input data is safe.

There's more...

To learn more about regular expressions, you can use the following sources:

- ▶ `http://www.php.net/manual/en/reference.pcre.pattern.syntax.php`
- ▶ *Mastering Regular Expressions*, by Jeffrey Friedl (`http://regex.info/`)

See also

- ▶ The recipe named *Configuring URL rules* in this chapter
- ▶ The recipe named *Creating URL rules for static pages* in this chapter

Creating URL rules for static pages

A website typically contains some static pages. Usually, they are /about, /contact, /tos, and so on, and it is common to handle these pages in a single controller action. Let's find a way to create URL rules for these types of pages.

Getting ready

1. Create a fresh Yii application using `yiic webapp` as described in the official guide and find your `protected/config/main.php`. It should contain the following:

```
// application components
'components'=>array(
    ...
    // uncomment the following to enable URLs in path-format
    /*
    'urlManager'=>array(
        'urlFormat'=>'path',
        'rules'=>array(
            '<controller:\w+>/<id:\d+>'=>'<controller>/view',
            '<controller:\w+>/<action:\w+>/<id:\
                d+>'=>'<controller>/<action>',
            '<controller:\w+>/<action:\w+>'=>'<controller>/<action>',
        ),
    ),
```

2. Delete everything from rules as we are going to start from scratch.

3. In your `protected/controllers`, create `WebsiteController` with the following code:

```
class WebsiteController extends CController
{
    public function actionPage($alias)
    {
        echo "Page is $alias.";
    }
}
```

4. Configure your application server to use clean URLs. If you are using Apache with `mod_rewrite` and `AllowOverride` turned on you should add the following lines to the `.htaccess` file under your webroot folder:

```
Options +FollowSymLinks
IndexIgnore */*
RewriteEngine on

# if a directory or a file exists, use it directly
RewriteCond %{REQUEST_FILENAME} !-f
RewriteCond %{REQUEST_FILENAME} !-d

# otherwise forward it to index.php
RewriteRule . index.php
```

How to do it...

The most straightforward way is defining a rule for each page:

```
'<alias:about>' => 'website/page',
'<alias:contact>' => 'website/page',
'<alias:tos>' => 'website/page',
```

Using regular expressions, we can compact it to a single rule:

```
'<alias:(about|contact|tos)>' => 'website/page',
```

Now, what if we want the URL to be /tos and an alias parameter to be terms_of_service?

No problem, we can use default parameters to achieve it:

```
'tos' => array('website/page', 'defaultParams' => array('alias' =>
'terms_of_service')),
```

OK. What if we have many pages and want to be able to dynamically create pages without adding more rules or changing existing ones?

We can achieve this with the following rule:

```
'<alias>' => 'website/page'
```

As this rule matches everything, we need to place it last, so it won't affect all other rules. In addition, default rules with one slug, such as controller name will stop working. To overcome this issue, we need to add default rules which we deleted in the *Getting ready* section of this recipe.

How it works...

Let's read rules we just wrote.

```
'<alias:about>' => 'website/page',
```

If the URL is /about, then pass it as the alias parameter to website/page.

```
'<alias:(about|contact|tos)>' => 'website/page',
```

If the URL is /about or /contact or /tos, then pass it as the alias parameter to website/page.

```
'tos' => array('website/page', 'defaultParams' => array('alias' =>
'terms_of_service')),
```

When the URL is /tos, pass terms_of_service as the alias parameter value.

This rule is a bit special because it uses default parameter option. Default parameter allows you to set a value that will be used if parameter with name specified is omitted. When you need to specify an option for the rule, you should use an array notation:

```
'pattern' => array('internal/route', 'option' => 'value', 'option' =>
'value', …),
```

 For a list of options you can set, refer to the following API page:

`http://www.yiiframework.com/doc/api/1.1/CUrlRule`

See also

▶ The recipe named *Configuring URL rules* in this chapter

▶ The recipe named *Using regular expressions in URL rules* in this chapter

Providing your own URL rules at runtime

When you are developing an application with pluggable module architecture, you most likely need to somehow inject your module-specific rules into an existing application.

Getting ready

1. Set up a new application using `yiic webapp`.

2. Add `.htaccess`, shown in official URL Management guide to your `webroot`.

3. Add `'showScriptName' => false` to your URL manager configuration.

4. Generate the `page` module using Gii.

5. Don't forget to add your new module to the modules list in your application configuration.

The Yii code generator is shown in the following screenshot:

How to do it...

1. Create `ModuleUrlManager.php` in your `protected/components` directory with the following code inside:

```php
<?php
class ModuleUrlManager
{
  static function collectRules()
  {
    if(!empty(Yii::app()->modules))
    {
      foreach(Yii::app()->modules as $moduleName => $config)
      {
        $module = Yii::app()->getModule($moduleName);
        if(!empty($module->urlRules))
        {
          Yii::app()->getUrlManager()->addRules
            ($module->urlRules);
        }
      }
    }
```

```
    return true;
  }
}
```

2. In your application configuration, add the following line:

```
'onBeginRequest' => array('ModuleUrlManager', 'collectRules'),
```

3. Now, in your page module, you can add custom rules. To do so, open `PageModule.php` and add:

```
public $urlRules = array(
  'test' => 'page/default/index',
);
```

4. To test if it works, open your browser and go to `http://example.com/test`. This page should look like the one shown in the following screenshot:

This is the view content for action "index". The action belongs to the controller "DefaultController" in the "page" module.

5. You still can override URL rules from your main application configuration file. So, what you specify in module's `urlRules` is used only when the main application rules are not matching.

How it works...

Let's review the `ModuleUrlManager::collectRules` method.

If there are modules defined in our application, then we are checking if `urlRules` public property exists. If it does, then there are some rules defined in the module and they are added using `CUrlManager::addRules`.

`CUrlManager::addRules` description says "In order to make the new rules effective, this method must be called before `CWebApplication::processRequest`".

Now, let's check how our application works. In our `index.php`, we have the following line:

```
Yii::createWebApplication($config)->run();
```

After being initialized with configuration, we are calling `CWebApplication::run()`:

```
public function run()
{
    if($this->hasEventHandler('onBeginRequest'))
        $this->onBeginRequest(new CEvent($this));
    $this->processRequest();
    if($this->hasEventHandler('onEndRequest'))
        $this->onEndRequest(new CEvent($this));
}
```

As we can see, there is an `onBeginRequest` event raised just before calling `processRequest`. That is why we are attaching our class method to it.

There's more...

As instantiating all application modules on every request is not good for performance, it is good to cache module rules. Caching strategy can vary depending on your application. Let's implement a simple one:

```php
<?php
class ModuleUrlManager
{
  static function collectRules()
  {
    if(!empty(Yii::app()->modules))
    {
      $cache = Yii::app()->getCache();

      foreach(Yii::app()->modules as $moduleName => $config)
      {
        $urlRules = false;

        if($cache)
          $urlRules = $cache->get('module.urls.'.$moduleName);

        if($urlRules===false){
          $urlRules = array();
          $module = Yii::app()->getModule($moduleName);
```

```
            if(isset($module->urlRules))
                $urlRules = $module->urlRules;

            if($cache)
                $cache->set('module.urls.'.$moduleName, $urlRules);
        }
        if(!empty($urlRules))
            Yii::app()->getUrlManager()->addRules($urlRules);
    }
}

    return true;
    }
}
```

This implementation caches URL rules per module. So, adding new modules is not a problem but changing existing ones requires you to flush cache manually using `Yii::app()->cache->flush()`.

See also

▶ The recipe named *Configuring URL rules* in this chapter

Using base controller

In many frameworks, the concept of a base controller that is being extended by other ones is described right in the guide. In Yii, it is not in the guide as you can achieve flexibility in many other ways. Still, using base controller is possible and can be useful.

Getting ready

A new application using `yiic webapp` is to be set up.

Let's say we want to add some controllers that will be accessible only when the user is logged in. We can surely set this constraint for each controller separately, but we will do it in a better way.

How to do it...

1. First, we will need a base controller that our user-only controllers will use. Let's create `SecureController.php` in `protected/components` with the following code:

    ```php
    <?php
    class SecureController extends Controller
    ```

```
    {
        public function filters()
        {
            return array(
                'accessControl',
            );
        }

        public function accessRules()
        {
            return array(
                array('allow',
                    'users'=>array('@'),
                ),
                array('deny',
                    'users'=>array('*'),
                ),
            );
        }
    }
```

2. Now, go to the Gii controller generator and enter `SecureController` into the `Base Class` field. You will get something like this:

```
class TestController extends SecureController
{
    public function actionIndex()
    {
        $this->render('index');
    }
    ...
}
```

3. Now, your `TestController` index will be only accessible if the user is logged in, even though we have not declared it explicitly in the `TestController` class.

How it works...

The trick is nothing more than a basic class inheritance. If filters or `accessRules` is not found in `TestController`, then it will be called from `SecureController`.

Using external actions

In Yii, you can define controller actions as separate classes and then connect them to your controllers. This way, you can reuse some common functionality.

For example, you can move backend for autocomplete fields to an action and save some time by not having to write it over and over again.

Another simple example that we will review is deleting a model.

Getting ready

1. Set up a new application using `yiic webapp`.

2. Create a DB schema with the following script:

```
CREATE TABLE `post` (
  `id` int(10) unsigned NOT NULL auto_increment,
  `created_on` int(11) unsigned NOT NULL,
  `title` varchar(255) NOT NULL,
  `content` text NOT NULL,
  PRIMARY KEY  (`id`)
);


CREATE TABLE `user` (
  `id` int(10) unsigned NOT NULL auto_increment,
  `username` varchar(200) NOT NULL,
  `password` char(40) NOT NULL,
  PRIMARY KEY  (`id`)
);
```

3. Generate `Post` and `User` models using Gii.

How to do it...

1. Let's write a usual delete action for posts first, as follows:

```
class PostController extends CController
{
  function actionIndex()
  {
    $posts = Post::model()->findAll();
    $this->render('index', array(
      'posts' => $posts,
    ));
```

```
    }

    function actionDelete($id)
    {
        $post = Post::model()->findByPk($id);
        if(!$post)
            throw new CHttpException(404);

        if($post->delete())
            $this->redirect('post/index');

        throw new CHttpException(500);
    }
}
```

We have defined two actions. One lists all posts and another deletes a post specified if it exists and redirects back to index action.

2. Now, let's do the same in a separate action class. Create DeleteAction.php in your protected/components directory as follows:

```
class DeleteAction extends CAction
{
    function run()
    {
        if(empty($_GET['id']))
            throw new CHttpException(404);

        $post = Post::model()->findByPk($_GET['id']);

        if(!$post)
            throw new CHttpException(404);

        if($post->delete())
            $this->redirect('post/index');

        throw new CHttpException(500);
    }
}
```

3. Let's use it inside our controller. Delete actionDelete, we will not need it anymore. Then, add the actions method:

```
class PostController extends CController
{
    function actions()
    {
```

```
        return array(
            'delete' => 'DeleteAction',
        );
    }

    ...


}
```

4. OK. Now, we are using external delete action for post controller, but what about the user controller? To use our `DeleteAction` with `UserController` we need to customize it first. We do this as follows:

```
class DeleteAction extends CAction
{
    public $pk = 'id';
    public $redirectTo = 'index';
    public $modelClass;

    function run()
    {
        if(empty($_GET[$this->pk]))
            throw new CHttpException(404);

        $model = CActiveRecord::model($this->modelClass)
          ->findByPk($_GET[$this->pk]);

        if(!$model)
            throw new CHttpException(404);

        if($model->delete())
            $this->redirect($this->redirectTo);

        throw new CHttpException(500);
    }
}
```

5. Now, we can use this action for both post controller and user controller. For post controller, we do this as follows:

```
class PostController extends CController
{
    function actions()
    {
        return array(
            'delete' => array(
```

```
                    'class' => 'DeleteAction',
                    'modelClass' => 'Post',
                );
            );
        }

        ...

    }
```

6. For user controller, we do this as follows:

```
class UserController extends CController
{
    function actions()
    {
        return array(
            'delete' => array(
                'class' => 'DeleteAction',
                'modelClass' => 'User',
            );
        );
    }

    ...

}
```

7. This way, you can save yourself a lot of time by implementing and reusing external actions for tasks of a similar type.

How it works...

Every controller can be built from external actions like a puzzle from pieces. The difference is that you can make external actions very flexible and reuse them in many places. In the final version of `DeleteAction`, we defined some public properties. As `DeleteAction` is a component, we can set its properties through config. In our case, we pass config into the `actions` controller method used to add actions to a module.

There's more...

For further information, refer to the following URLs:

▶ http://www.yiiframework.com/doc/api/CAction/
▶ http://www.yiiframework.com/doc/api/CController#actions-detail

Displaying static pages with CViewAction

If you have a few static pages and aren't going to change them very frequently, then it's not worth querying database and implementing a page management for them.

Getting ready

Set up a new application using `yiic webapp`.

How to do it...

1. We just need to connect `CViewAction` to our controller.

```
class SiteController extends CController
{
    function actions()
    {
        return array(
            'page'=>array(
                'class'=>'CViewAction',
            ),
        );
    }
}
```

2. Now, put your pages into `protected/views/site/pages`. Name them `about.php` and `contact.php`.

3. Now, you can try your pages by typing:

   `http://example.com/index.php?r=site/page&view=contact`

   Alternatively, you can type the following:

   `http://example.com/site/page/view/about`

   If you have configured clean URLs with path format.

How it works...

We are connecting external action named `CViewAction` that simply tries to find a view named the same as the `$_GET` parameter supplied. If it is there, it displays it. If not, then it will give you `404 Not found` page.

There's more...

There are some useful `CViewAction` parameters we can use. These are listed in the following table:

Parameter name	Description
basePath	It is a base path alias that is prepended to a view name. Default is `pages`. That means a page named faq.company will be translated to `protected/views/pages/faq/company.php`.
defaultView	It is a name of a page to render when there is no `$_GET` parameter supplied. Default is `index`.
layout	Layout used to render a page. By default, controller layout is used. If it is set to `null`, then no layout is applied.
renderAsText	If set to true, then the page will be rendered as is. Else, PHP inside will be executed.
viewParam	The name of the `$_GET` parameter used to pass page name to `CViewAction`. Default is `view`.

Further reading

For further information, refer to the following URL:

`http://www.yiiframework.com/doc/api/CViewAction`

See also

▶ The recipe named *Using external actions* in this chapter

Using flash messages

When you are editing a model with a form, when you are deleting a model, or doing any other operation, it is good to tell users if it went fine or if there was an error. Typically, after some kind of action, such as editing a form, a redirect will happen and we need to display a message on the page we want to go to. However, how to pass it from the current page to the redirect target and clean afterwards? Flash messages will help us.

Getting ready

Set up a new application using `yiic webapp`.

How to do it...

1. Let's create a `protected/controllers/WebsiteController.php` controller as follows:

```php
class WebsiteController extends CController
{
    function actionOk()
    {
        Yii::app()->user->setFlash('success', 'Everything went
            fine!');
        $this->redirect('index');
    }

    function actionBad()
    {
        Yii::app()->user->setFlash('error', 'Everything went
            wrong!');
        $this->redirect('index');
    }

    function actionIndex()
    {
        $this->render('index');
    }
}
```

2. Additionally, create the `protected/views/website/index.php` view as follows:

```php
<?php if(Yii::app()->user->hasFlash('success')):?>
<div class="flash-notice">
    <?php echo Yii::app()->user->getFlash('success')?>
</div>
<?php endif?>
<?php if(Yii::app()->user->hasFlash('error')):?>
<div class="flash-error">
    <?php echo Yii::app()->user->getFlash('error')?>
</div>
<?php endif?>
```

3. Now, if we go to `http://example.com/website/ok`, we'll be redirected to `http://example.com/website/index` and a success message will be displayed. Moreover, if we go to `http://example.com/website/bad`, we will be redirected to the same page, but with an error message. Refreshing the index page will hide the message.

How it works...

We are setting a flash message with `Yii::app()->user->setFlash('success', 'Everything went fine!')`, for example, calling `CWebUser::setFlash`. Internally, it is saving a message into a user state, so in the lowest level, our message is being kept in `$_SESSION` until `Yii::app()->user->getFlash('success')` is called and the `$_SESSION` key is deleted.

There's more...

The following URL contains an API reference of `CWebUser` and will help you to understand flash messages better:

`http://www.yiiframework.com/doc/api/CWebUser`

Using controller context in a view

Yii views are pretty powerful and have many features. One of them is that you can use controller context in a view. So, let's try it.

Getting ready

Set up a new application using `yiic webapp`.

How to do it...

1. Create a controller as follows:

```
class WebsiteController extends CController
{
    function actionIndex()
    {
        $this->pageTitle = 'Controller context test';
        $this->render('index');
    }

    function hello()
    {
        if(!empty($_GET['name']))
            echo 'Hello, '.$_GET['name'].'!';
    }
}
```

2. Now, we will create a view showing what we can do:

```
<h1><?php echo $this->pageTitle?></h1>
<p>Hello call. <?php $this->hello()?></p>
<?php $this->widget('zii.widgets.CMenu',array(
'items'=>array(
      array('label'=>'Home', 'url'=>array('index')),
      array('label'=>'Yiiframework home',
        'url'=>'http://yiiframework.ru/',
    ),
))?>
```

How it works...

We are using $this in a view to refer to a currently running controller. When doing it, we can call a controller method and access its properties. The most useful property is pageTitle which refers to the current page title and there are many built-in methods that are extremely useful in views such as renderPartials and widget.

There's more...

The following URL contains API documentation for CController where you can get a good list of methods you can use in your view:

```
http://www.yiiframework.com/doc/api/CController
```

Reusing views with partials

Yii supports partials, so if you have a block without much logic that you want to reuse or want to implement e-mail templates, partials are the right way to look.

Getting ready

1. Set up a new application using yiic webapp.

2. Create a WebsiteController as follows:

```
class WebsiteController extends CController
{
    function actionIndex()
    {
        $this->render('index');
    }
}
```

How to do it...

We will start with a reusable block. For example, we need to embed a YouTube video at several website pages. Let's implement a reusable template for it.

1. Create a view file named `protected/views/common/youtube.php` and paste an embed code from YouTube. You will get something like:

```
<object width="480" height="385"><param name="movie"
value="http://www.youtube.com/v/S6u7ylr0zIg?fs=1 "></
param><param name="allowFullScreen" value="true"></
param><param name="allowscriptaccess" value="always"></
param><embed src="http://www.youtube.com/v/S6u7ylr0zIg?fs=1"
type="application/x-shockwave-flash" allowscriptaccess="always"
allowfullscreen="true" width="480" height="385"></embed></object>
```

2. Now, we need to make it reusable. We want to be able to set video ID, width, and height. Let's make width and height optional, as follows:

```
<object width="<?php echo!empty($width) ? $width : 480?>"
height="<?php echo!empty($height) ? $height: 385?>"><param
name="movie" value="http://www.youtube.com/v/<?php echo
$id?>?fs=1 "></param><param name="allowFullScreen" value="true"></
param><param name="allowscriptaccess" value="always"></
param><embed src="http://www.youtube.com/v/<?php echo $id?>?fs=1"
type="application/x-shockwave-flash" allowscriptaccess="always"
allowfullscreen="true" width="<?php echo !empty($width) ? $width
: 480?>" height="<?php echo !empty($height) ? $height: 385?>"></
embed></object>
```

3. Now, you can use it in your `protected/views/website/index.php` like this:

```
<?php $this->renderPartial('////common/youtube', array(
    'id' => '8Rp-CaIKvQs', // you can get this id by simply looking
                            at video URL
    'width' => 320,
    'height' => 256,
))?>
```

Looks better, right? Note that we have used `//` to reference a view. This means that Yii will look for a view starting from `protected/views` not taking controller name into account.

4. Now, let's send some e-mails. As we are unable to write unique letters to thousands of users, we will use a template but will make it customized. Let's add a new method to `protected/controllers/WebsiteController.php` as follows:

```
class WebsiteController extends CController
{
    function actionSendmails()
```

```
    {
        $users = User::model->findAll();
        foreach($users as $user)
        {
            $this->sendEmail('welcome', $user->email, 'Welcome to the
                website!', array('user' => $user));
        }
        echo 'Emails were sent.';
    }

    function sendEmail($template, $to, $subject, $data)
    {
        mail($to, $subject, $this->renderPartial
            ('//email/'.$template, $data, true));
    }
}
```

5. Here is our template `protected/views/email/welcome.php`:

```
Hello <?php echo $user->name?>,

Welcome to the website!

You can go check our new videos section. There are funny raccoons.

Yours,
Website team.
```

How it works...

`CController::renderPartial` does the same template processing as
`CController::render` except the former does not use layout. As we can access current
controller in a view using `$this`, we can use its `renderPartial` to use view within another
view. `renderPartial` is also useful when dealing with AJAX as you don't need layout
rendered in this case.

There's more...

For further information, refer to the following URL:

http://www.yiiframework.com/doc/api/CController/#renderPartial-detail

See also

▶ The recipe named *Using controller context in a view* in this chapter

Using clips

One of the Yii features you can use in your views is **clips**. The basic idea is that you can record some output and then reuse it later in a view. A good example will be defining additional content regions for your layout and filling them elsewhere.

Getting ready

Set up a new application using `yiic webapp`.

How to do it...

1. For our example, we need to define two regions in our layout: `beforeContent` and `footer`. Open `protected/views/layouts/main.php` and insert the following just before the content output (`<?php echo $content; ?>`):

   ```
   <?php if(!empty($this->clips['beforeContent'])) echo
       $this->clips['beforeContent']?>
   ```

   Then, insert the following into `<div id="footer">`:

   ```
   <?php if(!empty($this->clips['footer'])) echo
       $this->clips['footer']?>
   ```

2. That is it. Now, we need to fill these regions somehow. We will use a controller action for the `beforeContent` region. Open `protected/controllers/SiteController.php` and add the following to `actionIndex`:

   ```
   $this->beginClip('beforeContent');
   echo 'Your IP is '.Yii::app()->request->userHostAddress;
   $this->endClip();
   ```

3. As for footer, we will set its content from a view. Open `protected/views/site/index.php` and add the following:

   ```
   <?php $this->beginClip('footer')?>
   This application was built with Yii.
   <?php $this->endClip()?>
   ```

4. Now, when you open your website's index page, you should get your IP just before the page content and "built with" note in the footer.

How it works...

We mark regions with the code that just checks for existence of a clip specified and, if clip exists, the code outputs it. Then, we record content for clips we defined using special controller methods named `beginClip` and `endClip`.

See also

▶ The recipe named *Using controller context in a view* in this chapter

Using decorators

In Yii, we can enclose content into a decorator. The common usage of decorators is layout. Yes, when you are rendering a view using the `render` method of your controller, Yii automatically decorates it with the main layout. Let's create a simple decorator that will properly format quotes.

Getting ready

Set up a new application using `yiic webapp`.

How to do it...

1. First, we will create a decorator file `protected/views/decorators/quote.php`:

   ```
   <div class="quote">
       &ldquo;<?php echo $content?>&rdquo;, <?php echo $author?>
   </div>
   ```

2. Now in `protected/views/site/index.php`, we will use our decorator:

   ```
   <?php $this->beginContent('//decorators/quote', array('author' =>
   'Edward A. Murphy'))?>
   If anything bad can happen, it probably will
   <?php $this->endContent()?>
   ```

3. Now, your homepage should include the following markup:

   ```
   <div class="quote">
       &ldquo;If anything bad can happen, it probably will&rdquo;,
   Edward A. Murphy
   </div>
   ```

How it works...

Decorators are pretty simple. Everything between `beginContent` and `endContent` is rendered into a `$content` variable and passed into a decorator template. Then, the decorator template is rendered and inserted in the place where `endContent` was called. We can pass additional variables into decorator using a second parameter of `beginContent`, such as the one we did for the author.

Note that we have used `//decorators/quote` as view path. This means that the view will be searched starting from either theme views root or application views root.

There's more...

The following URL provides more details about decorators:

`http://www.yiiframework.com/doc/api/CContentDecorator/`

See also

▶ The recipe named *Defining multiple layouts* in this chapter

▶ The recipe named *Using controller context in a view* in this chapter

Defining multiple layouts

Most applications use a single layout for all their views. However, there are situations when multiple layouts are needed. For example, an application can use different layouts at different pages: Two additional columns for blog, one additional column for articles, and no additional columns for portfolio.

Getting ready

Set up a new application using `yiic webapp`.

How to do it...

1. Create two layouts in `protected/views/layouts`: `blog` and `articles`. Blog will contain the following code:

```php
<?php $this->beginContent('//layouts/main')?>
<div>
<?php echo $content?>
</div>
<div class="sidebar tags">
   <ul>
      <li><a href="#php">PHP</a></li>
      <li><a href="#yii">Yii</a></li>
   </ul>
</div>
```

```
<div class="sidebar links">
    <ul>
        <li><a href="http://yiiframework.com/">Yiiframework</a></li>
        <li><a href="http://php.net/">PHP</a></li>
    </ul>
</div>
<?php $this->endContent()?>
```

2. Articles will contain the following code:

```
<?php $this->beginContent('//layouts/main')?>
<div>
<?php echo $content?>
</div>
<div class="sidebar toc">
    <ul>
        <li><a href="#intro">1. Introduction</a></li>
        <li><a href="#quick-start">2. Quick start</a></li>
    </ul>
</div>
<?php $this->endContent()?>
```

3. Create three controllers named `BlogController`, `ArticleController`, and `PortfolioController` with index actions in both:

```
class BlogController extends Controller
{
    function actionIndex()
    {
        $this->layout = 'blog';
        $this->render('//site/index');
    }
}


class ArticleController extends Controller
{
    function actionIndex()
    {
        $this->layout = 'articles';
        $this->render('//site/index');
    }
}


class PortfolioController extends Controller
{
    function actionIndex()
```

```
    {
        $this->render('//site/index');
    }
}
```

4. Now try `http://example.com/blog`, `http://example.com/article`, and `http://example.com/portfolio`.

How it works...

We defined two additional layouts for blog and articles. As we don't want to copy-paste common parts from the `main` layout, we apply additional layout decorators using `$this->beginContent` and `$this->endContent`, as shown on the following diagram:

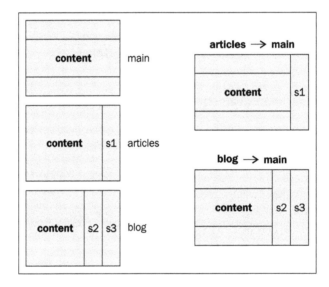

So, we are using a view rendered inside `articles` layout as `main`'s `$content`.

See also

▶ The recipe named *Using controller context in a view* in this chapter
▶ The recipe named *Using decorators* in this chapter

Paginating and sorting data

In latest Yii releases, accent was moved from using Active Record directly to grids, lists, and data providers. Still, sometimes it is better to use active record directly. Let's see how to list paginated AR records with ability to sort them.

Getting ready

1. Setup a new application using `yiic webapp`.

2. Create a database structure table `post` with `id` and `title` fields, add 10–20 records.

3. Generate `Post` model using Gii.

How to do it...

1. First, you need to create `protected/controllers/PostController.php`:

```
class PostController extends Controller
{
  function actionIndex()
  {
    $criteria = new CDbCriteria();
    $count=Post::model()->count($criteria);
    $pages=new CPagination($count);

    // elements per page
    $pages->pageSize=5;
    $pages->applyLimit($criteria);

    // sorting
    $sort = new CSort('Post');
    $sort->attributes = array(
        'id',
        'title',
    );
    $sort->applyOrder($criteria);

    $models = Post::model()->findAll($criteria);

    $this->render('index', array(
        'models' => $models,
        'pages' => $pages,
```

```
            'sort' => $sort,
        ));
    }
}
```

2. Now, let's implement `protected/views/post/index.php` as follows:

```
<p><?php echo $sort->link('id')?></p>
<p><?php echo $sort->link('title')?></p>
<ol>
<?php foreach($models as $model):?>
  <li>
    <h2><?php echo $model->id?> - <?php echo $model->title?></h2>
  </li>
<?php endforeach?>
</ol>

<?php $this->widget('CLinkPager', array(
    'pages' => $pages,
))?>
```

3. Try to load `http://example.com/post`. You should get a working pagination and links that allow sorting list by ID or by title.

How it works...

First, we get total models count and initialize new pagination component instance with it. Then, we use the `applyLimit` method to apply limit and offset to criteria we have used for count request. After that, we create sorter instance for the model, specifying model attributes we want to sort by and applying order conditions to criteria by calling `applyOrder`. Then, we pass modified criteria to `findAll`. At this step, we have models list, pages, data used for link pager, and sorter that we use to generate sorting links.

In a view, we are using data we gathered. First, we are generating links with `CSort::link` method. Then, we are listing models. Finally, using `CLinkPager` widgets we are rendering pagination control.

There's more...

Visit the following links to get more information about pagination and sorting:

▶ http://www.yiiframework.com/doc/api/CPagination/

▶ http://www.yiiframework.com/doc/api/CSort/

3
AJAX and jQuery

In this chapter, we will cover:

- ▶ Loading a block through AJAX
- ▶ Managing assets
- ▶ Including resources into the page
- ▶ Working with JSON
- ▶ Passing configuration from PHP to JavaScript
- ▶ Handling variable number of inputs

Introduction

Yii's client side is built with jQuery—the most widely used JavaScript library which is very powerful and simple to learn and use. In this chapter, we will focus on Yii-specific tricks rather than jQuery itself. If you need to learn more about jQuery, then please refer to its documentation at `http://docs.jquery.com/`.

Loading a block through AJAX

Nowadays, it's common when a part of a page is loaded asynchronously. Let's implement the quotes box which will display random quotes and will have the "Next quote" link to show the next one.

Getting ready

- ▶ Create a fresh Yii application using `yiic webapp` as described in the official guide
- ▶ Configure application to use clean URLs

How to do it...

Carry out the following steps:

1. Create a new controller named `protected/controllers/QuoteController.php` as follows:

```php
<?php
class QuoteController extends Controller
{
    private $quotes = array(
        array('Walking on water and developing software from a
specification are easy if both are frozen.', 'Edward V Berard'),
        array('It always takes longer than you expect, even when you
take into account Hofstadter&rsquo;s Law.', 'Hofstadter&rsquo;s
Law'),
        array('Always code as if the guy who ends up maintaining
your code will be a violent psychopath who knows where you live.',
'Rick Osborne'),
        array('I have always wished for my computer to be as easy to
use as my telephone; my wish has come true because I can no longer
figure out how to use my telephone.', 'Bjarne Stroustrup'),
        array('Java is to JavaScript what Car is to Carpet.', 'Chris
Heilmann'),
    );

    private function getRandomQuote()
    {
        return $this->quotes[array_rand($this->quotes, 1)];
    }

    function actionIndex()
    {
        $this->render('index', array(
            'quote' => $this->getRandomQuote()
        ));
    }

    function actionGetQuote()
    {
        $this->renderPartial('_quote', array(
            'quote' => $this->getRandomQuote(),
        ));
    }
}
```

2. We will require two views. The first is `protected/views/quote/index.php`:

```
<h2>Quote of the day</h2>
<div id="quote-of-the-day">
    <?php $this->renderPartial('_quote', array(
        'quote' => $quote,
    ))?>
</div>
<?php echo CHtml::ajaxLink('Next quote', array('getQuote'),
array('update' => '#quote-of-the-day'))?>
```

The second view named `protected/views/quote/_quote.php` is as follows:

```
&ldquo;<?php echo $quote[0]?>&rdquo;, <?php echo $quote[1]?>
```

3. That is it. Now, try to access your quote controller and click on the **Next quote** link, as shown in the following screenshot:

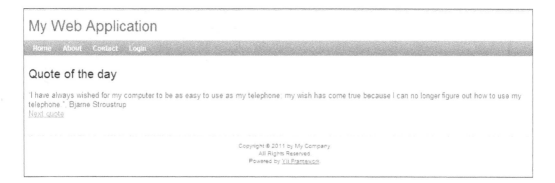

How it works...

First, we define a list of quotes in the controller's private property `$quotes` and create a method to get a random quote. In a real application, you will probably get a quote from a database using DAO or an active record.

Then, we define a view for the `index` action and `_quote` which is used in the `getQuote` action that renders it without layout and the `index` view as a partial. In the `index` action, we use `CHtml::ajaxLink` to create a link which makes a request to the `getQuote` action and updates the HTML element with the ID of `quote-of-the-day`. This is done with a response `CHtml::ajaxLink` that generates the following code in the resulting HTML page (reformatted):

```
<script type="text/javascript">
/*<![CDATA[*/
jQuery(function($) {
    jQuery('body').delegate('#yt0','click',function(){
```

```
        jQuery.ajax({
            'url':'/quote/getQuote',
            'cache':false,
            'success':function(html){
                jQuery("#quote-of-the-day").html(html)
            }
        });
        return false;
    });
});
/*]]>*/
</script>
```

As jQuery is being used, Yii includes it in the page automatically and does it only once, no matter how many times we are using it.

 You can see that Yii generated a #yt0 ID for us. That is great because you don't have to worry about setting IDs manually. Nevertheless, if you are loading a part of the page through AJAX and this part includes JavaScript-enabled widgets or CHtml AJAX helpers, then you need to set IDs manually because of possible IDs intersection.

There's more...

If you want to customize the success callback, then you can do this by setting it through a third parameter as follows:

```
<?php echo CHtml::ajaxLink('Next quote', array('getQuote'),
array('success' => 'js:function(data){
    alert(data);
}'))?>
```

 Note that we used the js: prefix, which is required when you want to use JavaScript instead of a string, as in this example.

In some cases, it is not desirable to allow a non-AJAX access to the getQuote action. There are two ways through which we can limit its usage to AJAX-only. First, you can use the built-in ajaxOnly filter as follows:

```
class QuoteController extends Controller
{
    function filters()
    {
```

```
        return array(
            'ajaxOnly + getQuote',
        );
    }
...
```

After adding this, ones who try to use the `getQuote` action directly will get an HTTP error: `400 Bad Request`.

The second way is to detect if request is made through AJAX with a special request method. For example, if we want to show the standard 404 "Not found" page, we can do this as follows:

```
function actionGetQuote()
{
    if(!Yii::app()->request->isAjaxRequest)
        throw new CHttpException(404);

    $this->renderPartial('_quote', array(
        'quote' => $this->getRandomQuote(),
    ));
}
```

Similarly, we can use one action to serve both AJAX and non-AJAX responses:

```
function actionGetQuote()
{
    $quote = $this->getRandomQuote();
    if(Yii::app()->request->isAjaxRequest)
    {
        $this->renderPartial('_quote', array(
            'quote' => $quote,
        ));
    }
    else
    {
        $this->render('index', array(
            'quote' => $quote,
        ));
    }
}
```

Prevent including a bundled jQuery

Sometimes, you need to suppress including a bundled jQuery. For example, if your project code relies on version specific functionality. To achieve this, you need to configure a `clientScript` application component using `protected/config/main.php` as follows:

```
return array(

    // …

    // application components
    'components'=>array(
        // …
        'clientScript' => array(
            'scriptMap' => array(
                'jquery.js'=>false,
                'jquery.min.js'=>false,
            ),
        ),
    ),

    // …
);
```

Further reading

For further information, refer to the following URLs:

▶ http://api.jquery.com/

▶ http://docs.jquery.com/Ajax/jQuery.ajax#options

▶ http://www.yiiframework.com/doc/api/CHtml#ajax-detail

▶ http://www.yiiframework.com/doc/api/CHtml#ajaxButton-detail

▶ http://www.yiiframework.com/doc/api/CHtml#ajaxSubmitButton-detail

▶ http://www.yiiframework.com/doc/api/CHtml#ajaxLink-detail

See also

▶ The recipes named *Managing assets* and *Working with JSON* in this chapter

▶ The recipe named *Passing configuration from PHP to JavaScript* in this chapter

Managing assets

An ability to manage assets is one of the greatest parts of Yii. It is especially useful in the following cases:

▶ When you want to implement an extension that stores its JavaScript, CSS, and images in its own folder and is not accessible from a browser

▶ When you need to pre-process your assets: combine JavaScript, compress it, and so on

▶ When you use assets multiple times per page and want to avoid duplicates

While the first two cases could be considered as bonus ones, the third one solves many widget reusing problems.

Let's create a simple Facebook event widget which will publish and use its own CSS, JavaScript, and an image.

Getting ready

▶ Create a fresh Yii application using `yiic webapp` as described in the official guide

▶ Check that `assets` directory under application's `webroot` (where `index.php` is) has write permissions; assets will be written there

▶ Generate and download a preloader image from `http://ajaxload.info/`

How to do it...

Let's do some planning first. In Yii, you can place your widgets virtually inside any directory and often, it is `protected/components`. It is acceptable to have one or two classes inside, but when the number of classes increases, it can create problems. Therefore, let's place our widget into `protected/extensions/facebook_events`. Create an `assets` directory inside the widget and put inside the `ajax-loader.gif` you have just downloaded. Also, create `facebook_events.css` and `facebook_events.js` in the same directory.

1. Therefore, let's start with the widget class itself `protected/extensions/facebook_events/EFacebookEvents.php`:

```php
<?php
class EFacebookEvents extends CWidget
{
    public $keyword;

    private $loadingImageUrl;
    protected $url = "https://graph.facebook.com/search?q=%s&type=
        event&callback=?";
```

```
    protected function getUrl()
    {
       return sprintf($this->url, urlencode($this->keyword));
    }

    public function init()
    {
       $assetsDir = dirname(__FILE__).'/assets';
       $cs = Yii::app()->getClientScript();

       $cs->registerCoreScript("jquery");

       // Publishing and registering JavaScript file
       $cs->registerScriptFile(
          Yii::app()->assetManager->publish(
             $assetsDir.'/facebook_events.js'
          ),
          CClientScript::POS_END
       );

       // Publishing and registering CSS file
       $cs->registerCssFile(
          Yii::app()->assetManager->publish(
             $assetsDir.'/facebook_events.css'
          )
       );

       // Publishing image. publish returns the actual URL
       // asset can be accessed with
       $this->loadingImageUrl = Yii::app()->assetManager->publish(
             $assetsDir.'/ajax-loader.gif'
       );
    }

    public function run()
    {
       $this->render("body", array(
          'url' => $this->getUrl(),
          'loadingImageUrl' => $this->loadingImageUrl,,
          'keyword' => $this->keyword,
       ));
    }
}
```

2. Now let's define body view we are using inside run method `protected/ extensions/ facebook_events/views/body.php`:

```php
<div class="facebook-events" data-url="<?php echo $url?>">
    <h2><?php echo $keyword?> events</h2>
    <div class="data">
        <?php echo CHtml::image($loadingImageUrl)?>
    </div>
</div>
```

3. We will need to put the following into `facebook_events.js`:

```javascript
jQuery(function($){
    $(".facebook-events").each(function(){
        var url = $(this).data("url");
        var container = $(".data", this);

        $.getJSON(url,function(json){
            var html = "<ul>";
            $.each(json.data,function(){
                html += "<li>"+
                    "<p><strong>" + this.name + "</strong>
                        </p><p>"+this.location
                    "</p></li>";
            });
            html += "</ul>";
            container.html(html);
        });
    });
});
```

4. Write the following in `facebook_events.css` created previously:

```css
.facebook-events {
    padding: 10px;
    width: 400px;
    float: left;
}

.facebook-events ul {
    padding: 0;
}

.facebook-events li {
    list-style: none;
    border: 1px solid #ccc;
    padding: 10px;
    margin: 2px;
}
```

5. That is it. Our widget is ready. Let's use it. Open your `protected/views/site/index.php` and add the following code to it:

```php
<?php $this->widget("ext.facebook_events.EFacebookEvents", array(
    'keyword' => 'php',
))?>

<?php $this->widget("ext.facebook_events.EFacebookEvents", array(
    'keyword' => 'jquery',
))?>
```

6. Now, it is time to check our application homepage. There should be two blocks with Facebook events named **php events** and **jquery events**, as shown in the following screenshot:

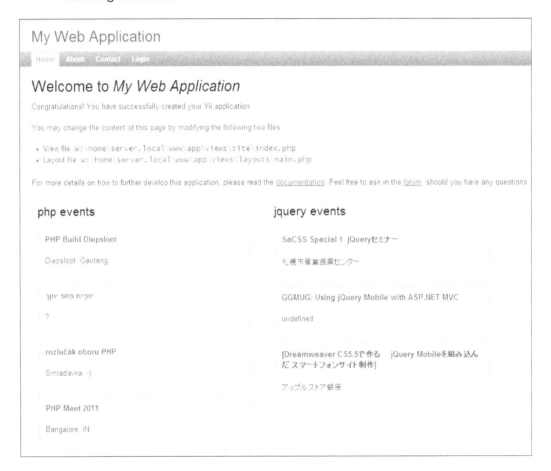

How it works...

When we use `$this->widget` in the `site/index` view, two `EFacebookEvents` methods are run: `init` which publishes assets and connects them to the page, and `run` which renders widget HTML. First, we use `CAssetManager::publish` to copy our file into the `assets` directory visible from the web. It returns URL that can be used to access the resource. In the case of JavaScript and CSS, we use `CClientScript` methods that add necessary `<script>` and `<style>` tags and prevent duplication. As for an image, we pass its URL to the `body` view that uses it to render a placeholder with `CHtml::image`. When JavaScript is loaded, it makes requests to Facebook API (described at `http://developers.facebook.com/docs/api`) and replaces placeholder with the actual data received.

There's more...

There is more about working with assets.

What is inside the assets directory?

Let's check our `assets` directory. It should look similar to the following:

```
assets
  1a6630a0\
    main.css
  2bb97318\
    pager.css
  4ab2ffe\
    jquery.js
    ...
```

Directories such as `1a6630a0` are used to prevent collisions of files with similar names from different directories. The name of the directory is a hash of complete path to the published asset directory. Therefore, assets from the same directory are copied to the same place. This means that if you publish both the image and the CSS file, you can reference images from CSS using relative paths.

Publishing an entire directory

Using `CAssetManager::publish`, you can publish an entire directory recursively. The difference is that single files are monitored after being published, whereas directories are not.

Further reading

For further information, refer to the following URL:

- ▶ `http://www.yiiframework.com/doc/api/CAssetManager`
- ▶ `http://www.yiiframework.com/doc/api/CClientScript`
- ▶ `http://www.yiiframework.com/doc/api/CHtml#asset`

See also

▶ The recipe named *Creating a widget* in *Chapter 8, Extending Yii*

Including resources into the page

Yii has a special class named `CClientScript` that can help to include scripts, CSS, and other resources into the page.

How to do it...

We will start with including a script. There are three types of scripts, namely, external scripts, core scripts, and inline scripts.

1. External script is a script located in a file and accessible through its own URL. For example, to include a script with URL `http://example.com/js/main.js`, you can use the following code:

```
Yii::app()->clientScript->registerScriptFile
   ("http://example.com/js/main.js");
```

2. In order to control the place where script will be inserted, you can pass one of the following constants as the second parameter:

`CClientScript::POS_HEAD`	In the head section right before the title element
`CClientScript::POS_BEGIN`	At the beginning of the body section
`CClientScript::POS_END`	At the end of the body section

3. Core scripts are the ones bundled with Yii, such as jQuery. You can include a core script in the following way:

```
Yii::app()->clientScript->registerCoreScript('jquery');
```

4. All packages are listed in `framework/web/js/packages.php`:

```
return array(
    'jquery'=>array(
       'js'=>array(YII_DEBUG ? 'jquery.js' : 'jquery.min.js'),
    ),
    'yii'=>array(
       'js'=>array('jquery.yii.js'),
       'depends'=>array('jquery'),
    ),
    'yiitab'=>array(
       'js'=>array('jquery.yiitab.js'),
```

```
        'depends'=>array('jquery'),
    ),
    'yiiactiveform'=>array(
        'js'=>array('jquery.yiiactiveform.js'),
        'depends'=>array('jquery'),
    ),
    'jquery.ui'=>array(
        'js'=>array('jui/js/jquery-ui.min.js'),
        'depends'=>array('jquery'),
    ),
    ...
```

5. In this list, keys of the array such as `jquery`, `yii`, `yiitab`, `yiiactiveform` are the names you can use with `registerClientScript` and the corresponding arrays are the real script file names relative to `framework/web/js/source` that are actually loaded.

6. Inline scripts are the scripts contained in a page body. Typically, these are ones different at every request. You can include these type of scripts in the following way:

    ```
    Yii::app()->clientScript->registerScript('myscript', 'echo "Hello,
    world!";', CClientScript::POS_READY);
    ```

    The first parameter is the unique script ID you have chosen. The second parameter is the script itself. The third one tells Yii where to include a script. Additionally there are two more positions to ones used for `registerScriptFile`:

    | CClientScript::POS_LOAD | In the `window.onload()` function |
    | CClientScript::POS_READY | In the jQuery's `ready` function |

Now, let's move on to CSS. There are two types of CSS: inline and external (no core type this time).

1. In order to include an external CSS, you can use the following code:

    ```
    Yii::app()->clientScript->registerCssFile
        ('http://example.com/css/main.css');
    ```

    Additionally, this method takes a second parameter which allows you to specify which media type you want to include CSS for, such as `screen` or `print`. There is no position parameter, as the only valid place to include a CSS is inside a `head` tag.

    Inline CSS should be avoided wherever possible, but in case you really need it, you can include it in the following way:

    ```
    Yii::app()->registerCss('myCSS', 'body {margin: 0; padding: 0}',
        'all');
    ```

2. In the preceding code, `myCSS` is the unique ID. Then, we have the actual CSS code and a media type.

How it works...

The Yii's `CClientScript` methods which we have reviewed do not include scripts and CSS instantly. Instead, resources are stored until application controller calls the `render` method. Then, it finds a proper place in layout and inserts all needed script and CSS blocks and tags. If we include a resource with the same name or URL twice, then it will be included only once. This allows us to efficiently use resources in a widget, view partial, or any reusable piece of code.

There's more

We have reviewed the most common resource types: JavaScript and CSS. However, there is more.

Using custom script packages

While using Yii, you can leverage package features to manage script dependencies in the same way core dependencies are managed. The feature is described well at the following API page:

```
http://www.yiiframework.com/doc/api/CClientScript#packages-detail
```

Registering linked resources

`CClientScript` offers another method that allows you to register a custom `<link` tag. For example, it can be useful to add an RSS link for a specific controller action as follows:

```
Yii::app()->clientScript->registerLinkTag(
    'alternate',
      'application/rss+xml',
      $this->createUrl('rss/articles')
);
```

Registering meta tags

In addition, `CClientScript` allows registering of meta tags such as `description` or `keywords` by using the `registerMetaTag` method. For example, in order to specify a document encoding, you can use the following code:

```
Yii::app()->clientScript->registerMetaTag(' text/html;charset=utf-8',
null, 'Content-Type');
```

Further reading

For further information, refer to the following URLs:

- ▶ `http://www.yiiframework.com/doc/api/CClientScript`
- ▶ `http://www.yiiframework.com/doc/guide/1.1/en/topics.performance`

See also

- ▶ The recipe named *Managing assets* in this chapter
- ▶ The recipe named *Loading a block through AJAX* in this chapter

Working with JSON

JSON is a very simple, compact, and therefore a widely used format for AJAX applications data exchange. Yii has a few handy ways to work with it. Therefore, let's create a simple application that will show news list and update it every two seconds.

Getting ready

1. Create a new application by using the `yiic webapp` tool.

2. Create and setup a new database.

3. Add a table named `news` with at least `id`, `created_on`, and `title` fields:

```
CREATE TABLE `news` (
  `id` int(11) unsigned NOT NULL AUTO_INCREMENT,
  `created_on` int(11) unsigned NOT NULL,
  `title` varchar(255) NOT NULL,
  PRIMARY KEY (`id`)
)
```

4. Generate a `News` model using Gii.

How to do it...

1. Create a new controller named `protected/controllers/NewsController.php` as follows:

```php
<?php
class NewsController extends Controller
{
    public function filters()
    {
        return array(
            'ajaxOnly + data',
```

```
            );
        }

        public function actionIndex()
        {
            $this->render('index');
        }

        public function actionData()
        {
            $criteria = new CDbCriteria();
            $criteria->order = 'created_on DESC';
            $criteria->limit = 10;
            $news = News::model()->findAll($criteria);

            echo CJSON::encode($news);
        }

        public function actionAddRandomNews()
        {
            $news = new News();
            $news->title = "Item #".rand(1, 10000);
            $news->created_on = time();
            $news->save();
            echo "OK";
        }
    }
```

2. Moreover, create a view named `protected/views/news/index.php` as follows:

```
<div class="news-list">
    Loading...
</div>

<?php Yii::app()->clientScript->registerCoreScript("jquery")?>
<script type="text/javascript">
    jQuery(function($) {
        var newsList = $('.news-list');

        function updateNews(){
            newsList.html("Loading...");
            $.ajax({
                url: "<?php echo $this->createUrl('data')?>",
                dataType: 'json',
                cache: false,
                success: function(data) {
                    var out = "<ol>";
                    $(data).each(function(){
```

```
            out+="<li>"+this.title+"</li>";
        });
        out += "</ol>";
        newsList.html(out);
    }
  });
}

updateNews();

setInterval(function(){
    updateNews()
}, 2000);
 });
</script>
```

3. Now, run the `index` action of the news controller and try to add a few records into the news database table by running the `addRandomNews` action. Do not refresh the `index` page. News added will appear on the index page once every two seconds, as shown in the following screenshot:

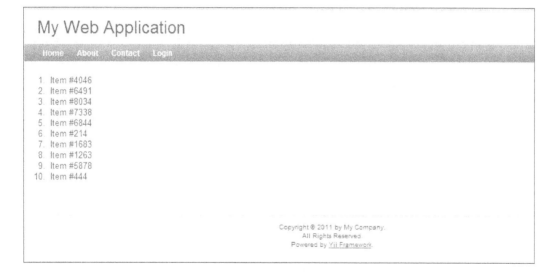

How it works...

The `index` action does nothing special. It simply renders a view that includes a `div` container and some JavaScript code. As we are using jQuery, we need to ensure it is included:

```
<?php Yii::app()->clientScript->registerCoreScript("jquery")?>
```

Then, we define a function named `updateNews` and run it every 2,000 milliseconds using the core JavaScript `setInterval` function. In `updateNews`, we make an AJAX request to the data action of the same controller, to process the JSON response and replace the current content of placeholder `div` with formatted data.

In `actionData`, we get the latest news and convert them to JSON format by passing the result to `CJSON::encode`.

There's more

For further information, refer to the following URLs:

▶ `http://api.jquery.com/category/ajax/`

▶ `http://www.yiiframework.com/doc/api/CJSON/`

▶ `http://www.yiiframework.com/doc/api/CClientScript/#registerCore Script-detail`

See also

▶ The recipe named *Loading a block through AJAX* in this chapter

Passing configuration from PHP to JavaScript

You can store application parameters in your configuration file `protected/config/main.php` that we can access using `Yii::app()->params['paramName']`. When your application uses the JavaScript code, it is handy to have these parameters available for it. Let's see how to do it in a simple and effective way.

Getting ready

1. Set up a fresh application using the `yiic webapp` tool. It should generate application parameters array in `protected/config/main.php`:

   ```
   'params'=>array(
       // this is used in contact page
       'adminEmail'=>'webmaster@example.com',
   ),
   ```

2. Add additional parameters as follows:

   ```
   'params'=>array(
       // this is used in contact page
       'adminEmail'=>'webmaster@example.com',
       'alert' => array(
   ```

```
        'enabled' => true,
        'message' => 'Hello there!',
    ),
),
```

How to do it...

1. Create a controller named `protected/controllers/AlertController.php` as follows:

```php
<?php
class AlertController extends Controller
{
  function actionIndex()
  {
    $config = CJavaScript::encode
      (Yii::app()->params->toArray());
    Yii::app()->clientScript->registerScript
      ('appConfig', "var config = ".$config.";",
      CClientScript::POS_HEAD););

    $this->render('index');
  }
}
```

2. Moreover, create view named `protected/views/alert/index.php` as follows:

```
<script>
    if(config && config.alert && config.alert.enabled &&
      config.alert.message){
        alert(config.alert.message);
    }
</script>
```

3. Now, if you will run the `alert` controller `index` action, you should get a standard JavaScript alert window saying **Hello there!**, as shown in the following screenshot:

How it works...

We use `CJavaScript::encode` that converts PHP data structures into JavaScript ones to turn Yii application parameters into a JavaScript array. Then, we register a script that assigns it to a global variable `config`. Then, in our view JavaScript code, we just use this global variable `config`.

See also

▶ The recipe named *Managing assets* in this chapter

▶ The recipe named *Loading a block through AJAX* in this chapter

Handling variable number of inputs

Sometimes an application requires a form with variable number of inputs. For example, a task management application can provide a screen where you can add one or more tasks to your task list. An example of such an application is shown in the following screenshot:

By default, the page will display one task and two buttons: **Add task** will add another empty task and **Save** will reload a form with all the tasks added. Let's check how we can solve it.

Getting ready

Create a fresh application using `yiic webapp`.

How to do it...

For our example, we will not save any data into the database. Instead, we will learn how to get a form with variable number of fields up and running, and how to collect data submitted with it.

1. Therefore, we will start with the task model. As we agreed not to use database, CFormModel will be enough. `protected/models/Task.php`:

```php
<?php
class Task extends CFormModel
{
   public $title;
   public $text;

   public function rules()
   {
      return array(
         array('title', 'required'),
         array('text', 'safe'),
      );
   }
}
```

2. Now, the controller `protected/controllers/TaskController.php`:

```php
<?php
class TaskController extends Controller
{
   public function filters()
   {
      return array(
         'ajaxOnly + field'
      );
   }

   public function actionIndex()
   {
      $models = array();

      if(!empty($_POST['Task']))
      {
         foreach($_POST['Task'] as $taskData)
```

```php
        {
            $model = new Task();
            $model->setAttributes($taskData);
            if($model->validate())
                $models[] = $model;
        }
    }

    if(!empty($models)){
        // We've received some models and validated them.
        // If you want to save the data you can do it here.
    }
    else
        $models[] = new Task();

    $this->render('index', array(
        'models' => $models,
    ));
}

public function actionField($index)
{
    $model = new Task();
    $this->renderPartial('_task', array(
        'model' => $model,
        'index' => $index,
    ));
}
}
```

3. Now, the `pretected/views/task/index.php` view:

```php
<div class="form">
<?php echo CHtml::beginForm()?>
    <ul class="tasks">
        <?php for($i=0; $i<count($models); $i++):?>
            <?php $this->renderPartial('_task', array(
                'model' => $models[$i],
                'index' => $i,
            ))?>
        <?php endfor ?>
    </ul>
    <div class="row buttons">
        <?php echo CHtml::button('Add task',
            array('class' => 'tasks-add'))?>
```

```php
<?php Yii::app()->clientScript->registerCoreScript
    ("jquery")?>
<script>
    $(".tasks-add").click(function(){
        $.ajax({
            success: function(html){
                $(".tasks").append(html);
            },
            type: 'get',
            url: '<?php echo $this->createUrl('field')?>',
            data: {
                index: $(".tasks li").size()
            },
            cache: false,
            dataType: 'html'
        });
    });
</script>
<?php echo CHtml::submitButton('Save')?>
    </div>
<?php echo CHtml::endForm()?>
</div>
```

4. Finally, a partial `protected/views/task/_task.php`:

```php
<li>
    <div class="row">
        <?php echo CHtml::activeLabel($model, "[$index]title")?>
        <?php echo CHtml::activeTextField($model, "[$index]title")?>
    </div>
    <div class="row">
        <?php echo CHtml::activeLabel($model, "[$index]text")?>
        <?php echo CHtml::activeTextArea($model, "[$index]text")?>
    </div>
</li>
```

5. That is it. Now run the `index` action of the `task` controller and check it in action, as shown in the following screenshot:

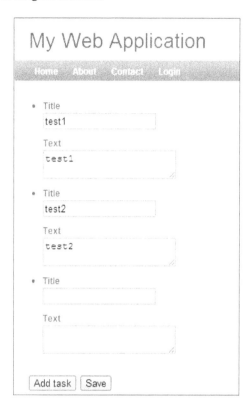

How it works...

Let's review how it works starting from the controller's `index` action. As we are working with more than one data item, we need to collect them accordingly. Same as with a single model, a form will pass its data in `$_POST['model_name']`. The only difference is that in our case, there will be an array of data items as follows:

```
if(!empty($_POST['Task']))
{
    foreach($_POST['Task'] as $taskData)
    {
        $model = new Task();
        $model->setAttributes($taskData);
        if($model->validate())
            $models[] = $model;
    }
}
```

For each data item, we are creating a `Task` model, setting its attributes with data item and if it is valid, storing a model into the `$models` array as follows:

```
if(!empty($models)){
    // We've received some models and validated them.
    // If you want to save the data you can do it here.
}
else
    $models[] = new Task();
```

If the `$models` array is not empty, then there is data passed from the form and it is valid. If there is no data in the `$models`, then we still need at least one item to show it in the form.

We are not actually saving data in this example. When we use Active Record models, we can actually save data using `$model->save()`.Then, we just render the `index` view when we render a form as follows:

```
<?php for($i=0; $i<count($models); $i++):?>
    <?php $this->renderPartial('_task', array(
        'model' => $models[$i],
        'index' => $i,
    ))?>
<?php endfor ?>
```

As there are many models, we need to render fields for each one. That is done in the `_task` view partial:

```
<li>
    <div class="row">
        <?php echo CHtml::activeLabel($model, "[$index]title")?>
        <?php echo CHtml::activeTextField($model, "[$index]title")?>
    </div>
    <div class="row">
        <?php echo CHtml::activeLabel($model, "[$index]text")?>
        <?php echo CHtml::activeTextArea($model, "[$index]text")?>
    </div>
</li>
```

Note how we use active labels and active fields. For each one, we specify a model and a name in format `[model_index]field_name`. The preceding code will generate the following HTML:

```
<li>
<div class="row">
    <label for="Task_0_title">Title</label>
    <input name="Task[0][title]" id="Task_0_title" type="text"
        value="" />
```

```
        </div>
        <div class="row">
            <label for="Task_0_text">Text</label>
            <textarea name="Task[0][text]" id="Task_0_text"></textarea></div>
        </li>
        <li>
            <div class="row">
                <label for="Task_1_title">Title</label>
                <input name="Task[1][title]" id="Task_1_title" type="text"
                        value="" />
            </div>
            <div class="row">
                <label for="Task_1_text">Text</label>
                <textarea name="Task[1][text]" id="Task_1_text">
        </textarea></div>
        </li>
```

Fields such as `Task[0][title]` are a special PHP feature. When submitted, parameters with such names are automatically parsed into PHP arrays.

Now, let's review how the **Add task** button works:

```
<?php echo CHtml::button('Add task', array('class' => 'tasks-add'))?>
<?php Yii::app()->clientScript->registerCoreScript("jquery")?>
<script>
    $(".tasks-add").click(function(){
        $.ajax({
            success: function(html){
                $(".tasks").append(html);
            },
            type: 'get',
            url: '<?php echo $this->createUrl('field')?>',
            data: {
                index: $(".tasks li").size()
            },
            cache: false,
            dataType: 'html'
        });
    });
</script>
```

We are adding a button with a class `tasks-add` and a jQuery script that attaches the `onClick` handler to it. On click, we send an AJAX request to the `field` action of our controller with parameter `index`. Parameter's value equals the number of data items in the form. The `field` action responds with a part of an HTML form that we append to what we already have.

There's more...

You can find additional information about handling multiple inputs in the official guide at the following URL:

`http://www.yiiframework.com/doc/guide/en/form.table`

See also

▶ The recipe named *Loading a block through AJAX* in this chapter

4
Working with Forms

In this chapter, we will cover:

- ▶ Writing your own validators
- ▶ Uploading files
- ▶ Adding CAPTCHA
- ▶ Customizing CAPTCHA
- ▶ Creating a custom input widget with CWidget

Introduction

Yii makes working with forms a breeze and the documentation on it is almost complete. Still, there are some areas that need clarification and examples. We will describe them in this chapter.

Writing your own validators

Yii provides a good set of built-in form validators which cover the most typical of developer needs and are highly configurable. However, in some cases, the developer may face a need to create a custom validator.

A good example would be the website ownership validation. For a few of their services, Google requires you to upload a file with the name and content specified to your website and then checks if it is there. We will do the same.

There are two ways to achieve it. First, you can use a class method as validator, and the second way is to create a separate class.

Create a new application using `yiic webapp` as described in the official guide.

1. We will start with the class method approach. First, we need to implement a form model. So, create `protected/models/SiteConfirmation.php` as follows:

```php
<?php
class SiteConfirmation extends CFormModel {
    public $url;

    public function rules()
    {
        return array(
            array('url', 'confirm'),
        );
    }

    public function confirm($attribute,$params)
    {
        $ch = curl_init();
        curl_setopt($ch, CURLOPT_URL, $this->url);
        curl_setopt($ch, CURLOPT_RETURNTRANSFER, 1);
        $output = curl_exec($ch);
        curl_close($ch);
        if(trim($output)!='code here')
            $this->addError('url','Please upload file first.');
    }
}
```

2. Now we will use our model from our test controller. Create `protected/controllers/TestController.php` as follows:

```php
<?php
class TestController extends CController
{
    function actionIndex()
    {
        $confirmation = new SiteConfirmation();
        $confirmation->url = 'http://yiicookbook.org/verify.html';
        if($confirmation->validate())
            echo 'OK';
        else
            echo 'Please upload a file.';
    }
}
```

3. Now try to run the test controller. You should get **OK** because there is a file with the `code here` text available from `http://yiicookbook.org/verify.html`. If you replace the confirmation URL with another one, then you get **Please upload file first** as there is no such file uploaded.

How it works...

In the `SiteConfirmation` model, we define a `$url` field and add a `rules` method that defines a single validation rule for this field. As there is no built-in validator named `confirm`, Yii assumes that we want to describe the validation rule in a method named `confirm`. In this method, we use standard PHP's `CURL` to get `verify.html` file contents from a remote host and compare its content with the `code here` string. If the file content is different, then we add an error using the `addError` method.

Optionally, we can use two validation method arguments: `$attribute` and `$params`. For example, if we specify the validation rule in the following way:

```
array('url', 'confirm', 'param1' => 'value1', 'param2' => 'value3'),
```

then we get the `$attribute` value set to `'url'` and the `$params` value set to the following:

```
array
(
    'param1' => 'value1'
    'param2' => 'value3'
)
```

There's more...

As we probably want to reuse this kind of validator, we will move its functionality from a model method to a separate class. So, create a file named `protected/components/RemoteFileValidator.php` as follows:

```php
<?php
class RemoteFileValidator extends CValidator
{
    public $content = '';

    protected function validateAttribute($object,$attribute)
    {
        $value=$object->$attribute;

        $ch = curl_init();
        curl_setopt($ch, CURLOPT_URL, $value);
        curl_setopt($ch, CURLOPT_RETURNTRANSFER, 1);
        $output = curl_exec($ch);
```

```
        curl_close($ch);

        if(trim($output)!=$this->content)
            $this->addError($object,$attribute,'Please upload file
                first.');
    }
}
```

The custom validator class should extend `CValidator` and implement its abstract `validateAttribute` method. Arguments passed on to it are `$object`, which is an instance of the model validated, and `$attribute` that contains validated attribute name. Parameters passed are assigned to corresponding public properties of the validator class.

That is it. Now, we will use it. In the `SiteConfirmation` model, we should change the validation rule to the following:

```
array('url', 'RemoteFileValidator', 'content' => 'code here'),
```

Here we have used an external validator name. If there is no method with the same name in the model and no same named built-in validator, then Yii will try to find an external validator class with the name or path alias specified.

The rest of the code stays untouched and now you can reuse the validator in other models.

Further reading

For further information, refer to the following URLs:

▶ `http://www.yiiframework.com/doc/api/CValidator/`

▶ `http://www.yiiframework.com/doc/api/CModel#rules-detail`

Uploading files

Handling file uploads is a pretty common task for a web application. Yii has some helpful classes built-in. Let's create a simple form that will allow uploading ZIP archives and storing them in `protected/uploads`.

Getting ready

▶ Create a fresh application using `yiic webapp`

▶ In your `protected` directory, create an `uploads` directory

How to do it...

1. We will start with the model, so create `protected/models/Upload.php` as follows:

```php
<?php
class Upload extends CFormModel
{
    public $file;

    public function rules()
    {
        return array(
            array('file', 'file', 'types'=>'zip'),
        );
    }
}
```

2. Now we will move on to the controller, so create `protected/controllers/UploadController.php`:

```php
<?php
class UploadController extends Controller
{
    function actionIndex()
    {
        $dir = Yii::getPathOfAlias('application.uploads');
        $uploaded = false;

        $model=new Upload();

        if(isset($_POST['Upload']))
        {
            $model->attributes=$_POST['Upload'];
            $file=CUploadedFile::getInstance($model,'file');
            if($model->validate()){
                $uploaded = $file->saveAs($dir.'/'.$file->getName());
            }
        }

        $this->render('index', array(
            'model' => $model,
            'uploaded' => $uploaded,
            'dir' => $dir,
        ));
    }
}
```

3. Finally, a view `protected/views/upload/index.php`:

```php
<?php if($uploaded):?>
<p>File was uploaded. Check <?php echo $dir?>.</p>
<?php endif ?>
<?php echo CHtml::beginForm('','post',array
    ('enctype'=>'multipart/form-data'))?>
    <?php echo CHtml::error($model, 'file')?>
    <?php echo CHtml::activeFileField($model, 'file')?>
    <?php echo CHtml::submitButton('Upload')?>
<?php echo CHtml::endForm()?>
```

4. That is it. Now run the upload controller and try uploading both ZIP archives and other files, as shown in the following screenshot:

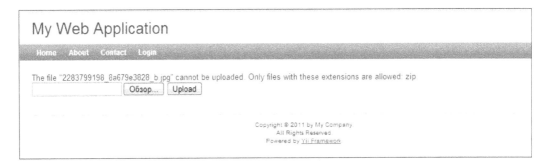

How it works...

The model we use is pretty simple. We define only one field named `$file` and a validation rule that uses file validator (`CFileValidator`) which reads "only zip files are allowed".

Controller is a bit more complicated. We will review it line by line:

```php
$dir = Yii::getPathOfAlias('application.uploads');
$uploaded = false;
$model=new Upload();
if(isset($_POST['Upload']))
{
$model->attributes=$_POST['Upload'];
```

`$dir` is a directory that will hold the ZIP archives uploaded. We set it to `protected/uploads` using an alias. `$uploaded` is a flag that determines if we need to display a success message. Then, we create a model instance and fill it with data from `$_POST` if form is submitted.

```php
$file=CUploadedFile::getInstance($model,'file');
if($model->validate()){
```

```
$file->saveAs($dir.'/'.$file->getName());
        $uploaded = true;
```

Then, we use `CUploadedFile::getInstance` that gives us access to use `CUploadedFile` instance. This class is a wrapper around the `$_FILE` array that PHP fills when the file is uploaded.

If we make sure that the file is a ZIP archive by calling the model's `validate` method, then we save the file using `CUploadedFile::saveAs`.

The rest is passing some values to the view:

```
<?php if($uploaded):?>
<p>File was uploaded. Check <?php echo $dir?>.</p>
<?php endif ?>
```

If there is a `$uploaded` flag set to `true`, then we display a message.

In order to upload a file, the HTML form must meet the following two important requirements:

1. Method should be set to `POST`.
2. The `enctype` attribute should be set to `'multipart/form-data'`.

We can generate such HTML using the `CHtml` helper or `CActiveForm` with `htmlOptions` set. This time, `CHtml` was used:

```
<?php echo CHtml::beginForm('','post',array('enctype'=>'multipart/
form-data'))?>
```

The rest is the standard form: We display an error and a field for model's `file` attribute and render a submit button.

There's more...

If you want to upload multiple files, then you should modify the code in the following way:

```
if(isset($_POST['Upload']))
{
    $model->attributes=$_POST['Upload'];
    $files=CUploadedFile::getInstance($model,'file');
    if($model->validate())
    {
        foreach($files as $file)
          $file->saveAs($dir.'/'.$file->getName());
```

In a view, you should echo file fields in the following way:

```php
<?php echo CHtml::activeFileField($model, "[0]file")?>
<?php echo CHtml::activeFileField($model, "[1]file")?>
<?php echo CHtml::activeFileField($model, "[2]file")?>
```

File validation

The file validator we use in a model allows us not only to limit files to a certain type, but also to set other limits, such as file size or number of files in case of a multiple file upload. For example, the following rule will only allow uploading images with file size less than one megabyte:

```php
array('file', 'file', 'types'=>'jpg, gif, png', 'maxSize' => 1048576),
```

Further reading

For further information, refer to the following URLs:

▶ http://www.yiiframework.com/doc/api/CFileValidator

▶ http://www.yiiframework.com/doc/api/CUploadedFile

See also

▶ The recipe named *Handling variable number of inputs* in *Chapter 3, AJAX and jQuery*

Adding CAPTCHA

Nowadays, on the Internet, if you leave a form without a spam protection, you will get a ton of spam data entered in a short time. Yii includes a CAPTCHA component that makes adding such a protection a breeze. The only problem is that there is no systematic guide on how to use it.

In the following example, we will add a CAPTCHA protection to a simple form.

Getting ready

1. Create a fresh application using `yiic webapp`
2. Create a form model named `protected/models/EmailForm.php` as follows:

```php
<?phpclass EmailForm extends CFormModel
{
    public $email;

    function rules(){
```

```php
        return array(
          array('email', 'email'),
        );
    }
}
```

3. Create a controller named `protected/controllers/EmailController.php` as follows:

```php
<?php
class EmailController extends Controller
{
    public function actionIndex()
    {
        $success = false;

        $model = new EmailForm();
        if(!empty($_POST['EmailForm']))
        {
            $model->setAttributes($_POST['EmailForm']);
            if($model->validate())
            {
                $success = true;
                // handle form here
            }
        }
        $this->render('index', array(
            'model' => $model,
            'success' => $success,
        ));
    }
}
```

4. Create a view named `protected/views/email/index.php` as follows:

```php
<?php if($success):?>
<p>Success!</p>
<?php endif?>

<?php echo CHtml::beginForm()?>
    <p>
        <?php echo CHtml::activeLabel($model, 'email')?>
        <?php echo CHtml::activeTextField($model, 'email')?>
        <?php echo CHtml::error($model, 'email')?>
    </p>
    <p>
        <?php echo CHtml::submitButton()?>
    </p>
<?php echo CHtml::endForm()?>
```

5. Now, we have an e-mail submission form which validates the e-mail field. Let's add CAPTCHA.

How to do it...

1. First, we need to customize the form model. We need to add `$verifyCode` which will hold the verification code entered and add a validation rule for it.

```php
<?php
class EmailForm extends CFormModel
{
    public $verifyCode;
    public $email;

    function rules(){
        return array(
         array('email', 'email'),
         array('verifyCode', 'captcha', 'allowEmpty'=>
           !CCaptcha::checkRequirements()),
        );
    }
}
```

2. Then, we need to add an external action to the controller. Add the following code to it:

```php
public function actions()
{
    return array(
        'captcha'=>array(
            'class'=>'CCaptchaAction',
        ),
    );
}
```

3. In a view, we need to show an additional field and the CAPTCHA image. The following code will do this for us:

```
<?php if(CCaptcha::checkRequirements() &&
    Yii::app()->user->isGuest):?>
  <p>
    <?php echo CHtml::activeLabelEx($model, 'verifyCode')?>
    <?php $this->widget('CCaptcha')?>
  </p>
  <p>
    <?php echo CHtml::activeTextField($model, 'verifyCode')?>
    <?php echo CHtml::error($model, 'verifyCode')?>
  </p>
<?php endif?>
```

4. That is it. Now, you can run the `email` controller and check CAPTCHA in action, as shown in the following screenshot:

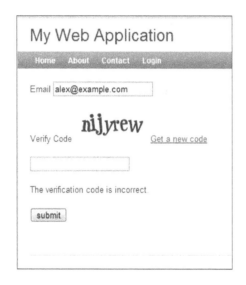

If there are no errors on the screen and no CAPTCHA field in the form, then most probably, you don't have the GD PHP extension installed and configured. GD is required for CAPTCHA because it generates images. We have added several `CCaptcha::checkRequirements()` checks, so the application will not use CAPTCHA if the image cannot be displayed, but will still work.

How it works...

In a view, we call the CCaptcha widget that renders the `<img` tag with a `src` attribute pointing to CCaptchaAction we added to the controller. In this action, an image with a random word is generated. The word generated is a code that the user should enter into the form. It is stored in a user session and an image is displayed to the user.

When the user enters the e-mail and verification code into the form, we assign these values to the form model and then validate it. For the verification of the code field, we use CCaptchaValidator. It gets the code from the user session and compares it to the code entered. If they don't match, then the model data is considered invalid.

There's more...

If you restrict access to controller actions by using the `accessRules` controller method, then don't forget to grant everyone access to it:

```
public function accessRules() {
    return array(
        // …
        array('allow',
            'actions'=>array('captcha'),
            'users'=>array('*'),
        ),
        array('deny',
            'users'=>array('*'),
        ),
    );
}
```

Further reading:

For further information, refer to the following URLs:

- http://www.yiiframework.com/doc/api/CCaptcha/
- http://www.yiiframework.com/doc/api/CCaptchaAction/
- http://www.yiiframework.com/doc/api/CCaptchaValidator/

See also

- The recipe named *Using external actions* in *Chapter 2, Router, Controller, and Views*
- The recipe named *Customizing CAPTCHA* in this chapter

Customizing CAPTCHA

A standard Yii CAPTCHA is good enough to protect you from spam, but there are situations where you may want to customize it, such as the following:

▶ You face a spam-bot that can read image text and need to add more challenge

▶ You want to make it more interesting or easier to enter the CAPTCHA text

In our example, we will modify Yii's CAPTCHA, so it will require the user to solve a really simple arithmetic puzzle instead of just repeating a text in an image.

Getting ready

As a starting point for this example, we will take the result of the *Adding CAPTCHA* recipe. Alternatively, you can take any form that uses CAPTCHA as we are not modifying the existing code a lot.

How to do it...

We need to customize `CCaptchaAction` which generates the code and renders its image representation. The code should be a random number and the representation should be an arithmetic expression which gives the same result.

1. Create `protected/components/MathCaptchaAction.php` as follows:

```php
<?phpclass MathCaptchaAction extends CCaptchaAction
{
    protected function generateVerifyCode()
    {
        return mt_rand((int)$this->minLength,
            (int)$this->maxLength);
    }

    public function renderImage($code)
    {
        parent::renderImage($this->getText($code));
    }

    protected function getText($code)
    {
        $code = (int)$code;
        $rand = mt_rand(1, $code-1);
        $op = mt_rand(0, 1);
        if($op)
```

```
                return $code-$rand.»+».$rand;
        else
                return $code+$rand.»-».$rand;
    }
}
```

2. Now, in our controller `actions` method, we need to replace `CCaptchaAction`
    with our own CAPTCHA action as follows:

```
public function actions()
{
    return array(
        'captcha'=>array(
            'class'=>'MathCaptchaAction',
            'minLength' => 1,
            'maxLength' => 10,
        ),
    );
}
```

3. Now, run your form and try the new CAPTCHA. It will show arithmetic expressions
    with numbers from 1 to 10 and will require entering an answer, as shown in the
    following screenshot:

We override two `CCaptchaAction` methods. In `generateVerifyCode`, we generate
a random number instead of text. As we need to render an expression instead of just
showing text, we override `renderImage`. The expression itself is generated in our custom
`getText` method.

There's more...

In order to learn more about CAPTCHA, you can use the following resources:

- ▶ `http://www.yiiframework.com/doc/api/CCaptcha/`
- ▶ `http://www.yiiframework.com/doc/api/CCaptchaAction/`
- ▶ `http://www.yiiframework.com/doc/api/CCaptchaValidator/`

See also

- ▶ The recipe named *Using external actions* in *Chapter 3, Router, Controller, and Views*
- ▶ The recipe named *Adding CAPTCHA* in this chapter

Creating a custom input widget with CInputWidget

Yii has a very good set of form widgets, but as every framework out there, Yii cannot have them all. In this recipe, we will learn how to create your own input widget. For our example, we will create a range input widget.

Getting ready

Create a fresh application by using `yiic webapp`.

How to do it...

We will start with the widget itself.

1. Create a widget class named `protected/components/RangeInputField.php` as follows:

```php
<?php
class RangeInputField extends CInputWidget
{
    public $attributeFrom;
    public $attributeTo;

    public $nameFrom;
    public $nameTo;

    public $valueFrom;
    public $valueTo;
```

```php
    function run()
    {
        if($this->hasModel())
        {
            echo CHtml::activeTextField
                ($this->model, $this->attributeFrom);
            echo ' &rarr; ';
            echo CHtml::activeTextField
                ($this->model, $this->attributeTo);
        }
        else {
            echo CHtml::textField($this->nameFrom, $this->valueFrom);
            echo ' &rarr; ';
            echo CHtml::textField($this->nameTo, $this->valueTo);
        }
    }
}
```

2. Now we need to test how it works. We will need a form model named `protected/models/RangeForm.php`:

```php
<?php
class RangeForm extends CFormModel
{
    public $from;
    public $to;

    function rules()
    {
        return array(
            array('from, to', 'numerical', 'integerOnly' => true),
            array('from', 'compare', 'compareAttribute' => 'to',
                'operator' => '<=', 'skipOnError' => true),
        );
    }
}
```

3. Now create a controller named `protected/controllers/RangeController.php` as follows:

```php
<?php
class RangeController extends Controller
{
    function actionIndex()
    {
        $success = false;
        $model = new RangeForm();
        if(!empty($_POST['RangeForm']))
        {
```

```php
        $model->setAttributes($_POST['RangeForm']);
        if($model->validate())
            $success = true;
    }

    $this->render('index', array(
        'model' => $model,
        'success' => $success,
    ));
    }
}
```

4. Create a view named `protected/views/range/index.php` as follows:

```php
<?php if($success):?>
<p>Success!</p>
<?php endif?>

<?php echo CHtml::errorSummary($model)?>
<?php echo CHtml::beginForm()?>
    <?php $this->widget('RangeInputField', array(
        'model' => $model,
        'attributeFrom' => 'from',
        'attributeTo' => 'to',
    ))?>
    <?php echo CHtml::submitButton('Submit')?>
<?php echo CHtml::endForm()?>
```

5. Now, run the `range` controller to see a widget in action, as shown in the following screenshot:

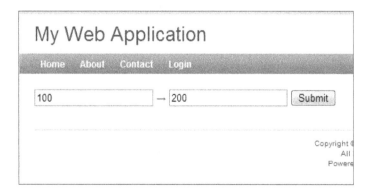

How it works...

A typical input widget can be used both with a model as an active field widget and without a model. Active field widget handles the value and validation automatically.

As there are two fields (`from` and `to`) in our widget, we define three pairs of public properties: `attribute`, `name`, and `value`. The `attribute` pair is used if there is a model passed to a widget; this means that the widget is used as an active input. The `name` and `value` pairs are used if you want to generate the input with custom names and values.

In our case, we simply override the `run` method to render two fields in a customized way. Actual field handling is delegated to `CHtml::activeTextField` and `CHtml::textField`.

In order to render a widget in a view, we use the `CController::widget` method as follows:

```php
<?php $this->widget('RangeInputField', array(
    'model' => $model,
    'attributeFrom' => 'from',
    'attributeTo' => 'to',
))?>
```

All options set in an array are assigned to the corresponding public properties of a widget.

There's more...

In order to learn more about widgets, you can use the following resources:

▶ http://www.yiiframework.com/doc/api/CInputWidget/

▶ http://www.yiiframework.com/doc/api/CWidget/

See also

▶ The recipe named *Configuring components* in *Chapter 1, Under the Hood*

▶ The recipe named *Configuring widget defaults* in *Chapter 1*

5
Testing your Application

In this chapter, we will cover:

- ▶ Setting up the testing environment
- ▶ Writing and running unit tests
- ▶ Using fixtures
- ▶ Testing the application with functional tests
- ▶ Generating code coverage reports

Introduction

In a small application, the value of testing can be unnoticeable. In large applications, it is different. When application grows and you start modifying your code, it becomes difficult not to break anything else relying on it. Even if you hire a team of professional testers, you are slowing the development a lot. However, automated testing can partially solve this problem.

Another application of automated testing is **TDD** (**Test Driven Development**). The idea is simple: When you know how a component will work, write down your requirements in a form of automated test prior to implementing a component. This way in the end, you will know if your component works as expected and will not have to write tests later.

Setting up the testing environment

In this recipe, we will prepare a testing environment that can be used to run automated test supports: unit tests and functional tests. Unit tests in Yii are based on **PHPUnit** and functional tests are based on selenium server. Additionally, you need **Xdebug** to generate code coverage reports.

Getting ready

▶ Make sure that you have properly configured PHP to work in a command-line mode.

▶ Use the `yiic webapp` tool to generate a fresh application.

How to do it...

We will start with PHPUnit.

1. To install it, we need to set up PEAR first. In most Linux environments, it is already set up, so you can skip this part if it already works.

2. To test if PEAR works, open console and type `pear`. You should get the following output:

```
D:\>pear
Commands:
build              Build an Extension From C Source
bundle             Unpacks a Pecl Package
channel-add        Add a Channel
channel-alias      Specify an alias to a channel name
channel-delete     Remove a Channel From the List
channel-discover   Initialize a Channel from its server
channel-info       Retrieve Information on a Channel
```

3. If you get the preceding output after running `pear`, then everything is OK. If not, then you need to install it by carrying out the following steps:

   ❑ Open `http://pear.php.net/go-pear` and save the content as a PHP file `go-pear.php`. Then, run it in the console with `php go-pear.php` and follow instructions.

   ❑ In Windows, it is useful to add the PEAR location to the `PATH` environment variable, so it can be used simply as `pear`.

4. Now, it is time to install the PHPUnit. Open the console and type the following:

```
pear channel-discover pear.phpunit.de
pear channel-discover components.ez.no
pear channel-discover pear.symfony-project.com
pear install phpunit/PHPUnit
```

5. Now, type `phpunit` and you should get the following output:

```
D:\>phpunit
PHPUnit 3.5.11 by Sebastian Bergmann.

Usage: phpunit [switches] UnitTest [UnitTest.php]
       phpunit [switches] <directory>

  --log-junit <file>       Log test execution in JUnit XML format to file.
  --log-tap <file>         Log test execution in TAP format to file.
  --log-dbus               Log test execution to DBUS.
  --log-json <file>        Log test execution in JSON format
```

6. Done. Now let's install the Selenium Server. There is no PEAR package for it, so go to `http://seleniumhq.org/download/` and download the latest release of the Selenium Server project. You should get an archive named like `selenium-server-standalone-2.0rc2.jar`.

7. In order to run the server, you should have the Java runtime environment installed. Go to the server directory and type the following:

   `java -jar selenium-server-standalone-2.0rc2.jar`

   You should get something similar to the following:

```
W:\usr\local\selenium>java -jar selenium-server-standalone-2.0rc2.jar
02:17:56.758 INFO - Java: Sun Microsystems Inc. 19.1-b02
02:17:56.760 INFO - OS: Windows 7 6.1 x86
02:17:56.773 INFO - v2.0 [rc2], with Core v2.0 [rc2]
02:17:57.094 INFO - RemoteWebDriver instances should connect to: http://127.0.0
1:4444/wd/hub
02:17:57.096 INFO - Version Jetty/5.1.x
02:17:57.098 INFO - Started HttpContext[/selenium-server/driver,/selenium-serve
/driver]
02:17:57.100 INFO - Started HttpContext[/selenium-server,/selenium-server]
02:17:57.100 INFO - Started HttpContext[/,/]
02:17:57.180 INFO - Started org.openqa.jetty.jetty.servlet.ServletHandler@112f6
4
02:17:57.181 INFO - Started HttpContext[/wd,/wd]
02:17:57.193 INFO - Started SocketListener on 0.0.0.0:4444
02:17:57.194 INFO - Started org.openqa.jetty.jetty.Server@ca2dce
```

8. That is it. The server is up and running. Now, we move onto Xdebug. Go to `http://www.xdebug.org/download.php` and download the latest binaries or the source for your platform. On Linux, the extension should be built from the source. Under Windows, you just put `dll` somewhere. Then, in your `php.ini` you need to add the following:

   ```
   [xdebug]
   zend_extension=c:/path/to/your/php_xdebug_version.dll
   ```

   If you are running Linux, then you should provide the absolute path to `php_xdebug_version.so` compiled according to `http://www.xdebug.org/docs/install`.

In order to test if Xdebug is installed, you can use `http://www.xdebug.org/find-binary.php`.

Now, you should have all tools up and running.

9. Now, we will review the application generated by using `yiic webapp`. Everything test-related was put under `protected/tests`:

```
fixtures
functional
report
unit
bootstrap.php
WebTestCase.php
phpunit.xml
```

Folders generated are used to store different tests, fixtures, and code coverage reports.

10. `bootstrap.php` is used to initialize Yii application environment to run tests in it:

```
// change the following paths if necessary
$yiit=dirname(__FILE__).'/../../../framework/yiit.php';
$config=dirname(__FILE__).'/../config/test.php';

require_once($yiit);
require_once(dirname(__FILE__).'/WebTestCase.php');

Yii::createWebApplication($config);
```

As we can see, it uses a separate configuration file under `protected/config/test.php`, so if you use database or cache, you need to configure it in this file.

11. `WebTestCase.php` is used as a base class for all functional tests. We need to edit it and set `TEST_BASE_URL` to the URL of your website. Finally, `phpunit.xml` is the standard PHPUnit configuration file. We don't need to touch it, unless you want to add more browsers for functional tests or to configure the global PHPUnit settings.

There's more...

In order to get a more detailed installation guide, you can refer to the following URLs:

- `http://pear.php.net/manual/en/installation.php`
- `http://phpunit.de/`
- `http://seleniumhq.org/docs/05_selenium_rc.html`

▶ The recipe named *Writing and running unit tests* in this chapter

▶ The recipe named *Using fixtures* in this chapter

▶ The recipe named *Testing the application with functional tests* in this chapter

▶ The recipe named *Generating code coverage reports* in this chapter

Writing and running unit tests

Unit testing is generally used to test relatively standalone components of application, such as API wrappers of different services or classes by implementing your own custom logic.

In this recipe, we will review the structure of a unit test, most useful methods of PHPUnit, and a way to run a test from yiic console.

As an example, we will follow the TDD approach to create a class that will generate an HTML markup from a limited amount of BBCode tags. For simplicity, we will support only [b], [i], and [url].

Getting ready

Make sure that you have a ready to use application and testing tools as described in *Setting up the testing environment* recipe in this chapter.

How to do it...

1. First, let's define the syntax and some use cases:

In	Out
[b]test[/b]	test
[i]test[/i]	test
[url]http://yiiframework.com/[/url]	<a href="http://yiiframework.com/">http://yiiframework.com/</a>
[url=http://yiiframework.com/]yiiframework.com[/url]	<a href="http://yiiframework.com/">yiiframework.com</a>
[b]test1[/b] [b]test2[/b]	test1 test2
[b] [i]test[/i] [/b]	test

2. We will call our class `EBBCode` and its method to convert BBCode to HTML
`EBBCode::process`, and write unit tests. Create a test file `protected/tests/
unit/BBCodeTest.php` as follows:

```php
<?php
class BBCodeTest extends CTestCase
{
  private function process($bbCode)
  {
    $bb = new EBBCode();
    return $bb->process($bbCode);
  }

  function testSingleTags()
  {
    $this->assertEquals('<strong>test</strong>',
      $this->process('[b]test[/b]'));
    $this->assertEquals('<em>test</em>',
      $this->process('[i]test[/i]'));
    $this->assertEquals(
            '<a href="http://yiiframework.com/">
                http://yiiframework.com/</a>',
            $this->process('[url]http://yiiframework.com/[/url]')
        );
        $this->assertEquals(
            '<a href="http://yiiframework.com/">
                yiiframework.com</a>',
            $this->process
        ('[url=http://yiiframework.com/]yiiframework.com[/url]')
        );
  }

  function testMultipleTags()
  {
    $this->assertEquals(
      '<strong>test1</strong> <strong>test2</strong>',
      $this->process('[b]test1[/b] [b]test2[/b]')
    );
    $this->assertEquals(
        '<strong><em>test</em></strong>',
        $this->process('[b][i]test[/i][/b]')
    );
  }
}
```

3. Here we run the BBCode converter with different input strings and check if the output matches with what we are expecting. Now, we will run a test and make sure it fails. Open the console and type the following:

```
cd path/to/protected/tests
phpunit unit/BBCodeTest.php
```

You should get an output similar to the following screenshot:

```
D:\web\home\yiicmf\www\protected\tests>phpunit unit/BBCodeTest.php
PHPUnit 3.5.11 by Sebastian Bergmann.

EE

Time: 1 second, Memory: 4.75Mb

There were 2 errors:

1) BBCodeTest::testSingleTags
include(EBBCode.php): failed to open stream: No such file or directory

D:\web\home\yiicmf\framework\YiiBase.php:396
D:\web\home\yiicmf\framework\YiiBase.php:396
D:\web\home\yiicmf\www\protected\tests\unit\BBCodeTest.php:6
D:\web\home\yiicmf\www\protected\tests\unit\BBCodeTest.php:12

2) BBCodeTest::testMultipleTags
include(EBBCode.php): failed to open stream: No such file or directory

D:\web\home\yiicmf\framework\YiiBase.php:396
D:\web\home\yiicmf\framework\YiiBase.php:396
D:\web\home\yiicmf\www\protected\tests\unit\BBCodeTest.php:6
D:\web\home\yiicmf\www\protected\tests\unit\BBCodeTest.php:28

FAILURES!
Tests: 2, Assertions: 0, Errors: 2.

D:\web\home\yiicmf\www\protected\tests>
```

4. EE means that there are two tests and two errors each marked with E and a summary at the end doubles it with a readable text. In the middle, there are errors telling us why tests have failed. In our case, both tests failed because we have not created any implementation yet.

5. Now, we will fix it. As the error states, we need an EBBCode.php file with an EBBCode class inside. Create one in protected/components/EBBCode.php as follows:

```php
<?php
class EBBCode
{
}
```

Run tests again. Tests are still failing, but this time we have a different error, as seen in the following screenshot:

```
D:\web\home\yiicmf\www\protected\tests>phpunit unit/BBCodeTest.php
PHPUnit 3.5.11 by Sebastian Bergmann.


Fatal error: Call to undefined method EBBCode::process() in D:\web\home\yiicmf\w
ww\protected\tests\unit\BBCodeTest.php on line 7
```

6. It tells us to create a method named `EBBCode::process`. Create it and run tests again. The output will be different again because we did what was instructed by the test:

```
D:\web\home\yiicmf\www\protected\tests>phpunit unit/BBCodeTest.php
PHPUnit 3.5.11 by Sebastian Bergmann.

FF

Time: 1 second, Memory: 5.00Mb

There were 2 failures:

1) BBCodeTest::testSingleTags
Failed asserting that two strings are equal.
--- Expected
+++ Actual
@@ @@
-<strong>test</strong>
+

D:\web\home\yiicmf\www\protected\tests\unit\BBCodeTest.php:12

2) BBCodeTest::testMultipleTags
Failed asserting that two strings are equal.
--- Expected
+++ Actual
@@ @@
-<strong>test1</strong> <strong>test2</strong>
+

D:\web\home\yiicmf\www\protected\tests\unit\BBCodeTest.php:29

FAILURES!
Tests: 2, Assertions: 2, Failures: 2.

D:\web\home\yiicmf\www\protected\tests>
```

7. So, now there are no fatal errors and PHPUnit tells us that for input string provided at line 12 of BBCodeTest.php, we should get output as **\<strong\>test\</strong\>**, but we got an empty string. So, let's do some implementation to fix it:

```php
<?php
class EBBCode
{
  function process($string)
  {
    $preg = array(
      '~\[~\[b\](.*)\[/b\]~i' => '<strong>$1</strong>',
      '~\[i\](.*)\[/i\]~i' => '<em>$1</em>',
      '~\[url\](.*)\[/url\]~i' => '<a href="$1">$1</a>',
      '~\[url=([^]]+)\](.*)\[/url\]~i' => '<a href="$1">$2</a>',
    );
    return preg_replace(array_keys($preg), array_values($preg),
        $string);
  }
}
```

8. Now, the test output should be similar to the one shown in the following screenshot:

```
D:\web\home\yiicmf\www\protected\tests>phpunit unit/BBCodeTest.php
PHPUnit 3.5.11 by Sebastian Bergmann.

.F

Time: 0 seconds, Memory: 5.00Mb

There was 1 failure:

1) BBCodeTest::testMultipleTags
Failed asserting that two strings are equal.
--- Expected
+++ Actual
@@ @@
-<strong>test1</strong> <strong>test2</strong>
+<strong>test1[/b] [b]test2</strong>

D:\web\home\yiicmf\www\protected\tests\unit\BBCodeTest.php:29

FAILURES!
Tests: 2, Assertions: 5, Failures: 1.

D:\web\home\yiicmf\www\protected\tests>
```

9. **.F** (in the preceding screenshot) means that one test passed and one failed. As we can see in the error message, nested tags were processed wrong. So, we will fix this by using a non-greedy modifier for regular expressions as follows:

```php
<?php
class EBBCode
{
  function process($string)
  {
    $preg = array(
      '~\[b\](.*?)\[/b\]~i' => '<strong>$1</strong>',
      '~\[i\](.*?)\[/i\]~i' => '<em>$1</em>',
      '~\[url\](.*?)\[/url\]~i' => '<a href="$1">$1</a>',
      '~\[url=([^]]+)\](.*?)\[/url\]~i' => '<a href="$1">$2</a>',
    );
    return preg_replace(array_keys($preg),
      array_values($preg), $string);
  }
}
```

10. Now, test results are the ones we'd like to see:

```
D:\web\home\yiicmf\www\protected\tests>phpunit unit/BBCodeTest.php
PHPUnit 3.5.11 by Sebastian Bergmann.

..

Time: 0 seconds, Memory: 4.75Mb

OK (2 tests, 6 assertions)

D:\web\home\yiicmf\www\protected\tests>
```

11. All tests passed which means that we have the `BBCode` class implemented in the right way, or at least in the way we have planned.

The preceding process, which allowed us to create a test that fails to implement the functionality that passes it, is called a **Test Driven Development** or **TDD**. It allows you to implement exactly what is planned and be sure that it will not break in the future.

How it works...

The `CTestCase` class we have used is a wrapper around PHPUnit `PHPUnit_Framework_TestCase`. It does not provide any additional functionality, but it is used to initialize the PHPUnit class loader. We have defined two methods with names starting with `test`. This means that they will be run as test methods. Inside, we are performing the same processing with a different input and comparing the output with the result expected by using the `PHPUnit_Framework_TestCase::assertEquals` method. This method simply checks if two values are equal. If they are not, an error is generated and the test method is considered as failed.

There's more...

If you need to check different assertion types, then you can use additional `PHPUnit_Framework_TestCase` methods, such as `assertTrue`, `assertFileExists`, or `assertRegExp`.

There are more features in PHPUnit which are described in the official documentation at the following URL:

`http://www.phpunit.de/manual/current/en/`

See also

▶ The recipe named *Setting up the testing environment* in this chapter

Using fixtures

Unit tests perform their job just fine when you test the class logic. However, when it comes to classes that work with environment and data, it becomes a little complicated. What data should we test against? How to get the same environment each time a test is being executed?

In order to be useful, a unit test should be repeatable. That is why we need to reset the data state on every test run. In PHPUnit, we can do this by using a feature named **fixtures**. When it comes to database, Yii have a helpful database fixtures addition.

For our example, we will test a coupon system which handles the coupon codes registration. The coupon will be stored in a database table named `coupon` having two columns: `id` and `description`. For simplicity, coupon component simply deletes the already registered coupon record and echoes its description.

▶ Make sure that you have a ready to use application and testing tools as described in the *Setting up the testing environment* recipe in this chapter.

▶ Create an active record model for coupon `protected/models/Coupon.php` as follows:

```php
<?php
class Coupon extends CActiveRecord
{
    public static function model($className=__CLASS__)
    {
        return parent::model($className);
    }

    public function tableName() {
        return 'coupon';
    }

    public function rules() {
        return array(
            array('description', 'required'),
        );
    }
}
```

▶ Create a coupon manager class `protected/components/CouponManager.php` as follows:

```php
<?php
class CouponManager
{
    function registerCoupon($code)
    {
        $coupon = Coupon::model()->findByPk($code);
        if(!$coupon)
            return false;

        echo "Coupon registered. $coupon->description";
        return $coupon->delete();
    }
}
```

How to do it...

OK, now we will write tests. Inside `protected/tests/unit`, create `CouponTest.php`. We will need two test cases.

1. The first case will test the existing coupon code handling and the second case will test the non-existing coupon code handling. In addition, we need to configure a database, create tables, and insert data in the tables prior to the execution of the test. In the end, we will have the following code:

```php
<?php
class CouponTest extends CDbTestCase
{
  public $fixtures = array(
    'coupon' => 'Coupon',
  );

  public static function setUpBeforeClass()
  {
    if(!extension_loaded('pdo') ||
      !extension_loaded('pdo_sqlite'))
    markTestSkipped('PDO and SQLite extensions are required.');

    $config=array(
      'basePath'=>dirname(__FILE__),
      'components'=>array(
        'db'=>array(
          'class'=>'system.db.CDbConnection',
          'connectionString'=>'sqlite::memory:',
        ),
        'fixture'=>array(
          'class'=>'system.test.CDbFixtureManager',
        ),
      ),
    );

    Yii::app()->configure($config);

    $c = Yii::app()->getDb()->createCommand();
    $c->createTable('coupon', array(
      'id' => 'varchar(255) PRIMARY KEY NOT NULL',
      'description' => 'text',
    ));
  }
```

```
      public static function tearDownAfterClass()
      {
        if(Yii::app()->getDb())
          Yii::app()->getDb()->active=false;
      }

      protected function setUp()
      {
        parent::setUp();
        $_GET['existing_code'] = 'discount_for_me';
        $_GET['non_existing_code'] = 'non_existing';
      }

      public function testCodeAcceptance()
      {
        $cm = new CouponManager();
        $this->assertTrue($cm->registerCoupon
          ($_GET['existing_code']));
        $this->assertFalse((boolean)Coupon::model()->findByPk
          ($_GET['existing_code']));
      }

      public function testCodeNotFound()
      {
        $countBefore = Coupon::model()->count();

        $cm = new CouponManager();
        $this->assertFalse($cm->registerCoupon
          ($_GET['non_existing_code']));

        $countAfter = Coupon::model()->count();
        $this->assertEquals($countBefore, $countAfter);
      }
    }
```

2. Also, we need to define fixtures in `protected/tests/fixtures/coupon.php` as follows:

```php
<?php
return array(
    array(
        'id' => 'free_book',
        'description' => 'Choose one book for free!',
    ),
    array(
```

```
        'id' => 'merry_christmas',
        'description' => '5% Christmas discount!',
    ),
    array(
        'id' => 'discount_for_me',
        'description' => '5% discount special for you!',
    ),
);
```

Here, id and description keys corresponding to table or active record model fields and values are to be filled to these fields when the fixture is applied.

3. Now, try to run the test from the console as follows:

```
cd path/to/protected/tests
phpunit unit/CouponTest.php
```

You should now get the following output:

```
D:\web\home\yiicmf\www\protected\tests>phpunit unit/CouponTest.php
PHPUnit 3.5.11 by Sebastian Bergmann.

Coupon registered. 5% discount special for you!..

Time: 0 seconds, Memory: 6.50Mb

OK (2 tests, 4 assertions)

D:\web\home\yiicmf\www\protected\tests>_
```

How it works...

We will review the test execution flow. This time, we used a few special PHPUnit fixture methods named setUpBeforeClass and setUp. The setUpBeforeClass method executes once after the test class is instantiated and typically used to initialize things common for all test methods of this class. In our case, we check if we have PDO and SQLite required to run this test:

```
if(!extension_loaded('pdo') || !extension_loaded('pdo_sqlite'))
    markTestSkipped('PDO and SQLite extensions are required.');
```

We then create a configuration test application and apply the following:

```
$config=array(
    'basePath'=>dirname(__FILE__),
    'components'=>array(
        'db'=>array(
            'class'=>'system.db.CDbConnection',
```

```
            'connectionString'=>'sqlite::memory:',
        ),
        'fixture'=>array(
            'class'=>'system.test.CDbFixtureManager',
        ),
    ),
);
```

```
    Yii::app()->configure($config);
```

We use an in-memory SQLite database to speed tests up and avoid creating and deleting database files. In addition, we connect a `fixture` component which we use to fill data.

Now, it is time to create the database schema. In our case, it is the `coupon` table:

```
$c = Yii::app()->getDb()->createCommand();
$c->createTable('coupon', array(
    'id' => 'varchar(255) PRIMARY KEY NOT NULL',
    'description' => 'text',
));
```

That is it. The test class is created and PHPUnit starts to execute test methods one by one. Before each test method execution, it calls `setUp`. In our case, it is simple:

```
parent::setUp();
$_GET['existing_code'] = 'discount_for_me';
$_GET['non_existing_code'] = 'non_existing';
```

`parent::setUp` refers to `CDbTestCase::setup` that reads data from fixtures and places it into the tables or models. Both fixtures and models are defined in the `$fixtures` property as follows:

```
public $fixtures = array(
    'coupon' => 'Coupon',
);
```

This means that fixtures are read from `protected/tests/fixtures/coupon.php` and applied to the `Coupon` model. In order to apply fixtures to the table without using a model, we can define a `$fixtures` property in the following way:

```
public $fixtures = array(
    'coupon' => ':coupon',
);
```

Then, we set the environment with `$_GET` variables. Similarly, you can set cookies, server variables, class properties, and so on.

After executing `testCodeAcceptance` and before the `testCodeNotFound` method execution, `setUp` is executed again restoring the coupon table data from the fixture.

Finally, when all test methods have been executed, we need to close the connection. We do this in the `tearDownAfterClass` method executed just before the class is destroyed.

There's more...

We have used Yii database fixtures and it allowed the data not to be cleaned up manually on each execution. If we need to clean up data, then we can use the PHPUnit `teardown` method that is executed after each test method execution.

You can refer to the following sources to get more information about fixtures:

- `http://www.phpunit.de/manual/current/en/fixtures.html`
- `http://www.yiiframework.com/doc/guide/en/test.fixture`

See also

- The recipe named _Setting up the testing environment_ in this chapter

Testing the application with functional tests

While unit tests are used to test standalone components or component groups, functional tests allow testing the complete application like black box testing. We don't know what is inside and can only provide an input and get/verify the output. In our case, the input is actions the user carries out in a browser, such as clicking on buttons or links, loading pages, and so on, and the output is what happens in the browser.

For our example, we will create a simple "check all" widget with a single button that checks and unchecks all checkboxes on the current page.

Getting ready

- Make sure that you have a ready-to-use application and testing tools as described in the _Setting up the testing environment_ recipe in this chapter
- Don't forget to run the server
- Drop the widget code into `protected/components/ECheckAllWidget.php` as follows:

```php
<?php
class ECheckAllWidget extends CWidget
{
    public $checkedTitle = 'Uncheck all';
```

```php
        public $uncheckedTitle = 'Check all';

        public function run()
        {
            Yii::app()->clientScript->registerCoreScript('jquery');
            echo CHtml::button($this->uncheckedTitle, array(
                'id' => 'button-'.$this->id,
                'class' => 'check-all-btn',
                'onclick' => '
                    switch($(this).val())
                    {
                        case "'.$this->checkedTitle.'":
                            $(this).val("'.$this->uncheckedTitle.'");
                            $("input[type=checkbox]").attr("checked",
                                false);
                        break;
                        case "'.$this->uncheckedTitle.'":
                            $(this).val("'.$this->checkedTitle.'");
                            $("input[type=checkbox]").attr("checked", true);
                        break;
                    }
                '
            ));
        }
    }
```

▶ Now create `protected/controllers/CheckController.php` as follows:

```php
<?php
class CheckController extends Controller
{
    function actionIndex()
    {
        $this->render('index');
    }
}
```

▶ In addition, create a view `protected/views/check/index.php` as follows:

```php
<?php $this->widget('ECheckAllWidget')?>

<?php echo CHtml::checkBox('test1', true)?>
<?php echo CHtml::checkBox('test2', false)?>
<?php echo CHtml::checkBox('test3', true)?>
<?php echo CHtml::checkBox('test4', false)?>
<?php echo CHtml::checkBox('test5', true)?>
<?php echo CHtml::checkBox('test6', true)?>
```

How to do it...

Let's imagine how we would test it manually:

- ▶ Load the page
- ▶ Verify that the button title is "Check all"
- ▶ Click on a button once
- ▶ Verify that all checkboxes are checked and the button title is "Uncheck all"
- ▶ Click on a button again
- ▶ Verify that all checkboxes are unchecked and the button title is "Check all"

Now, we will implement the functional test doing exactly that.

1. Create `protected/tests/functional/CheckAllWidgetTest.php` as follows:

```php
<?php
class CheckAllWidgetTest extends WebTestCase
{
    public function testWidget()
    {
        $this->open('check/index');
        $this->assertEquals("Check all",
            $this->getAttribute("class=check-all-btn@value"));

        $this->click("class=check-all-btn");
        $this->assertChecked("css=input[type=checkbox]");
        $this->assertEquals("Uncheck all",
            $this->getAttribute("class=check-all-btn@value"));

        $this->click("class=check-all-btn");
        $this->assertNotChecked("css=input[type=checkbox]");
        $this->assertEquals("Check all",
            $this->getAttribute("class=check-all-btn@value"));
    }
}
```

2. Now open the console:

```
cd path/to/protected/tests
phpunit functional/CheckAllWidgetTest.php
```

You should get the following output:

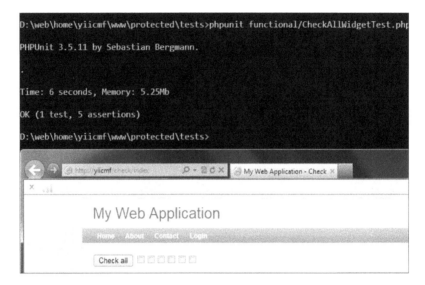

3. Now, try to break a widget and run the test again. For example, you can comment the `onclick` handler:

```
D:\web\home\yiicmf\www\protected\tests>phpunit functional/CheckAllWidgetTest.php

PHPUnit 3.5.11 by Sebastian Bergmann.

F

Time: 5 seconds, Memory: 5.25Mb

There was 1 failure:

1) CheckAllWidgetTest::testWidget
Current URL: http://yiicmf/check/index

Failed asserting that two strings are equal.
--- Expected
+++ Actual
@@ @@
-Uncheck all
+Check all

D:\web\home\yiicmf\www\protected\tests\functional\CheckAllWidgetTest.php:11

FAILURES!
Tests: 1, Assertions: 3, Failures: 1.
```

This means that your widget does not work as expected. In this case, the test failed on line 11.

```
$this->assertEquals("Uncheck all",
  $this->getAttribute("class=check-all-btn@value"));
```

Actual value was still "Check all" but test expected "Uncheck all".

How it works...

PHPUnit starts executing all methods named like `testSomething` one by one. As we have only one method, it executes `testWidget`:

```
$this->open('check/index');
```

It opens a page we created for testing:

```
$this->assertEquals("Check all", $this->getAttribute
  ("class=check-all-btn@value"));
```

It gets button text and checks if it equals the string provided. The `getAttribute` searches for a DOM element with a class `check-all-btn` and returns its `value` attribute text.

```
$this->click("class=check-all-btn");
```

It clicks an element with class `check-all-btn`. That is the button.

```
$this->assertChecked("css=input[type=checkbox]");
```

The `assertChecked` and `assertNotChecked` methods are used to find whether a checkbox is checked. This time we use a CSS selector `input[type=checkbox]` to get all checkboxes.

Inside, we call methods such as `getAttribute` or `assertChecked`, and pass it to the Selenium Server that does the actual work and returns the result.

There's more...

In order to learn more about the functional testing, you can refer to the following resources:

- `http://www.yiiframework.com/doc/guide/en/test.functional`
- `http://www.phpunit.de/manual/current/en/selenium.html`
- `http://seleniumhq.org/docs/05_selenium_rc.html`
- `http://seleniumhq.org/docs/04_selenese_commands.html`

See also

- ▶ The recipe named *Setting up the testing environment* in this chapter
- ▶ The recipe named *Writing and running unit tests* in this chapter

Generating code coverage reports

It is very important to know how well your application is tested. If you wrote all tests by yourself, then you can probably guess it, but if there is a team or you are working on a relatively old project, guessing will not work. Fortunately, there is a way to generate code coverage reports using PHPUnit and Xdebug. This report gives information about how well the application is tested, which lines are being executed while running tests, and which are not.

As an example, we will generate a report for the Yii framework core base classes.

Getting ready

The Yii framework core tests are not included into release distributions, so we need to check it out from the SVN repository.

 Make sure that your test environment is setup properly.

How to do it...

1. Go to `http://code.google.com/p/yii/source/checkout` and follow the given instructions to check out the trunk code using either command line or one of the GUI clients, such as SmartSVN or TortoiseSVN.

2. In the console, enter the following:

   ```
   cd path/to/checked/out/code/tests/ phpunit --coverage-html reports
   framework/base
   ```

3. After the report is generated, go to `path/to/checked/out/code/tests/ reports` and open `index.html` in your browser.

How it works...

The code coverage report that was generated can tell us how well the project was tested and which parts required more testing to be done.

The code coverage report is generated based only on tests you have run. It is better to run the complete test pack for the project to get the actual information, but for simplicity and speed, only a few tests of the Yii framework code were executed.

The first report page gives us an overview: which files were tested, how many lines, methods, and classes were executed. As we are interested in covering as much code as we can, things to look for are displayed in red and yellow. In the following screenshot, we can see that more tests for **CApplication** and **CStatePersister** need to be written:

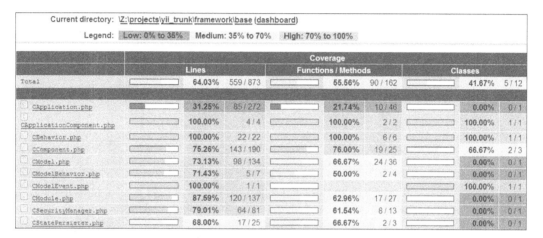

If we click on a class name, for example, on **CComponent**, then we get more details. The following screenshot shows the class level report:

Moreover, the actual code shows what is covered in green:

```
109         :        public function __get(
110    11   :        {
111    11   :            $getter='get'.$nam
112    11   :            if(method_exists($
113     2   :                return $this->
114     2   :            else if(strncasecm
115         :            {
116     1   :                // duplicating
117     1   :                $name=strtolow
118     1   :                if(!isset($thi
119     1   :                    $this->_e[
120         :                    return $this->
121     1   :                }
122     1   :                else if(isset($thi
123     1   :                    return $this->
124     1   :                else if(is_array($
125     0   :                {
126         :                    foreach($this-
127     0   :                    {
128     0   :                        if($object
129     0   :                            return
130     0   :                    }
131     1   :                }
132     1   :                throw new CExcepti
133         :                    array('{class}
134         :            }
135         :
136         :            /**
137         :             * Sets value of a com
                         * Do not call this me
```

If we click on the **dashboard** link on the main report page, then we get a handy summary showing most risky untested classes and methods, as shown in the following screenshot:

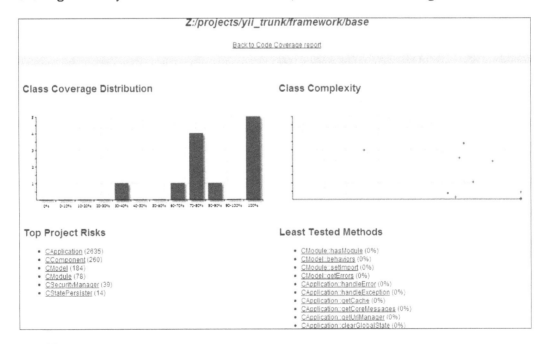

There's more...

In order to learn more about the code coverage, refer to the PHPUnit manual at the following URLs:

- ▶ `http://www.phpunit.de/manual/current/en/code-coverage-analysis.html`
- ▶ `http://www.phpunit.de/manual/current/en/selenium.html`

See also

- ▶ The recipe named *Setting up the testing environment* in this chapter

6
Database, Active Record, and Model Tricks

In this chapter, we will cover:

- ▶ Getting data from a database
- ▶ Defining and using multiple DB connections
- ▶ Using scopes to get models for different languages
- ▶ Processing model fields with AR event-like methods
- ▶ Applying markdown and HTML
- ▶ Highlighting code with Yii
- ▶ Automating timestamps
- ▶ Setting author automatically
- ▶ Implementing single table inheritance
- ▶ Using CDbCriteria

Introduction

There are three main methods to work with database in Yii: Active Record, query builder, and direct SQL queries through DAO. All three are different in terms of syntax, features, and performance.

In this chapter, we will learn how to work with the database efficiently, when to use models and when not to, how to work with multiple databases, how to automatically pre-process Active Record fields, and how to use powerful database criteria.

In this chapter, we will use Sakila sample database Version 0.8 available at the official MySQL website: `http://dev.mysql.com/doc/sakila/en/sakila.html`.

Getting data from a database

Most applications today use databases. Be it a small website or a social network, at least some parts are powered by databases. Yii introduces three ways which allow you to work with databases:

- ▶ Active Record
- ▶ Query builder
- ▶ SQL via DAO

We will use all these methods to get data from the `film`, `film_actor`, and `actor` tables and show it in a list. We will measure the execution time and memory usage to determine when to use these methods.

Getting ready

- ▶ Create a new application by using `yiic webapp` as described in the official guide at the following URL:

  `http://www.yiiframework.com/doc/guide/en/quickstart.first-app`

- ▶ Download Sakila database from the following URL:

  `http://dev.mysql.com/doc/sakila/en/sakila.html`

  Execute the downloaded SQLs: first schema then data

- ▶ Configure the DB connection in `protected/config/main.php` to use `sakila` database

- ▶ Use Gii to create models `actor` and `field` tables

How to do it...

1. We will create `protected/controllers/DbController.php` as follows:

```php
<?php
class DbController extends Controller
{
  protected function afterAction($action)
  {
```

```
    $time = sprintf('%0.5f', Yii::getLogger()
        ->getExecutionTime());
    $memory = round(memory_get_peak_usage()/(1024*1024),2)."MB";
    echo "Time: $time, memory: $memory";
    parent::afterAction($action);
}

public function actionAr()
{
    $actors = Actor::model()->findAll(array('with' => 'films',
        'order' => 't.first_name, t.last_name, films.title'));
    echo '<ol>';
    foreach($actors as $actor)
    {
        echo '<li>';
        echo $actor->first_name.' '.$actor->last_name;
        echo '<ol>';
        foreach($actor->films as $film)
        {
            echo '<li>';
            echo $film->title;
            echo '</li>';
        }
        echo '</ol>';
        echo '</li>';
    }
    echo '</ol>';
}

public function actionQueryBuilder()
{
    $rows = Yii::app()->db->createCommand()
        ->from('actor')
        ->join('film_actor', 'actor.actor_id=film_actor.actor_id')
        ->leftJoin('film', 'film.film_id=film_actor.film_id')
        ->order('actor.first_name, actor.last_name, film.title')
        ->queryAll();

    $this->renderRows($rows);
}

public function actionSql()
{
    $sql = "SELECT *
```

```
          FROM actor a
            JOIN film_actor fa ON fa.actor_id = a.actor_id
            JOIN film f ON fa.film_id = f.film_id
            ORDER BY a.first_name, a.last_name, f.title";

          $rows = Yii::app()->db->createCommand($sql)->queryAll();

          $this->renderRows($rows);
      }

      public function renderRows($rows)
      {
        $lastActorName = null;

        echo '<ol>';
        foreach($rows as $row)
        {
          $actorName = $row['first_name'].' '.$row['last_name'];
          if($actorName!=$lastActorName){
            if($lastActorName!==null){
              echo '</ol>';
              echo '</li>';
            }

            $lastActorName = $actorName;
            echo '<li>';
            echo $actorName;
            echo '<ol>';
          }
          echo '<li>';
          echo $row['title'];
          echo '</li>';
        }
        echo '</ol>';
      }
  }
```

Here we have three actions corresponding to three different methods of getting data from a database.

2. After running the preceding `db/ar`, `db/queryBuilder`, and `db/sql` actions, you should get a tree showing 200 actors and 1,000 films they have acted in, as shown in the following screenshot:

```
 36. THEORY MERMAID
 37. TITANIC BOONDOCK
 38. UNFORGIVEN ZOOLANDER
 39. WAGON JAWS
 40. YOUTH KICK
199. JULIA FAWCETT
      1. BERETS AGENT
      2. BOILED DARES
      3. CHISUM BEHAVIOR
      4. CLOSER BANG
      5. DAY UNFAITHFUL
      6. HOPE TOOTSIE
      7. LUKE MUMMY
      8. MULAN MOON
      9. OPUS ICE
     10. POLLOCK DELIVERANCE
     11. RIDGEMONT SUBMARINE
     12. SHANGHAI TYCOON
     13. SHAWSHANK BUBBLE
     14. THEORY MERMAID
     15. WAIT CIDER
200. THORA TEMPLE
      1. AFRICAN EGG
      2. BADMAN DAWN
      3. BLANKET BEVERLY
      4. CANDIDATE PERDITION
      5. CAROL TEXAS
      6. CHRISTMAS MOONSHINE
      7. GALAXY SWEETHEARTS
      8. HOCUS FRIDA
      9. INSIDER ARIZONA
     10. INTERVIEW LIAISONS
     11. JADE BUNCH
     12. LOVER TRUMAN
     13. LOVERBOY ATTACKS
     14. MADISON TRAP
     15. RANDOM GO
     16. TELEGRAPH VOYAGE
     17. TROJAN TOMORROW
     18. VIRGINIAN PLUTO
     19. WARDROBE PHANTOM
     20. WRONG BEHAVIOR

Time: 0.67937, memory: 17.08MB
```

At the bottom, there are statistics that give information about the memory usage and execution time. Absolute numbers can be different if you run this code, but the difference between methods used should be about the same:

Method	Memory usage, megabytes	Execution time, seconds
Active Record	19.74	1.14109
Query Builder	17.98	0.35732
SQL (DAO)	17.74	0.35038

How it works...

Let's review the preceding code.

The `actionAr` action method gets model instances by using the Active Record approach. We start with the `Actor` model generated with Gii to get all actors and specify `'with' =>` `'films'` to get corresponding films using a single query or eager loading through relation which Gii built for us from `InnoDB` table foreign keys. Then, we simply iterate over all actors and for each actor—over each film. For each item, we print its name.

`actionQueryBuilder` uses query builder. First, we create a query command for the current DB connection with `Yii::app()->db->createCommand()`. Then, we add query parts one by one with `from`, `join`, and `leftJoin`. These methods escape values, tables, and field names automatically. `queryAll` returns an array of raw database rows. Each row is also an array indexed with result field names. We pass the result to `renderRows` that renders it.

With `actionSql`, we do the same except two things: we pass SQL directly instead of adding its parts one by one and we escape values manually with `Yii::app()->db->quoteValue` before using them in the query string.

`renderRows` renders the query builder and DAO raw row requires you to add more checks and generally feels unnatural compared to rendering Active Record result.

As we can see, all these give the same result in the end but have different performance, syntax, and extra features. We will do a comparison and figure out when to use which method:

Method	Active Record	Query Builder	SQL (DAO)
Syntax	Will do SQL for you.	Clean API, suitable for building query on the fly.	Good for complex SQL
	Gii will generate models and relations for you.		Manual values and keywords quoting.
	Works with models, completely OO-style, and very clean API.	Produces raw data arrays as the result.	Not very suitable for building query on the fly.
	Produces array of properly nested models as the result.		Produces raw data arrays as results.
Performance	Higher memory usage and execution time compared to SQL and query builder.	OK.	OK.
Extra features	Quotes values and names automatically.	Quotes values and names automatically.	None.
	Behaviors.		
	Before/after hooks.		
	Validation.		

Method	Active Record	Query Builder	SQL (DAO)
Best for	Prototyping selects. Update, delete, and create actions for single models (model gives a huge benefit when using with forms).	Working with large amounts of data, building queries on the fly.	Complex queries you want to do with pure SQL and have maximum possible performance.

There's more...

In order to learn more about working with databases in Yii, refer to the following resources:

- `http://www.yiiframework.com/doc/guide/en/database.dao`
- `http://www.yiiframework.com/doc/guide/en/database.query-builder`
- `http://www.yiiframework.com/doc/guide/en/database.ar`
- `http://www.yiiframework.com/doc/guide/en/database.ar`

See also

- The recipe named *Defining and using multiple DB connections* in this chapter
- The recipe named *Using CDbCriteria* in this chapter

Defining and using multiple DB connections

Multiple database connections are not used too often for new standalone web applications. However, when you are building an add-on application for an existing system, you will most probably need another database connection.

From this recipe, you will learn how to define multiple DB connections and use them with DAO, query builder, and Active Record models.

Getting ready

- Create a new application by using `yiic webapp` as described in the official guide at the following URL:

  `http://www.yiiframework.com/doc/guide/en/quickstart.first-app`

- Create two MySQL databases named `db1` and `db2`
- Create a table named `post` in `db1` as follows:

```
DROP TABLE IF EXISTS `post`;
CREATE TABLE IF NOT EXISTS `post` (
  `id` INT(10) UNSIGNED NOT NULL AUTO_INCREMENT,
```

```
    `title` VARCHAR(255) NOT NULL,
    `text` TEXT NOT NULL,
    PRIMARY KEY  (`id`)
);
```

▶ Create a table named `comment` in db2 as follows:

```
DROP TABLE IF EXISTS `comment`;
CREATE TABLE IF NOT EXISTS `comment` (
    `id` INT(10) UNSIGNED NOT NULL AUTO_INCREMENT,
    `text` TEXT NOT NULL,
    `postId` INT(10) UNSIGNED NOT NULL,
    PRIMARY KEY  (`id`)
);
```

How to do it...

1. We will start with configuring DB connections. Open `protected/config/main.php` and define a primary connection as described in the guide:

```
'db'=>array(
    'connectionString' => 'mysql:host=localhost;dbname=db1',
    'emulatePrepare' => true,
    'username' => 'root',
    'password' => '',
    'charset' => 'utf8',
),
```

2. Then copy it, rename the 'db' component to 'db2' and change the connection string accordingly. Also, you need to add the class name as follows:

```
'db2'=>array(
    'class'=>'CDbConnection',
    'connectionString' => 'mysql:host=localhost;dbname=db2',
    'emulatePrepare' => true,
    'username' => 'root',
    'password' => '',
    'charset' => 'utf8',
),
```

3. That is it. Now, you have two database connections and can use them with DAO and query builder as follows:

```
$db1Rows = Yii::app()->db->createCommand($sql)->queryAll();
$db2Rows = Yii::app()->db2->createCommand($sql)->queryAll();
```

Now, what if we need to use Active Record models? This is a little tricky, but still possible.

1. First, we need to create models with Gii. As the connection to `db1` is primary, we have no problems in generating and using `Post`.

2. In order to generate the `Comment` model, we need to temporarily make `db2` as our primary connection as follows:

```
/*'db'=>array(
    'connectionString' => 'mysql:host=localhost;dbname=db1',
    'emulatePrepare' => true,
    'username' => 'root',
    'password' => '',
    'charset' => 'utf8',
),*/
'db'=>array(
    'class'=>'system.db.CDbConnection',
    'connectionString' => 'mysql:host=localhost;dbname=db2',
    'emulatePrepare' => true,
    'username' => 'root',
    'password' => '',
    'charset' => 'utf8',
),
```

3. Then, generate the `Comment` model as usual, uncomment `db`, and restore the `db2` configuration. We have a model, but have not specified that it should use the `db2` connection. Add the following to `protected/models/Comment.php` as follows:

```
class Comment extends CActiveRecord
{
    // …
    public function getDbConnection()
    {
        return Yii::app()->db2;
    }
    // …
}
```

4. That is it. Now, you can use the `Comment` model as usual. Create `protected/controllers/DbtestController.php` as follows:

```
<?php
class DbtestController extends CController
{
    public function actionIndex()
    {
        $post = new Post();
        $post->title = "Post #".rand(1, 1000);
```

```
        $post->text = "text";
        $post->save();

        echo '<h1>Posts</h1>';

        $posts = Post::model()->findAll();
        foreach($posts as $post)
        {
            echo $post->title."<br />";
        }

        $comment = new Comment();
        $comment->postId = $post->id;
        $comment->text = "comment #".rand(1, 1000);
        $comment->save();

        echo '<h1>Comments</h1>';

        $comments = Comment::model()->findAll();
        foreach($comments as $comment)
        {
            echo $comment->text."<br />";
        }
    }
}
```

5. Run `dbtest/index` multiple times and you should see records added to both databases, as shown in the following screenshot:

Posts

Post #40
Post #230
Post #710
Post #445
Post #744

Comments

comment #340
comment #765
comment #107
comment #535
comment #685

How it works...

In Yii, you can add and configure your own components through the configuration file. For non-standard components, such as db2, you have to specify the component class. Similarly, you can add db3, db4, or any other component, for example, facebookApi. The remaining array key-value pairs are assigned to the component's public properties respectively.

There's more...

Depending on the RDBMS used, there are additional things we can do to make it easier to use multiple databases.

Cross-database relations

If you are using MySQL, then it is possible to create cross-database relations for your models. In order to do this, you should prefix the Comment model's table name with database name as follows:

```
class Comment extends CActiveRecord
{
    //…
    public function tableName()
    {
        return 'db2.comment';
    }
    //…
}
```

Now, if you have a comments relation defined in the Post model relations method, then you can use the following code:

```
$posts = Post::model()->with('comments')->findAll();
```

Further reading

For further information, refer to the following URL:

http://www.yiiframework.com/doc/api/CActiveRecord

See also

▶ The recipe named *Getting data from a database* in this chapter

Using scopes to get models for different languages

Internationalizing your application is not an easy task: You need to translate interfaces, translate messages, format dates properly, and so on. Yii helps you to do it by giving access to **CLDR** (**Unicode Common Locale Data Repository**) data and providing translation and formatting tools. When it comes to applications with data in multiple languages, you have to find your own way.

From this recipe, you will learn a possible way to get a handy model function that will help to get blog posts for different languages.

Getting ready

▶ Create a new application by using `yiic webapp` as described in the official guide at the following URL:

`http://www.yiiframework.com/doc/guide/en/quickstart.first-app`

▶ Set up the database connection and create a table named `post` as follows:

```
DROP TABLE IF EXISTS `post`;
CREATE TABLE IF NOT EXISTS `post` (
    `id` INT(10) UNSIGNED NOT NULL AUTO_INCREMENT,
    `lang` VARCHAR(5) NOT NULL DEFAULT 'en',
    `title` VARCHAR(255) NOT NULL,
    `text` TEXT NOT NULL,
    PRIMARY KEY (`id`)
);

INSERT INTO `post`(`id`,`lang`,`title`,`text`)
VALUES (1,'en_us','Yii news','Text in English'),
(2,'de','Yii Nachrichten','Text in Deutsch');
```

▶ Generate Post model using Gii

How to do it...

1. Add the following methods to `protected/models/Post.php` as follows:

```
class Post extends CActiveRecord
{
    public function defaultScope()
    {
        return array(
```

```
                'condition' => "lang=:lang",
                'params' => array(
                    ':lang' => Yii::app()->language,
                ),
            );
        }

    public function lang($lang){
        $this->getDbCriteria()->mergeWith(array(
            'condition' => "lang=:lang",
            'params' => array(
                ':lang' => $lang,
            ),
        ));
        return $this;
    }
}
```

2. That is it. Now, we can use our model. Create `protected/controllers/DbtestController.php` as follows:

```php
<?php
class DbtestController extends CController
{
    public function actionIndex()
    {
        // Get posts written in default application language
        $posts = Post::model()->findAll();

        echo '<h1>Default language</h1>';
        foreach($posts as $post)
        {
            echo '<h2>'.$post->title.'</h2>';
            echo $post->text;
        }

        // Get posts written in German
        $posts = Post::model()->lang('de')->findAll();

        echo '<h1>German</h1>';
        foreach($posts as $post)
        {
            echo '<h2>'.$post->title.'</h2>';
            echo $post->text;
        }
    }
}
```

3. Now, run `dbtest/index` and you should get an output similar to the one shown in the following screenshot:

Default language

Yii news

Text in English

German

Yii Nachrichten

Text in Deutsch

How it works...

We have used Yii Active Record scopes in the preceding code. `defaultScope` returns the default condition or criteria that will be applied to all the `Post` model query methods. As we need to specify the language explicitly, we create a named scope named `lang` which accepts the language name. With `$this->getDbCriteria()`, we get the model's criteria in its current state and then merge it with the new condition. As the condition is exactly the same as in `defaultScope`, except the parameter value, it overrides the default one.

In order to support chained calls, `lang` returns the model instance by itself.

There's more...

For further information, refer to the following URLs:

- `http://www.yiiframework.com/doc/guide/en/database.ar`
- `http://www.yiiframework.com/doc/api/CDbCriteria/`

See also

- The recipe named *Getting data from a database* in this chapter
- The recipe named *Using CDbCriteria* in this chapter
- The recipe named *Processing model fields with AR events* in this chapter

Processing model fields with AR event-like methods

Active record implementation in Yii is very powerful and has many features. One of these features is **event-like methods** that you can use to pre-process model fields before putting them into the database or getting them from a database, deleting data related to the model, and so on.

In this recipe, we will "linkify" all URLs in the post text and will list all existing active record event-like methods.

Getting ready

▶ Create a new application by using `yiic webapp` as described in the official guide at the following URL:

`http://www.yiiframework.com/doc/guide/en/quickstart.first-app`

▶ Set up a database connection and create a table named `post` as follows:

```
DROP TABLE IF EXISTS `post`;
CREATE TABLE IF NOT EXISTS `post` (
  `id` INT(10) UNSIGNED NOT NULL AUTO_INCREMENT,
  `title` VARCHAR(255) NOT NULL,
  `text` TEXT NOT NULL,
  PRIMARY KEY (`id`)
);
```

▶ Generate the `Post` model using Gii

How to do it...

1. Add the following method to `protected/models/Post.php` as follows:

```
protected function beforeSave()
{
    $this->text = preg_replace('~((?:https?|ftps?)://.*?)( |$)~iu',
'<a href="\1">\1</a>\2', $this->text);
    return parent::beforeSave();
}
```

2. That is it. Now, try saving a post containing a link. Create `protected/controllers/TestController.php` as follows:

```php
<?php
class TestController extends CController
{
    function actionIndex()
    {
        $post=new Post();
        $post->title='links test';
        $post->text='test http://www.yiiframework.com/ test';
        $post->save();
        print_r($post->text);
    }
}
```

3. Run `test/index`. You should get the following:

test http://www.yiiframework.com/ test

How it works...

`beforeSave` is implemented in the `CActiveRecord` class and executed just before saving a model. By using a regular expression, we replace everything that looks like a URL with a link that uses this URL and calls the parent implementation, so real events are raised properly. In order to prevent saving, you can return `false`.

There's more...

There are more event-like methods available as shown in the following table:

Method name	Description
`afterConstruct`	Called after a model instance is created by the new operator
`beforeDelete/afterDelete`	Called before/after deleting a record
`beforeFind/afterFind`	Method is invoked before/after each record is instantiated by a find method
`beforeSave/afterSave`	Method is invoked before/after saving a record successfully
`beforeValidate/afterValidate`	Method is invoked before/after validation ends

Further reading

In order to learn more about using event-like methods in Yii, you can refer to the following URLs:

▶ `http://www.yiiframework.com/doc/api/CActiveRecord/`

▶ `http://www.yiiframework.com/doc/api/CModel`

See also

▶ The recipe named *Using Yii events* in *Chapter 1, Under the Hood*

▶ The recipe named *Applying markdown and HTML* in this chapter

▶ The recipe named *Highlighting code with Yii* in this chapter

▶ The recipe named *Automating timestamps* in this chapter

▶ The recipe named *Setting author automatically* in this chapter

Applying markdown and HTML

When we create web applications, we will certainly have to deal with creating content. Of course, we can create it with pure text or HTML, but text is often too simple and HTML is too complex and insecure. That is why special markup languages such as BBCode, Textile, and markdown are used.

In this recipe, we will learn how to create a model which will automatically convert markdown to HTML when it is being saved.

Getting ready

▶ Create a new application by using `yiic webapp` as described in the official guide at the following URL:

`http://www.yiiframework.com/doc/guide/en/quickstart.first-app`

▶ Set up a database connection and create a table named `post` as follows:

```sql
DROP TABLE IF EXISTS `post`;
CREATE TABLE IF NOT EXISTS `post` (
    `id` INT(10) UNSIGNED NOT NULL AUTO_INCREMENT,
    `title` VARCHAR(255) NOT NULL,
    `text` TEXT NOT NULL,
    `html` TEXT NOT NULL,
    PRIMARY KEY (`id`)
);
```

▶ Generate the `Post` model using Gii

How to do it...

1. Open the `protected/models/Post.php` file and add the following method:

```
protected function beforeValidate()
{
    $parser=new CMarkdownParser();
    $this->html=$parser->transform($this->text);
    return parent::beforeValidate();
}
```

2. Now the `Post` model can be used transparently. Create `protected/controllers/TestController.php` as follows:

```php
<?php
class TestController extends CController
{
    function actionIndex()
    {
        $post = new Post();
        $post->title = "I promise to share my opinion on Yii
            framework";
        $post->text = "Recently I've started using [Yii
            framework](http://www.yiiframework.com/) and definitely
            will share my opinion as soon as I'll have some more free
            time.";
        $post->save();

        echo "<h1>$post->title</h1>";
        echo $post->html;
    }
}
```

3. That is it. Now run `test/index`. You should get the following:

I promise to share my opinion on Yii framework

Recently I've started using Yii framework and definitely will share my opinion as soon as I'll have some more free time.

Text marked up with markdown you have set for the `text` value will be automatically converted to HTML, ready to be displayed, and will be saved in the `html` database field. Therefore, `html` should be used at the "display post" screen and the markdown `text` should be used at "create post" or "edit post" screens.

How it works...

In the preceding code, we override `CActiveRecord::beforeValidate` to pre-process the data we have from the user input. This method is executed just before the validation that is called when we use `$post->save()`.

Yii includes a wrapper around "PHP Markdown Extra" markdown parser. `CMarkdownParser` is used mainly in the Yii documentation and we can surely use it in our applications.

Converting text from one format to another requires more CPU and memory resources, so should be avoided if possible. That is why we are not applying markdown on the fly and doing it only one time when saving a post.

When we edit `post`, we need to get the markdown source somehow. For this reason, we save both the markdown source and the produced HTML into a database. Alternatively, we can use a markdown parser on viewing `post` and cache results until `post` is altered.

There's more...

In order to learn more about markdown, and how it can be used to build the Yii documentation, you can refer to the following resources:

Markdown syntax

- ▶ http://daringfireball.net/projects/markdown/syntax
- ▶ http://michelf.com/projects/php-markdown/extra/

Yii markdown wrapper and usage

- ▶ http://www.yiiframework.com/doc/api/CMarkdownParser/
- ▶ http://code.google.com/p/yiidoc/

See also

- ▶ The recipe named *Processing model fields with AR event-like methods* in this chapter
- ▶ The recipe named *Highlighting code* in this chapter
- ▶ The recipe named *Automating timestamps* in this chapter
- ▶ The recipe named *Setting an author automatically* in this chapter

Highlighting code with Yii

If you are posting code, be it company's internal wiki or a public developer's blog, it is always better to have the syntax highlighted, so ones who read the code will feel comfortable.

Yii has Pear `Text_Highlighter` code-highlighting class bundled. It is used to highlight Yii definitive guide examples and we can use it to do the same for our application.

In this recipe, we will create a simple application that will allow adding, editing, and viewing code snippets.

Getting ready

▶ Create a new application by using `yiic webapp` as described in the official guide at the following URL:

   `http://www.yiiframework.com/doc/guide/en/quickstart.first-app`

▶ Set up a database connection and create a table named `snippet` as follows:

```
CREATE TABLE `snippet` (
  `id` int(11) unsigned NOT NULL auto_increment,
  `title` varchar(255) NOT NULL,
  `code` text NOT NULL,
  `html` text NOT NULL,
  `language` varchar(20) NOT NULL,
  PRIMARY KEY  (`id`)
);
```

▶ Generate a `Snippet` model by using Gii

How to do it...

1. First, we will tweak the `protected/models/Snippet.php` model code. Change rules method to the following:

```
public function rules()
{
  return array(
    array('title, code, language', 'required'),
    array('title', 'length', 'max'=>255),
    array('language', 'length', 'max' => 20),
  );
}
```

2. Add methods to the same `Snippet` model:

```php
protected function afterValidate()
{
    $highlighter = new CTextHighlighter();
    $highlighter->language = $this->language;
    $this->html = $highlighter->highlight($this->code);

    return parent::afterValidate();
}

public function getSupportedLanguages()
{
    return array(
        'php' => 'PHP',
        'css' => 'CSS',
        'html' => 'HTML',
        'javascript' => 'JavaScript',
    );
}
```

3. The model is ready. Now we will create a controller. Therefore, create `protected/controllers/SnippetController.php` as follows:

```php
<?php
class SnippetController extends CController
{
    public function actionIndex()
    {
        $criteria = new CDbCriteria();
        $criteria->order = 'id DESC';
        $models = Snippet::model()->findAll();
        $this->render('index', array(
            'models' => $models,
        ));
    }

    public function actionView($id)
    {
        $model = Snippet::model()->findByPk($id);
        if(!$model)
            throw new CException(404);

        $this->render('view', array(
            'model' => $model,
        ));
```

```
        }

        public function actionAdd()
        {
            $model = new Snippet();
            $data = Yii::app()->request->getPost('Snippet');
            if($data)
            {
                $model->setAttributes($data);
                if($model->save())
                    $this->redirect(array('view', 'id' => $model->id));
            }
            $this->render('add', array(
                'model' => $model,
            ));
        }

        public function actionEdit($id){
            $model = Snippet::model()->findByPk($id);
            if(!$model)
                throw new CHttpException(404);

            $data = Yii::app()->request->getPost('Snippet');
            if($data)
            {
                $model->setAttributes($data);
                if($model->save())
                    $this->redirect(array('view', 'id' => $model->id));
            }
            $this->render('edit', array(
                'model' => $model,
            ));
        }
    }
```

4. Now views; create `protected/views/snippet/index.php` as follows:

```
<h2>Snippets</h2>
<?php echo CHtml::link('Add snippet', array('add'))?>
<ol>
<?php foreach($models as $model):?>
    <li>
        <?php echo CHtml::link(
```

```
        CHtml::encode($model->title),
        array('view', 'id' => $model->id)
    )?>
  </li>
<?php endforeach?>
</ol>
```

5. Create `protected/views/snippet/view.php` as follows:

```
<h2><?php echo CHtml::link('Snippets', array('index'))?> → <?php
    echo CHtml::encode($model->title)?>
</h2>
<?php echo CHtml::link('Edit', array
    ('edit', 'id' => $model->id))?>
<div>
    <?php echo $model->html?>
</div>
```

6. Create `protected/views/snippet/add.php` as follows:

```
<h2><?php echo CHtml::link('Snippets', array('index'))?> → Add
    snippet
</h2>
<?php $this->renderPartial('_form', array('model' => $model))?>
```

7. Create `protected/views/snippet/edit.php` as follows:

```
<h2><?php echo CHtml::link('Snippets', array('index'))?> → Edit
    snippet
</h2>
<?php $this->renderPartial('_form', array('model' => $model))?>
```

8. Create `protected/views/snippet/_form.php` as follows:

```
<?php echo CHtml::beginForm()?>
<ul>
  <li>
    <?php echo CHtml::activeLabel($model, 'title')?>
    <?php echo CHtml::activeTextField($model, 'title')?>
  </li>
  <li>
    <?php echo CHtml::activeLabel($model, 'code')?>
    <?php echo CHtml::activeTextArea($model, 'code')?>
  </li>
  <li>
    <?php echo CHtml::activeLabel($model, 'language')?>
```

```
        <?php echo CHtml::activeDropDownList($model, 'language',
            $model->getSupportedLanguages())?>
    </li>
    <li>
        <?php echo CHtml::submitButton('Save')?>
    </li>
</ul>
<?php echo CHtml::endForm()?>
```

9. That is it. Now run the snippet controller and try creating code snippets, as shown in the following screenshot:

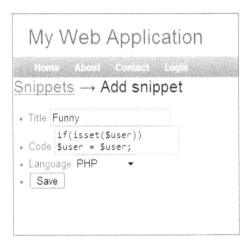

10. When it is viewed, it will look similar to the following:

How it works...

The snippet model's function is used to store the code and snippet title. Additionally, we have added the `html` and `language` fields. The first one (`html`) is used to store HTML representing the highlighted code and the `language` field is used for the snippet language (PHP, HTML, CSS, JavaScript, and so on). We need to store these, as we need them when we edit the the snippet.

As we remove the safe rule from the `Snippet` model, we make `title`, `code`, and `language` as the required fields. There is no rule for `html` which means that it cannot be set through the form directly.

The `afterValidate` method—as its name states—is executed after the validation gives us no errors. In this method, we transform the code which is stored in the `code` field to HTML representing the highlighted code in the `html` field by using the Yii's `CTextHighlighter` class and passing the `language` value to it.

 Note that you need to define CSS with `php-hl-*` classes defined to get highlighting. You can get the default style from `framework/vendors/TextHighlighter/highlight.css`.

`getSupportedLanguages` returns languages we want to support in the value-label array. We use this method in the snippet form.

There's more...

In order to learn more about code highlighting, you can use the following resources:

Yii code highlighter

► `http://www.yiiframework.com/doc/api/CTextHighlighter`
► `http://pear.php.net/package/Text_Highlighter/`

More code highlighters

If `Text_Highlighter` bundled with Yii does not fit your needs, then there are many code highlighters available on the Internet. A few good examples are:

► `http://qbnz.com/highlighter/`
► `http://softwaremaniacs.org/soft/highlight/en/`

See also

▶ The recipe named *Processing model fields with AR event-like methods* in this chapter

▶ The recipe named *Applying markdown and HTML* in this chapter

▶ The recipe named *Automating timestamps* in this chapter

▶ The recipe named *Setting an author automatically* in this chapter

Automating timestamps

Almost every model representing content should have creation and modification dates to show the content actuality, revisions, and so on. In Yii, there are two good ways to automate this, which are as follows:

▶ Overriding `beforeValidate`

▶ Using `CTimestampBehavior` behavior from Zii

We will see how to apply these to blog posts. We will use UNIX timestamps to store the date and time.

Getting ready

▶ Create a new application by using `yiic webapp` as described in the official guide at the following URL:

```
http://www.yiiframework.com/doc/guide/en/quickstart.first-app
```

▶ Set up a database connection and create a table named `post` as follows:

```
DROP TABLE IF EXISTS `post`;
CREATE TABLE IF NOT EXISTS `post` (
  `id` INT(10) UNSIGNED NOT NULL AUTO_INCREMENT,
  `title` VARCHAR(255) NOT NULL,
  `text` TEXT NOT NULL,
  `created_on` INT(10) UNSIGNED NOT NULL,
  `modified_on` INT(10) UNSIGNED NOT NULL,
  PRIMARY KEY (`id`)
);
```

▶ Generate a `Post` model using Gii

▶ Remove everything about `created_on` and `modified_on` from the `rules` method of the model

How to do it...

1. We will start with overriding the `beforeValidate` method. Open `protected/models/Post.php` and add the following method:

```php
protected function beforeValidate()
{
    if($this->getIsNewRecord())
        $this->created_on = time();

    $this->modified_on = time();

    return true;
}
```

2. Now add the following code to the new controller and run it:

```php
$post = new Post();
$post->title = "test title";
$post->text = "test text";
$post->save();
echo date('r', $post->created_on);
```

3. You should get a date and time. Since we have simply created a post, it will be about the current date and time. Another method is to use `CTimestampBehavior`. Delete the `Post` model and generate it one more time by using Gii. Remove everything about `created_on` and `modified_on` from the `rules` method of the model. Add the following method to the model:

```php
public function behaviors()
{
    return array(
        'timestamps' => array(
            'class' => 'zii.behaviors.CTimestampBehavior',
            'createAttribute' => 'created_on',
            'updateAttribute' => 'modified_on',
            'setUpdateOnCreate' => true,
        ),
    );
}
```

How it works...

The `beforeValidate` method executes just before the model validation starts. In this method, `modified_on` is always filled and `created_on` is filled only if the model is new, that means only when we are creating a post.

When we use the ready behavior from Zii, we specify `createAttribute` and `updateAttribute` to match the field names we have chosen. `setUpdateOnCreate` triggers filling `modified_on` when a record is inserted. The rest is done by the `behavior` function.

There's more...

In order to learn more about `CTimestampBehavior`, refer to the following API page:

`http://www.yiiframework.com/doc/api/CTimestampBehavior/`

See also

- ► The recipe named *Processing model fields with AR event-like methods* in this chapter
- ► The recipe named *Applying markdown and HTML* in this chapter
- ► The recipe named *Highlighting code with Yii* in this chapter
- ► The recipe named *Setting an author automatically* in this chapter

Setting an author automatically

Almost all applications which involve multiple content authors should have a way to track who created the content or who is the owner.

From this recipe, you will learn how to automate this by using a model. We assume that the application uses `CUserIdentity` to manage authorization and that `Yii::app()->user->id` returns integer user ID. We don't need to change the original post author if someone else edited it.

Getting ready

- ► Create a new application by using `yiic webapp` as described in the official guide at the following URL:

  `http://www.yiiframework.com/doc/guide/en/quickstart.first-app`

- ► Set up a database connection and create a table named `post` as follows:

  ```
  DROP TABLE IF EXISTS `post`;
  CREATE TABLE IF NOT EXISTS `post` (
    `id` INT(10) UNSIGNED NOT NULL AUTO_INCREMENT,
    `title` VARCHAR(255) NOT NULL,
    `text` TEXT NOT NULL,
    `author_id` INT(10) UNSIGNED NOT NULL,
    PRIMARY KEY (`id`)
  );
  ```

- ► Generate the `Post` model using Gii

How to do it...

1. Add the following method to the `protected/models/Post.php` model as follows:

```
protected function beforeValidate()
{
    if(empty($this->author_id))
        $this->author_id = Yii::app()->user->id;

    return parent::beforeValidate();
}
```

2. That is it. Now we will test it. So, create `protected/controllers/TestController.php` as follows:

```php
<?php
class TestController extends CController
{
    public function actionIndex()
    {
        $post = Post::model()->find();
        if(!$post)
            $post = new Post();

        $post->title = 'test';
        $post->text = 'test';
        $post->save();
        echo $post->author_id;
    }
}
```

3. Now log in and execute `test/index`. You should get an ID of the currently logged in user. Log in as another user and execute the code again. This time, you should get the same ID, which is exactly what we have planned.

How it works...

The `beforeValidate` method executes just before the model validation starts. In this method, we set the `author_id` value to `Yii::app()->user->id` only if the author ID is empty. Most likely, it will be post creation, but can also be when the original author is deleted (if you have properly set the foreign key with the on delete cascade option).

See also

- ▶ The recipe name *Processing model fields with AR event-like methods* in this chapter
- ▶ The recipe name *Applying markdown and HTML* in this chapter
- ▶ The recipe name *Highlighting code with Yii* in this chapter
- ▶ The recipe name *Automating timestamps* in this chapter

Implementing single table inheritance

Relational databases do not support inheritance. If we need to store inheritance in the database, then we should somehow support it through code. This code should be efficient, so it should generate as less JOINs as possible. A common solution to this problem was described by Martin Fowler and named **single table inheritance**.

When we use this pattern, we store all the class tree data in a single table and use the `type` field to determine a model for each row.

As an example, we will implement the single table inheritance for the following class tree:

```
Car
  |- SportCar
  |- FamilyCar
```

Getting ready

- ▶ Create a new application by using `yiic webapp` as described in the official guide
- ▶ Create and set up a database. Add the following table:

```sql
CREATE TABLE `car` (
    `id` int(10) UNSIGNED NOT NULL AUTO_INCREMENT,
    `name` varchar(255) NOT NULL,
    `type` varchar(100) NOT NULL,
    PRIMARY KEY (`id`)
);

INSERT INTO `car` (`name`, `type`)
VALUES ('Ford Focus', 'family'),
('Opel Astra', 'family'),
('Kia Ceed', 'family'),
('Porsche Boxster', 'sport'),
('Ferrari 550', 'sport');
```

How to do it...

1. First, we will create the car model `protected/models/Car.php` as follows:

```php
<?php
class Car extends CActiveRecord
{
    public static function model($className=__CLASS__)
    {
        return parent::model($className);
    }

    public function tableName()
    {
        return 'car';
    }

    protected function instantiate($attributes)
    {
        switch($attributes['type'])
        {
            case 'sport':
                $class='SportCar';
            break;
            case 'family':
                $class='FamilyCar';
            break;
            default:
                $class=get_class($this);
        }
        $model=new $class(null);
        return $model;
    }
}
```

2. Then, we implement `protected/models/SportCar.php` as follows:

```php
<?php
class SportCar extends Car
{
    public static function model($className=__CLASS__)
    {
        return parent::model($className);
    }
```

```php
   public function defaultScope()
   {
      return array(
         'condition'=>"type='sport'",
      );
   }
}
```

3. Also implement `protected/models/FamilyCar.php` as follows:

```php
<?php
class FamilyCar extends Car
{
   public static function model($className=__CLASS__)
   {
      return parent::model($className);
   }

   public function defaultScope()
   {
      return array(
         'condition'=>"type='family'",
      );
   }
}
```

4. Now create `protected/controllers/TestController.php` as follows:

```php
<?php
class TestController extends CController
{
   public function actionIndex()
   {
      echo "<h1>All cars</h1>";
      $cars = Car::model()->findAll();
      foreach($cars as $car)
      {
         // Each car can be of class Car, SportCar or FamilyCar
         echo get_class($car).' '.$car->name."<br />";
      }

      echo "<h1>Sport cars only</h1>";
      $sportCars = SportCar::model()->findAll();
      foreach($sportCars as $car)
      {
```

```
            // Each car should be SportCar
            echo get_class($car).' '.$car->name."<br />";
        }
    }
}
```

5. Run `test/index` and you should get the following output:

All cars

FamilyCar Ford Focus
FamilyCar Opel Astra
FamilyCar Kia Ceed
SportCar Porsche Boxster
SportCar Ferrari 550

Sport cars only

SportCar Porsche Boxster
SportCar Ferrari 550

How it works...

The base model `Car` is a typically used Yii AR model except two added methods. `tableName` explicitly declares the table name to be used for the model. For the `Car` model alone, this does not make sense but for child models, it will return the same `car` table which is just what we want—a single table for the entire class tree. `instantiate` is used by AR internally to create a model instance from the raw data when we call methods, such as `Car::model()->findAll()`. We use a switch statement to create different classes based on the `type` attribute and use the same class if the attribute value is either not specified or points to the non-existing class.

`SportCar` and `FamilyCar` models simply set the default AR scope, so when we find models with `SportCar::model()->` methods, we will get the `SportCar` model only.

There's more...

Use the following references to learn more about the single table inheritance pattern and Yii Active Record implementation:

▶   http://martinfowler.com/eaaCatalog/singleTableInheritance.html
▶   http://www.yiiframework.com/doc/api/CActiveRecord/

See also

▶ The recipe named *Using scopes to get models for different languages* in this chapter

Using CDbCriteria

When we use Yii's Active Record methods such as `findAll` or `find`, we can pass criteria as a parameter. It can be an array or an instance of the `CDbCriteria` class. This class represents query criteria, such as conditions, ordering by, limit/offset, and so on.

How to do it...

Usually, the criteria class is used as shown in the following example:

```
$criteria = new CDbCriteria();
$criteria->limit = 10;
$criteria->order= 'id DESC';
$criteria->with = array('comments');
$criteria->compare('approved', 1);
$criteria->addInCondition('id', array(4, 8, 15, 16, 23, 42));
$posts = Post::model()->findAll($criteria);
```

How it works...

Internally, the criteria class does not build any queries by itself, but it stores only data and allows us to modify it. The actual work is being done inside AR methods where criteria are being used.

The preceding code can be read as follows:

> *Get 10 posts along with comments from approved posts with ID equals to 4, 8, 15, 16, 23 or 42 ordered by the ID descendant.*

> *Or*

```
SELECT *
FROM post p
JOIN comment c ON p.id = c.post_id
WHERE p.approved = 1
AND p.id IN (4, 8, 15, 16, 23, 42)
ORDER BY p.id DESC
LIMIT 10
```

There's more...

For further information, refer to the following URLs:

- ▶ http://www.yiiframework.com/doc/api/CDbCriteria/
- ▶ http://www.yiiframework.com/doc/api/CPagination/
- ▶ http://www.yiiframework.com/doc/api/CSort/

See also

- ▶ The recipe named *Getting data from a database* in this chapter

7
Using Zii Components

In this chapter, we will cover:

- ▶ Using data providers
- ▶ Using grids
- ▶ Using lists
- ▶ Creating custom grid columns

Introduction

Yii have a useful library called Zii. It's bundled with framework and includes some classes aimed to make the developer's life easier. Its most handy components are grids and lists which allow you to build data in both the admin and user parts of a website in a very fast and efficient way. In this chapter you'll learn how to use and adjust these components to fit your needs. Also you'll learn about data providers. They are part of the core framework, not Zii, but since they are used extensively with grids and lists, we'll review them here.

We'll use Sakila sample database version 0.8 available from official MySQL website: `http://dev.mysql.com/doc/sakila/en/sakila.html`.

Using data providers

Data providers are used to encapsulate common data model operations such as sorting, pagination and querying. They are used with grids and lists extensively. Because both widgets and providers are standardized, you can display the same data using different widgets and you can get data for a widget from various providers. Switching providers and widgets is relatively transparent.

Currently there are CActiveDataProvider, CArrayDataProvider, and CSqlDataProvider implemented to get data from ActiveRecord models, arrays, and SQL queries respectively.

Let's try all these providers to fill a grid with data.

Getting ready

▶ Create a new application using yiic webapp as described in the official guide.

▶ Download the Sakila database from http://dev.mysql.com/doc/sakila/en/sakila.html and execute the downloaded SQLs: first schema then data.

▶ Configure the DB connection in protected/config/main.php.

▶ Use Gii to create a model for the film table.

How to do it...

1. Let's start with a view for a grid controller. Create protected/views/grid/index.php:

```php
<?php $this->widget('zii.widgets.grid.CGridView',
  array('dataProvider' => $dataProvider,
))?>
```

2. Then create a protected/controllers/GridController.php:

```php
<?php
class GridController extends Controller
{
  public function actionAR()
  {
    $dataProvider = new CActiveDataProvider('Film', array(
      'pagination'=>array(
        'pageSize'=>10,
      ),
      'sort'=>array(
        'defaultOrder'=> array('title'=>false),
      )
    ));

    $this->render('index', array(
      'dataProvider' => $dataProvider,
    ));
  }
```

```php
public function actionArray()
{
  $yiiDevelopers = array(
    array(
      'name'=>'Qiang Xue',
      'id'=>'2',
      'forumName'=>'qiang',
      'memberSince'=>'Jan 2008',
      'location'=>'Washington DC, USA',
      'duty'=>'founder and project lead',
      'active'=>true,
    ),
    array(
      'name'=>'Wei Zhuo',
      'id'=>'3',
      'forumName'=>'wei',
      'memberSince'=>'Jan 2008',
      'location'=>'Sydney, Australia',
      'duty'=>'project site maintenance and development',
      'active'=>true,
    ),
    array(
      'name'=>'Sebastián Thierer',
      'id'=>'54',
      'forumName'=>'sebas',
      'memberSince'=>'Sep 2009',
      'location'=>'Argentina',
      'duty'=>'component development',
      'active'=>true,
    ),
    array(
      'name'=>'Alexander Makarov',
      'id'=>'415',
      'forumName'=>'samdark',
      'memberSince'=>'Mar 2010',
      'location'=>'Russia',
      'duty'=>'core framework development',
      'active'=>true,
    ),
    array(
      'name'=>'Maurizio Domba',
      'id'=>'2650',
      'forumName'=>'mdomba',
      'memberSince'=>'Aug 2010',
```

```
                  'location'=>'Croatia',
                  'duty'=>'core framework development',
                  'active'=>true,
              ),
              array(
                  'name'=>'Y!!',
                  'id'=>'1644',
                  'forumName'=>'Y!!',
                  'memberSince'=>'Aug 2010',
                  'location'=>'Germany',
                  'duty'=>'core framework development',
                  'active'=>true,
              ),
              array(
                  'name'=>'Jeffrey Winesett',
                  'id'=>'15',
                  'forumName'=>'jefftulsa',
                  'memberSince'=>'Sep 2010',
                  'location'=>'Austin, TX, USA',
                  'duty'=>'documentation and marketing',
                  'active'=>true,
              ),
              array(
                  'name'=>'Jonah Turnquist',
                  'id'=>'127',
                  'forumName'=>'jonah',
                  'memberSince'=>'Sep 2009 - Aug 2010',
                  'location'=>'California, US',
                  'duty'=>'component development',
                  'active'=>false,
              ),
              array(
                  'name'=>'István Beregszászi',
                  'id'=>'1286',
                  'forumName'=>'pestaa',
                  'memberSince'=>'Sep 2009 - Mar 2010',
                  'location'=>'Hungary',
                  'duty'=>'core framework development',
                  'active'=>false,
              ),
          );
```

```
  $dataProvider = new CArrayDataProvider(
    $yiiDevelopers, array(
    'sort'=>array(
      'attributes'=>array('name', 'id', 'active'),
      'defaultOrder'=>array('active' => true, 'name' => false),
    ),
    'pagination'=>array(
      'pageSize'=>10,
    ),
  ));

  $this->render('index', array(
    'dataProvider' => $dataProvider,
  ));
}

public function actionSQL()
{
  $count=Yii::app()->db->createCommand('SELECT COUNT(*)
    FROM film')->queryScalar();
  $sql='SELECT * FROM film';
  $dataProvider=new CSqlDataProvider($sql, array(
    'keyField'=>'film_id',
    'totalItemCount'=>$count,
    'sort'=>array(
      'attributes'=>array('title'),
      'defaultOrder'=>array('title' => false),
    ),
    'pagination'=>array(
      'pageSize'=>10,
    ),
  ));

  $this->render('index', array(
    'dataProvider' => $dataProvider,
  ));
}
}
```

3. Now run `grid/aR`, `grid/array` and `grid/sql` actions and try using the grids.

Customer	Store	First Name	Last Name	Email	Address	
1	1	MARY	SMITH	MARY.SMITH@sakilacustomer.org	5	
2	1	PATRICIA	JOHNSON	PATRICIA.JOHNSON@sakilacustomer.org	6	
3	1	LINDA	WILLIAMS	LINDA.WILLIAMS@sakilacustomer.org	7	
4	2	BARBARA	JONES	BARBARA.JONES@sakilacustomer.org	8	
5	1	ELIZABETH	BROWN	ELIZABETH.BROWN@sakilacustomer.org	9	
6	2	JENNIFER	DAVIS	JENNIFER.DAVIS@sakilacustomer.org	10	
7	1	MARIA	MILLER	MARIA.MILLER@sakilacustomer.org	11	
8	2	SUSAN	WILSON	SUSAN.WILSON@sakilacustomer.org	12	
9	2	MARGARET	MOORE	MARGARET.MOORE@sakilacustomer.org	13	
10	1	DOROTHY	TAYLOR	DOROTHY.TAYLOR@sakilacustomer.org	14	

Advanced Search

Displaying 1-10 of 599 result(s)

Go to page   < Previous   **1** 2 3 4 5 6 7 8 9 10   Next >

How it works...

The view is pretty simple and stays the same for all data providers. We are calling the grid widget and passing the data provider instance to it.

Let's review actions one by one starting with `actionAR`:

```
$dataProvider = new CActiveDataProvider('Film', array(
  'pagination'=>array(
    'pageSize'=>10,
  ),
  'sort'=>array(
    'defaultOrder'=>array('title'=>false),
  )
));
```

`CActiveDataProvider` works with active record models. Model class is passed as a first argument of class constructor. Second argument is an array that defines class public properties. In the code above, we are setting pagination to 10 items per page and default sorting by title.

Note that instead of using a string we are using an array where keys are column names and values are true or false. `true` means order is DESC while `false` means that order is ASC. Defining the default order this way allows Yii to render a triangle showing sorting direction in the column header.

In `actionArray` we are using `CArrayDataProvider` that can consume any array.

```
$dataProvider = new CArrayDataProvider($yiiDevelopers, array(
  'sort'=>array(
    'attributes'=>array('name', 'id', 'active'),
    'defaultOrder'=>array('active' => true, 'name' => false),
  ),
  'pagination'=>array(
    'pageSize'=>10,
  ),
));
```

First argument accepts an associative array where keys are column names and values are corresponding values. Second argument accepts an array with the same options as in `CActiveDataProvider` case.

In `actionSQL`, we are using `CSqlDataProvider` that consumes the SQL query and modifies it automatically allowing pagination. First argument accepts a string with SQL and a second argument with data provider parameters. This time we need to supply `calculateTotalItemCount` with total count of records manually. For this purpose we need to execute the extra SQL query manually. Also we need to define `keyField` since the primary key of this table is not `id` but `film_id`.

To sum up, all data providers are accepting the following properties:

`pagination`	`CPagination` object or an array of initial values for new instance of `CPagination`.
`sort`	`CSort` object or an array of initial values for new instance of `CSort`.
`totalItemCount`	We need to set this only if the provider, such as `CSqlDataProvider`, does not implement the `calculateTotalItemCount` method.

There's more...

You can use data providers without any special widgets. Replace `protected/views/grid/index.php` content with the following:

```php
<?php foreach($dataProvider->data as $film):?>
  <?php echo $film->title?>
<?php endforeach?>

<?php $this->widget('CLinkPager',array(
  'pages'=>$dataProvider->pagination))?>
```

Further reading

To learn more about data providers refer to the following API pages:

- ▶ `http://www.yiiframework.com/doc/api/CDataProvider`
- ▶ `http://www.yiiframework.com/doc/api/CActiveDataProvider`
- ▶ `http://www.yiiframework.com/doc/api/CArrayDataProvider`
- ▶ `http://www.yiiframework.com/doc/api/CSqlDataProvider`
- ▶ `http://www.yiiframework.com/doc/api/CSort`
- ▶ `http://www.yiiframework.com/doc/api/CPagination`

See also

- ▶ The recipe named *Using grids* in this chapter
- ▶ The recipe named *Using lists* in this chapter

Using grids

Zii grids are very useful to quickly create efficient application admin pages or any pages you need to manage data on.

Let's use Gii to generate a grid, see how it works, and how we can customize it.

Getting ready

Carry out the following steps:

- ▶ Create a new application using `yiic webapp` as described in the official guide.
- ▶ Download the Sakila database from `http://dev.mysql.com/doc/sakila/en/sakila.html`. Execute the downloaded SQLs: first schema then data.
- ▶ Configure the DB connection in `protected/config/main.php`.
- ▶ Use Gii to create models for `customer`, `address`, and `city` tables.

How to do it...

1. Open Gii, select Crud Generator, and enter `Customer` into the Model Class field. Press Preview and then Generate.

2. Gii will generate a controller in `protected/controllers/CustomerController.php` and a group of views under `protected/views/customer/`.

3. Run `customer` controller and go to Manage Customer link. After logging in you should see the grid generated:

Advanced Search

Displaying 1-10 of 599 result(s)

Customer	Store	First Name	Last Name	Email	Address	
1	1	MARY	SMITH	MARY.SMITH@sakilacustomer.org	5	
2	1	PATRICIA	JOHNSON	PATRICIA.JOHNSON@sakilacustomer.org	6	
3	1	LINDA	WILLIAMS	LINDA.WILLIAMS@sakilacustomer.org	7	
4	2	BARBARA	JONES	BARBARA.JONES@sakilacustomer.org	8	
5	1	ELIZABETH	BROWN	ELIZABETH.BROWN@sakilacustomer.org	9	
6	2	JENNIFER	DAVIS	JENNIFER.DAVIS@sakilacustomer.org	10	
7	1	MARIA	MILLER	MARIA.MILLER@sakilacustomer.org	11	
8	2	SUSAN	WILSON	SUSAN.WILSON@sakilacustomer.org	12	
9	2	MARGARET	MOORE	MARGARET.MOORE@sakilacustomer.org	13	
10	1	DOROTHY	TAYLOR	DOROTHY.TAYLOR@sakilacustomer.org	14	

Go to page: < Previous 1 2 3 4 5 6 7 8 9 10 Next >

How it works...

Let's start with the `admin` action of `customer` controller:

```
public function actionAdmin()
{
  $model=new Customer('search');
  $model->unsetAttributes();  // clear any default values
  if(isset($_GET['Customer']))
    $model->attributes=$_GET['Customer'];

  $this->render('admin',array(
    'model'=>$model,
  ));
}
```

`Customer` model is created with `search` scenario, all attribute values are cleaned up, and then filled up with data from `$_GET`. On the first request `$_GET` is empty but when you are changing the page, or filtering by first name attribute using the input field below the column name, the following GET parameters are passed to the same action via an AJAX request:

```
Customer[address_id] =
Customer[customer_id] =
Customer[email] =
```

```
Customer[first_name] = alex
Customer[last_name] =
Customer[store_id] =
Customer_page = 2
ajax = customer-grid
```

Since scenario is `search`, the corresponding validation rules from `Customer::rules` are applied. For the search scenario, Gii generates a `safe` rule that allows to mass assigning for all fields:

```
array('customer_id, store_id, first_name, last_name, email, address_
id, active, create_date, last_update', 'safe',
'on'=>'search'),
```

Then model is passed to a view `protected/views/customer/admin.php`. It renders advanced search form and then passes the model to the grid widget:

```php
<?php $this->widget('zii.widgets.grid.CGridView', array(
  'id'=>'customer-grid',
  'dataProvider'=>$model->search(),
  'filter'=>$model,
  'columns'=>array(
    'customer_id',
    'store_id',
    'first_name',
    'last_name',
    'email',
    'address_id',
    /*
    'active',
    'create_date',
    'last_update',
    */
    array(
      'class'=>'CButtonColumn',
    ),
  ),
)); ?>
```

Columns used in the grid are passed to `columns`. When just a name is passed, the corresponding field from data provider is used.

Also we can use custom column represented by a class specified. In this case we are using `CButtonColumn` that renders view, update and delete buttons that are linked to the same named actions and are passing row ID to them so action can be done to a model representing specific row from database.

`filter` property accepts a model filled with data. If it's set, a grid will display multiple text fields at the top that the user can fill to filter the grid.

The `dataProvider` property takes an instance of data provider. In our case it's returned by the model's `search` method:

```
public function search()
{
  // Warning: Please modify the following code to remove attributes
     that
  // should not be searched.

  $criteria=new CDbCriteria;

  $criteria->compare('customer_id',$this->customer_id);
  $criteria->compare('store_id',$this->store_id);
  $criteria->compare('first_name',$this->first_name,true);
  $criteria->compare('last_name',$this->last_name,true);
  $criteria->compare('email',$this->email,true);
  $criteria->compare('address_id',$this->address_id);
  $criteria->compare('active',$this->active);
  $criteria->compare('create_date',$this->create_date,true);
  $criteria->compare('last_update',$this->last_update,true);

  return new CActiveDataProvider(get_class($this), array(
    'criteria'=>$criteria,
  ));
}
```

This method is called after the model was filled with `$_GET` data from the filtering fields so we can use field values to form the criteria for the data provider. In this case all numeric values are compared exactly while string values are compared using partial match.

There's more...

Code generated by Gii can be useful in a lot of simple cases but often we need to customize it.

Using data from related Active Record models

In the code, the generated grid displays the store and address IDs instead of corresponding values. Let's fix the address and display city, district, and address instead of just ID.

1. We have the following relations in the `Customer` model:

```
public function relations()
{
  // NOTE: you may need to adjust the relation name and
     the related
```

```
    // class name for the relations automatically generated below.
    return array(
      'address' => array(self::BELONGS_TO, 'Address', 'address_id'),
      'store' => array(self::BELONGS_TO, 'Store', 'store_id'),
      'payments' => array(self::HAS_MANY, 'Payment', 'customer_id'),
      'rentals' => array(self::HAS_MANY, 'Rental', 'customer_id'),
    );
  }
```

2. We need to load `address` data along with the model. That means we have to add these to the `with` part of the criteria passed to the data provider in `Customer::search`. Since the address includes city ID, we need to load the city data using the city relation of the `Address` model.

```
public function search()
{
    // Warning: Please modify the following code to remove
    //attributes that should not be searched.

    $criteria=new CDbCriteria;

    $criteria->with = array('address' => array(
      'with' => 'city'
    )); …
```

> Each relation used in the `with` part of the criteria can be specified in the way shown above where key is the relation name and value is an array representing criteria. These criteria will be applied to the related model.

3. Now let's modify the columns list passed to a grid in `protected/views/customer/admin.php`:

```
'columns'=>array(
    'customer_id',
    'store_id',
    'first_name',
    'last_name',
    'email',
    array(
      'name'=>'address',
      'value'=>'$data->address->address.",
        ".$data->address->city->city.",
        ".$data->address->district',
    ),
```

4. In the preceding code, we are using a relation name of `name` and setting `value` to a string consisting of address, city, and district.

   Now check the grid. It should now list address, city, and district in the address field.

Customer	Store	First Name	Last Name	Email	Address	
1	1	MARY	SMITH	MARY.SMITH@sakilacustomer.org	1913 Hanoi Way, Sasebo, Nagasaki	🔍 ✎ ✖
2	1	PATRICIA	JOHNSON	PATRICIA.JOHNSON@sakilacustomer.org	1121 Loja Avenue, San Bernardino, California	🔍 ✎ ✖
3	1	LINDA	WILLIAMS	LINDA.WILLIAMS@sakilacustomer.org	692 Joliet Street, Athenai, Attika	🔍 ✎ ✖
4	2	BARBARA	JONES	BARBARA.JONES@sakilacustomer.org	1566 Inegl Manor, Myingyan, Mandalay	🔍 ✎ ✖
5	1	ELIZABETH	BROWN	ELIZABETH.BROWN@sakilacustomer.org	53 Idfu Parkway, Nantou, Nantou	🔍 ✎ ✖
6	2	JENNIFER	DAVIS	JENNIFER.DAVIS@sakilacustomer.org	1795 Santiago de Compostela Way, Laredo, Texas	🔍 ✎ ✖
7	1	MARIA	MILLER	MARIA.MILLER@sakilacustomer.org	900 Santiago de Compostela Parkway, Kragujevac, Central Serbia	🔍 ✎ ✖
8	2	SUSAN	WILSON	SUSAN.WILSON@sakilacustomer.org	478 Joliet Way, Hamilton, Hamilton	🔍 ✎ ✖
9	2	MARGARET	MOORE	MARGARET.MOORE@sakilacustomer.org	613 Korolev Drive, Masqat, Masqat	🔍 ✎ ✖
10	1	DOROTHY	TAYLOR	DOROTHY.TAYLOR@sakilacustomer.org	1531 Sal Drive, Esfahan, Esfahan	🔍 ✎ ✖

Displaying 1-10 of 599 result(s)

Go to page. < Previous 1 2 3 4 5 6 7 8 9 10 Next >

5. The only problems now are that address is not sortable and filtering using address does not work.

   Let's fix the sorting first. In the `Customer::search` method we need to create `CSort` instance, configure it, and pass it to the data provider:

```
$sort = new CSort;
$sort->attributes = array(
  'address' => array(
    'asc' => 'address, city, district',
    'desc' => 'address DESC, city DESC, district DESC',
  ),
```

```
  '*',
);
return new CActiveDataProvider(get_class($this), array(
  'criteria'=>$criteria,
  'sort'=>$sort,
));
```

`CSort::attributes` accepts a list of sortable attributes. We want all `Customer` attributes to be sortable so we are adding * to the list. Additionally we are specifying SQL for both ascending and descending sorting of the `address` attribute.

That's it. Sorting should work.

6. Now let's fix filtering. First we need to add `address` to the safe attributes list in the model's `rules` method. Then we are replacing comparison in `Customer::search`:

```
$criteria->compare('address_id',$this->address_id);
```

should be replaced with:

```
$criteria->compare('address',$this->address,true);
$criteria->compare('district',$this->address,true,"OR");
$criteria->compare('city',$this->address,true,"OR");
```

7. When a user enters `california` in the address filter field, the three compares above will result in SQL like the following:

```
WHERE address LIKE '%california%'
OR district LIKE '%california%'
OR city LIKE '%california%'
```

Displaying 1-10 of 11 result(s)

Customer	Store	First Name	Last Name	Email	Address ▲	
					california	
2	1	PATRICIA	JOHNSON	PATRICIA.JOHNSON@sakilacustomer.org	1121 Loja Avenue, San Bernardino, California	🔍 ✎ ✖
51	1	ALICE	STEWART	ALICE.STEWART@sakilacustomer.org	1135 Izumisano Parkway, Fontana, California	🔍 ✎ ✖
488	2	SHANE	MILLARD	SHANE.MILLARD@sakilacustomer.org	184 Mandaluyong Street, La Paz, Baja California Sur	🔍 ✎ ✖
420	1	JACOB	LANCE	JACOB.LANCE@sakilacustomer.org	1866 al-Qatif Avenue, El Monte, California	🔍 ✎ ✖
593	2	RENE	MCALISTER	RENE.MCALISTER@sakilacustomer.org	1895 Zhezqazghan Drive, Garden Grove, California	🔍 ✎ ✖
214	1	KRISTIN	JOHNSTON	KRISTIN.JOHNSTON@sakilacustomer.org	226 Brest Manor, Sunnyvale, California	🔍 ✎ ✖
182	1	RENEE	LANE	RENEE.LANE@sakilacustomer.org	533 al-Ayn Boulevard, Compton, California	🔍 ✎ ✖
14	2	BETTY	WHITE	BETTY.WHITE@sakilacustomer.org	770 Bydgoszcz Avenue, Citrus Heights, California	🔍 ✎ ✖
343	1	DOUGLAS	GRAF	DOUGLAS.GRAF@sakilacustomer.org	785 Vaduz Street, Mexicali, Baja California	🔍 ✎ ✖
112	2	ROSA	REYNOLDS	ROSA.REYNOLDS@sakilacustomer.org	793 Cam Ranh Avenue, Lancaster, California	🔍 ✎ ✖

Go to page < Previous 1 2 Next >

Further reading

To learn more about grids and its properties refer to the following resources:

- ▶ http://www.yiiframework.com/doc/api/CGridView
- ▶ http://www.yiiframework.com/doc/api/CDbCriteria
- ▶ http://www.yiiframework.com/doc/api/CSort

See also

- ▶ The recipe named *Using data providers* in this chapter
- ▶ The recipe named *Using lists* in this chapter
- ▶ The recipe named *Creating custom grid columns* in this chapter

Using lists

Zii lists are a good tool to display data from any data provider to end users while handling pagination and sorting automatically. `CListView` is very customizable so it allows building any type of list page.

Let's use Gii to generate a list, see how it works, and how we can customize it.

Getting ready

▶ Create a new application using `yiic webapp` as described in the official guide.

▶ Download the Sakila database from `http://dev.mysql.com/doc/sakila/en/sakila.html`. Execute the downloaded SQLs: first schema then data.

▶ Configure the DB connection in `protected/config/main.php`.

▶ Use Gii to create models for `customer`, `store`, `address`, and `city` tables.

How to do it...

1. Open Gii, select Crud Generator, and enter `Customer` into the Model Class field. Press Preview and then Generate.

2. Gii will generate a controller in `protected/controllers/CustomerController.php` and a group of views under `protected/views/customer/`.

3. Run, `index` action of `customer` controller to see the customers list in action.

Displaying 1-10 of 599 result(s)

Customer: 1
Store: 1
First Name: MARY
Last Name: SMITH
Email: MARY SMITH@sakilacustomer org
Address: 5
Active: 1

Customer: 2
Store: 1
First Name: PATRICIA

How it works...

Let's start with the `index` action of `Customer` controller:

```
public function actionIndex()
{
```

```
$dataProvider=new CActiveDataProvider('Customer');
$this->render('index',array(
  'dataProvider'=>$dataProvider,
));
}
```

It's very simple: new active data provider for the `Customer` model is created and passed into the `protected/views/customer/index.php` view where it is used in the `CListView` widget:

```
<?php $this->widget('zii.widgets.CListView', array(
  'dataProvider'=>$dataProvider,
  'itemView'=>'_view',
)); ?>
```

`itemView` specifies a view partially used to render each data row. In our case it's `protected/views/customer/_view.php` that lists all attribute names and values like the following:

```
<b><?php echo CHtml::encode($data->getAttributeLabel(
  'first_name')); ?>:</b>
  <?php echo CHtml::encode($data->first_name); ?>
```

`$data` in the code above refers to a model representing a data row that came from the data provider.

There's more...

If you are using lists in real applications, most likely you'll want to customize them.

Adding sorting

Let's add ability to sort by last name and email. To implement it we need to define `sortableAttributes` property:

```
<?php $this->widget('zii.widgets.CListView', array(
  'dataProvider'=>$dataProvider,
  'itemView'=>'_view',
  'sortableAttributes'=>array(
    'last_name',
    'email',
  ),
)); ?>
```

Customizing templates

Let's add pagination and sorter at the top and the bottom, and remove the summary. To implement all these we need to customize just one widget property called `template`:

```php
<?php $this->widget('zii.widgets.CListView', array(
  'dataProvider'=>$dataProvider,
  'itemView'=>'_view',
  'sortableAttributes'=>array(
    'last_name',
    'email',
  ),
  'template' => '{sorter} {pager} {items} {sorter} {pager}',
)); ?>
```

Sort by: Last Name Email

Go to page « Previous **1** 2 3 4 5 6 7 8 9 10 Next >

Customer: 1
Store: 1
First Name: MARY
Last Name: SMITH
Email: MARY.SMITH@sakilacustomer.org
Address: 5
Active: 1

Customer: 2
Store: 1
First Name: PATRICIA
Last Name: JOHNSON
Email: PATRICIA.JOHNSON@sakilacustomer.org

Customizing markup and data displayed

Let's tweak list markup and templates starting with the widget parameters:

```php
<?php $this->widget('zii.widgets.CListView', array(
  'dataProvider'=>$dataProvider,
  'itemView'=>'_view',
  'itemsTagName' => 'ol',
  'itemsCssClass' => 'customers',
  'sortableAttributes'=>array(
    'last_name',
    'email',
  ),
  'template' => '{sorter} {pager} {items} {sorter} {pager}',
)); ?>
```

`itemsTagName` defines a tag that will be used as a base tag for a list. In this case the list is ordered so we are using `ol`. `itemsCssClass` sets a class for this `ol`.

We need to modify `protected/views/customer/_view.php`:

```
<li>
  <h2>
    <?php
    $title = CHtml::encode($data->first_name.' '.$data->last_name);
    echo CHtml::link($title, array('view', 'id'=>
      $data->customer_id));
    ?>
  </h2>

  <ul>
    <li>
      <strong><?php echo CHtml::encode($data->
        getAttributeLabel('store_id')); ?>:</strong>
      <?php echo CHtml::encode($data->store->
        address->address.', '.$data->store->address->city->city.',
        '.$data->store->address->district); ?>
    </li>
    <li>
      <strong><?php echo CHtml::encode($data->
        getAttributeLabel('email')); ?>:</strong>
      <?php echo CHtml::encode($data->email); ?>
    </li>
    <li>
      <strong><?php echo CHtml::encode($data->
        getAttributeLabel('address_id')); ?>:</strong>
      <?php echo CHtml::encode($data->address->address.',
        '.$data->address->city->city.',
        '.$data->address->district); ?>
    </li>
    <li>
      <strong><?php echo CHtml::encode($data->
        getAttributeLabel('active')); ?>:</strong>
      <?php echo $data->active ? 'Yes' : 'No'; ?>
    </li>
  </ul>
</li>
```

Let's apply some CSS. Create `protected/assets/customers.css`:

```
ol.customers {
  list-style: none;
  margin: 1em 0;
}

ol.customers>li {
  margin: 1em;
  padding:1em;
  background: #fcfcfc;
  border: 1px solid #9aafe5;
}
```

Then you need to add the following to `protected/views/customer/_view.php`:

```
<?php Yii::app()->clientScript->registerCssFile(
  Yii::app()->assetManager->publish(Yii::getPathOfAlias('application.
assets').
  '/customers.css'))?>
```

After applying styles, the list will look like this:

Further reading

To learn more about lists refer to the following API page:

▶ `http://www.yiiframework.com/doc/api/CListView/`

See also

▶ The recipe named *Using data providers* in this chapter

Creating custom grid columns

Most of the time you don't need to create your own grid column types since the ones included in Yii are pretty flexible and are suitable for most use cases. Still, there are situations when you need to create a custom column.

Let's create a custom grid column that will allow a toggling Y/N value that will change the corresponding model value via AJAX.

Getting ready

- ▶ Create a new application using `yiic webapp` as described in the official guide.
- ▶ Download the Sakila database from `http://dev.mysql.com/doc/sakila/en/sakila.html`. Execute the downloaded SQLs: first schema then data.
- ▶ Configure the DB connection in `protected/config/main.php`.
- ▶ Use Gii to create model for the customer `table`.
- ▶ Open Gii, select "Crud Generator" and enter `Customer` into the "Model Class" field. Press "Preview" and then "Generate".
- ▶ Gii will generate the controller in `protected/controllers/CustomerController.php` and a group of views under `protected/views/customer/`.
- ▶ Run customer controller and go to the "Manage Customer" link. After logging in you should see the grid generated.

How to do it...

In the table we have an `active` field that we want to toggle with the flag column. Column should display Y or N depending on what the value is and should allow toggling of the value by clicking on it. Grid should stay on the same page.

1. Let's create `protected/components/FlagColumn.php`:

```php
<?php
class FlagColumn extends CGridColumn
{
    public $name;
    public $sortable=true;
    public $callbackUrl = array('flag');
    private $_flagClass = "flag_link";

    public function init() {
        parent::init();
```

```php
    $cs=Yii::app()->getClientScript();
    $gridId = $this->grid->getId();
    $script = <<<SCRIPT
    jQuery(".{$this->_flagClass}").live("click", function(e){
      e.preventDefault();
      var link = this;
      $.ajax({
        dataType: "json",
        cache: false,
        url: link.href,
        success: function(data){
          $('#$gridId').yiiGridView.update('$gridId');
        }
      });
    });
    SCRIPT;
    $cs->registerScript(__CLASS__.$gridId.'#flag_link', $script);
  }

  protected function renderDataCellContent($row, $data) {
    $value=CHtml::value($data,$this->name);

    $this->callbackUrl['pk'] = $data->primaryKey;
    $this->callbackUrl['name'] = urlencode($this->name);
    $this->callbackUrl['value'] = (int)empty($value);

    $link = CHtml::normalizeUrl($this->callbackUrl);

    echo CHtml::link(!empty($value) ? 'Y' : 'N', $link, array(
      'class' => $this->_flagClass,
    ));
  }

  protected function renderHeaderCellContent()
  {
    if($this->grid->enableSorting && $this->sortable &&
      $this->name!==null)
      echo $this->grid->dataProvider->getSort()->link(
        $this->name,$this->header);
    else if($this->name!==null && $this->header===null)
    {
      if($this->grid->dataProvider instanceof CActiveDataProvider)
        echo CHtml::encode($this->grid->dataProvider->
          model->getAttributeLabel($this->name));
      else
        echo CHtml::encode($this->name);
```

```
    }
    else
      parent::renderHeaderCellContent();
  }
}
```

2. Now in `protected/controllers/CustomerController.php` we need to implement `actionFlag`:

```php
public function actionFlag($pk, $name, $value){
  $model = $this->loadModel($pk);
  $model->{$name} = $value;
  $model->save(false);

  if(!Yii::app()->request->isAjaxRequest){
    $this->redirect('admin');
  }
}
```

3. Finally we need to use it in a grid, `protected/views/customer/admin.php`:

```php
...
<?php $this->widget('zii.widgets.grid.CGridView', array(
  'id'=>'customer-grid',
  'dataProvider'=>$model->search(),
  'filter'=>$model,
  'columns'=>array(
    'customer_id',
    'store_id',
    'first_name',
    'last_name',
    'email',
    'address_id',
    array(
      'class' => 'FlagColumn',
      'name' => 'active',
    ),
    /*
    'create_date',
    'last_update',
    */
    array(
      'class'=>'CButtonColumn',
    ),
  ),
)); ?>
...
```

4. Now check the grid. It should contain an `Active` column with `Y` and `N` as values:

Customer	Store	First Name	Last Name	Email	Address	Active	
						Displaying 1-10 of 599 result(s)	
1	1	MARY	SMITH	MARY.SMITH@sakilacustomer.org	5	Y	🔍 ✏ ✖
2	1	PATRICIA	JOHNSON	PATRICIA.JOHNSON@sakilacustomer.org	6	N	🔍 ✏ ✖
3	1	LINDA	WILLIAMS	LINDA.WILLIAMS@sakilacustomer.org	7	Y	🔍 ✏ ✖
4	2	BARBARA	JONES	BARBARA.JONES@sakilacustomer.org	8	Y	🔍 ✏ ✖
5	1	ELIZABETH	BROWN	ELIZABETH.BROWN@sakilacustomer.org	9	N	🔍 ✏ ✖
6	2	JENNIFER	DAVIS	JENNIFER.DAVIS@sakilacustomer.org	10	Y	🔍 ✏ ✖
7	1	MARIA	MILLER	MARIA.MILLER@sakilacustomer.org	11	N	🔍 ✏ ✖
8	2	SUSAN	WILSON	SUSAN.WILSON@sakilacustomer.org	12	Y	🔍 ✏ ✖
9	2	MARGARET	MOORE	MARGARET.MOORE@sakilacustomer.org	13	Y	🔍 ✏ ✖
10	1	DOROTHY	TAYLOR	DOROTHY.TAYLOR@sakilacustomer.org	14	Y	🔍 ✏ ✖

Go to page < Previous **1** 2 3 4 5 6 7 8 9 10 Next >

How it works...

When calling a grid widget we can pass an array specifying column class and setting public properties of this class.

```
'columns'=>array(
  'customer_id',
  'store_id',
  'first_name',
  'last_name',
  'email',
  'address_id',
  array(
    'class' => 'FlagColumn',
    'name' => 'active',
  ),
```

In the code above we are using `FlagColumn` class and setting its `name` property to active.

```
class FlagColumn extends CGridColumn
```

A grid column should extend `CGridColumn` and implement at least the `renderDataCellContent` method:

```
protected function renderDataCellContent($row, $data) {
  $value=CHtml::value($data,$this->name);
```

```
$this->callbackUrl['pk'] = $data->primaryKey;
$this->callbackUrl['name'] = urlencode($this->name);
$this->callbackUrl['value'] = (int)empty($value);

$link = CHtml::normalizeUrl($this->callbackUrl);

echo CHtml::link(!empty($value) ? 'Y' : 'N', $link, array(
  'class' => $this->_flagClass,
));
}
```

Everything echoed in this method will be displayed as the cell content. $row is a row number, $data is a model instance representing a row. Using CHtml::value we are getting the value of active field and passing its name and value along with the model primary key to CHtml::normalizeUrl to create a link to the flag action.

Now we need to add some AJAX. We are doing it in the init method:

```
public function init() {
  parent::init();
  $cs=Yii::app()->getClientScript();
  $gridId = $this->grid->getId();
  $script = <<<SCRIPT
jQuery(".{$this->_flagClass}").live("click", function(e){
  e.preventDefault();
  var link = this;
  $.ajax({
    dataType: "json",
    cache: false,
    url: link.href,
    success: function(data){
      $('#$gridId').yiiGridView.update('$gridId');
    }
  });
});
SCRIPT;
  $cs->registerScript(__CLASS__.$gridId.'#flag_link', $script);
}
```

For each link we've created in the renderDataCellContent method, we are adding a click event handler. live usage is needed to handle the grid's AJAX pagination properly. On clicking we are making an AJAX request to flag action. On success we are refreshing the grid.

Action itself is very straightforward. We are getting the model instance, setting a field, and saving the model.

To support sorting, `FlagColumn` implements another method:

```
protected function renderHeaderCellContent()
{
  if($this->grid->enableSorting && $this->sortable &&
    $this->name!==null)
    echo $this->grid->dataProvider->getSort()->link(
      $this->name,$this->header);
  else if($this->name!==null && $this->header===null)
  {
    if($this->grid->dataProvider instanceof CActiveDataProvider)
      echo CHtml::encode($this->grid->dataProvider->
        model->getAttributeLabel($this->name));
    else
      echo CHtml::encode($this->name);
  }
  else
    parent::renderHeaderCellContent();
}
```

This is the exact copy of the method named `CDataProvider`. If both grid and column sorting are enabled, we are displaying a link to sort a grid.

There's more...

For further Information refer to:

- `http://www.yiiframework.com/doc/api/CGridColumn`
- `http://www.yiiframework.com/doc/api/CButtonColumn`
- `http://www.yiiframework.com/doc/api/CCheckBoxColumn`
- `http://www.yiiframework.com/doc/api/CDataColumn`
- `http://www.yiiframework.com/doc/api/CLinkColumn`

See also

- The recipe named *Using grids* in this chapter

8
Extending Yii

In this chapter, we will cover:

- ▶ Creating model behaviors
- ▶ Creating components
- ▶ Creating reusable controller actions
- ▶ Creating reusable controllers
- ▶ Creating a widget
- ▶ Creating CLI commands
- ▶ Creating filters
- ▶ Creating modules
- ▶ Creating a custom view renderer
- ▶ Making extensions distribution-ready

Introduction

In this chapter, we will show not only how to implement your own Yii extension but how to make your extension reusable and useful for the community. In addition, we will focus on many things you should do in order to make your extension as efficient as possible.

Creating model behaviors

There are many similar solutions in today's web applications. Leading products such as Google's Gmail are defining nice UI patterns. One of these is soft delete. Instead of a permanent deletion with tons of confirmations, Gmail allows to immediately mark messages as deleted and then easily undo it. The same behavior can be applied to any object such as blog posts, comments, and so on.

Let's create a behavior that will allow marking models as deleted, restoring models, selecting not yet deleted models, deleted models, and all models. In this recipe we'll follow a test driven development approach to plan the behavior and test if the implementation is correct.

Getting ready

Carry out the following steps:

▶ Create a database and add a post table to your database:

```
CREATE TABLE `post` (
  `id` int(11) NOT NULL auto_increment,
  `text` text,
  `title` varchar(255) default NULL,
  `is_deleted` tinyint(1) NOT NULL default '0',
  PRIMARY KEY  (`id`)
)
```

▶ Configure Yii to use this database in your primary application (`protected/config/main.php`).

▶ Make sure the `test` application have the same settings (`protected/config/test.php`).

▶ Uncomment the `fixture` component in the `test` application settings.

▶ Use Gii to generate the `Post` model.

How to do it...

1. Let's prepare a test environment first starting with defining fixtures for the Post model in `protected/tests/fixtures/post.php`:

```php
<?php
return array(
  array(
    'id' => 1,
    'title' => 'post1',
    'text' => 'post1',
    'is_deleted' => 0,
  ),
  array(
    'id' => 2,
    'title' => 'post2',
    'text' => 'post2',
    'is_deleted' => 1,
  ),
  array(
```

```
    'id' => 3,
    'title' => 'post3',
    'text' => 'post3',
    'is_deleted' => 0,
  ),
  array(
    'id' => 4,
    'title' => 'post4',
    'text' => 'post4',
    'is_deleted' => 1,
  ),
  array(
    'id' => 5,
    'title' => 'post5',
    'text' => 'post5',
    'is_deleted' => 0,
  ),
);
```

2. Then, we need to create a test case `protected/tests/unit/soft_delete/`
    `SoftDeleteBehaviorTest.php`:

```php
<?php
class SoftDeleteBehaviorTest extends CDbTestCase
{
  protected $fixtures = array(
    'post' => 'Post',
  );

  function testRemoved()
  {
    $postCount = Post::model()->removed()->count();
    $this->assertEquals(2, $postCount);
  }

  function testNotRemoved()
  {
    $postCount = Post::model()->notRemoved()->count();
    $this->assertEquals(3, $postCount);
  }

  function testRemove()
  {
    $post = Post::model()->findByPk(1);
    $post->remove()->save();
```

```
    $this->assertNull(Post::model()->notRemoved()->findByPk(1));
  }

  function testRestore()
  {
    $post = Post::model()->findByPk(2);
    $post->restore()->save();

    $this->assertNotNull(Post::model
      ()->notRemoved()->findByPk(2));
  }

  function testIsDeleted()
  {
    $post = Post::model()->findByPk(1);
    $this->assertFalse($post->isRemoved());

    $post = Post::model()->findByPk(2);
    $this->assertTrue($post->isRemoved());
  }
}
```

3. Now we need to implement `behavior`, attach it to the model, and make sure the test passes. Create a new directory under `protected/extensions` named `soft_delete`. Under this directory, create `SoftDeleteBehavior.php`. Let's attach the behavior to `Post` model first:

```
class Post extends CActiveRecord
{
  // ...

  public function behaviors()
  {
    return array(
      'softDelete' => array(
        'class' => 'ext.soft_delete.SoftDeleteBehavior'
      ),
    );
  }

  // ...
```

4. Now let's implement `protected/extensions/soft_delete/`
   `SoftDeleteBehavior.php`:

```php
<?php
class SoftDeleteBehavior extends CActiveRecordBehavior
{
  public $flagField = 'is_deleted';

  public function remove()
  {
    $this->getOwner()->{$this->flagField} = 1;
    return $this->getOwner();
  }

  public function restore()
  {
    $this->getOwner()->{$this->flagField} = 0;
    return $this->getOwner();
  }

  public function notRemoved()
  {
    $criteria = $this->getOwner()->getDbCriteria();
    $criteria->compare($this->flagField, 0);
    return $this->getOwner();
  }

  public function removed()
  {
    $criteria = $this->getOwner()->getDbCriteria();
    $criteria->compare($this->flagField, 1);
    return $this->getOwner();
  }

  public function isRemoved()
  {
    return (boolean)$this->getOwner()->{$this->flagField};
  }
}
```

   Run the test and make sure it passes.

5. That's it. We've created reusable behavior and can use it for all future projects by just connecting it to a model.

How it works...

Let's start with the test case. Since we want to use a set of models, we are defining fixtures. Fixture set is put into the DB each time the test method is executed. To use fixtures, the test class should be inherited from `CDbTestCase` and have public `$fixtures` declared:

```
protected $fixtures = array(
  'post' => 'Post',
);
```

In the preceding definition, `post` is the name of the file with fixture definitions and `Post` is the name of the model that fixtures will be applied to.

First, we are testing `removed` and `notRemoved` custom named scopes. First, we should limit the find result to removed items only, and second to non-removed items. Since we know which data we will get from fixtures, we can test for count of removed and non-removed items like the following:

```
$postCount = Post::model()->removed()->count();
$this->assertEquals(2, $postCount);
```

Then we are testing the `remove` and `restore` methods. The following is remove method test:

```
$post = Post::model()->findByPk(1);
$post->remove()->save();

$this->assertNull(Post::model()->notRemoved()->findByPk(1));
```

We are getting the item by `id`, removing it, and then trying to get it again using the `notRemoved` named scope. Since it's removed we should get `null` as result.

Finally, we are testing the `isRemoved` method that just returns the corresponding column value as Boolean.

Now let's move to the interesting implementation details. Since we are implementing the Active Record model behavior, we need to extend from `CActiveRecordBehavior`. In behavior, we can add our own methods that will be mixed into the model that behavior is attached to. We are using it to add `remove/restore/isRemoved` methods and `removed/notRemoved` named scopes:

```
public function remove()
{
  $this->getOwner()->{$this->flagField} = 1;
  return $this->getOwner();
}
public function removed()
{
```

```
    $criteria = $this->getOwner()->getDbCriteria();
    $criteria->compare($this->flagField, 1);
    return $this->getOwner();
}
```

In both methods, we are using the `getOwner` method to get the object the behavior is attached to. In our case it's a model so we can work with its data or change its finder criteria. We are returning the model instance to allow chained method calls like:

```
$post->remove()->save();
```

There's more...

There are more things that should be mentioned in this recipe.

CActiveRecordBehavior and CModelBehavior

Sometimes we need to get some more flexibility in a behavior such as reacting to model events. Both `CActiveRecordBehavior` and `CModelBehavior` are adding event-like methods we can override to handle model events. For example, if we need to handle cascade delete in a behavior we can do it by overriding the `afterDelete` method.

More behavior types

Behavior can be attached not only to a model but to any component. Each behavior inherits from `CBehavior` class so we can use its methods:

- ▶ `getOwner` to get the component that the behavior is attached to.
- ▶ `getEnabled` and `setEnabled` to check if behavior is enabled and set its state.
- ▶ `attach` and `detach` can be correspondingly used to initialize behavior and clean up temporary data created during behavior usage.

Further reading

To learn more about behaviors refer to the following API pages:

- ▶ http://www.yiiframework.com/doc/api/CActiveRecordBehavior
- ▶ http://www.yiiframework.com/doc/api/CModelBehavior
- ▶ http://www.yiiframework.com/doc/api/CBehavior

See also

- ▶ *Making extensions distribution-ready in this chapter*

Creating components

If you have some code that looks like it can be reused but you don't know if it's a behavior, widget, or something else, most probably it's a component. Component should be inherited from CComponent or CApplicationComponent. Later on the component can be attached to the application and configured using protected/config/main.php configuration file. That's the main benefit compared to using just a plain PHP class. Additionally we are getting behaviors, events, getters, and setters support.

For our example, we'll implement a simple EImageManager application component that will be able to resize images using the GD library, attach it to the application, and use it.

Getting ready

You will need to install the GD PHP extension to see image resizing in action.

How to do it...

Carry out the following steps:

1. Create protected/components/EImageManager.php:

```php
<?php
class EImageManager extends CApplicationComponent
{
  protected $image;
  protected $width;
  protected $height;

  protected $newWidth;
  protected $newHeight;

  public function resize($width = false, $height = false){
    if($width!==false) $this->newWidth = $width;
    if($height!==false) $this->newHeight = $height;

    return $this;
  }

  public function load($filePath)
  {
    list($this->width, $this->height, $type) =
      getimagesize($filePath);

    switch ($type)
    {
```

```php
    case IMAGETYPE_GIF:
      $this->image = imagecreatefromgif($filePath);
    break;
    case IMAGETYPE_JPEG:
      $this->image = imagecreatefromjpeg($filePath);
    break;
    case IMAGETYPE_PNG:
      $this->image = imagecreatefrompng($filePath);
    break;
    default:
      throw new CException('Unsupported image type ' . $type);
  }

  return $this;
}

public function save($filePath)
{

  $ext = pathinfo($filePath, PATHINFO_EXTENSION);

  $newImage = imagecreatetruecolor($this->newWidth,
    $this->newHeight);
  imagecopyresampled($newImage, $this->image, 0, 0, 0, 0,
    $this->newWidth, $this->newHeight, $this->width,
    $this->height);

  switch($ext)
  {
    case 'jpg':
    case 'jpeg':
      imagejpeg($newImage, $filePath);
    break;
    case 'png':
      imagepng($newImage, $filePath);
    break;
    case 'gif':
      imagegif($newImage, $filePath);
    break;
    default:
      throw new CException("Unsupported image type ", $ext);
  }
```

```
      imagedestroy($newImage);

      if(!is_file($filePath))
         throw new CException("Failed to write image.");
   }

   function __destruct()
   {
      imagedestroy($this->image);
   }
}
```

2. Now we need to attach our component to the application. In `protected/config/main.php` we need to add the following:

```
...
// application components
'components'=>array(
   'image' => array(
      'class' => 'EImageManager',
   ),
...
```

3. Now we can use it like the following:

```
Yii::app()->image
   ->load(Yii::getPathOfAlias('webroot').'/src.png')
   ->resize(100,100)
   ->save(Yii::getPathOfAlias('webroot').'/dst.png');
```

How it works...

To be able to attach a component to an application it needs to be extended from `CApplicationComponent`. Attaching is as simple as adding a new array to the `components` section of configuration. There, a `class` value specifies the component's class and all other values are set to a component through the corresponding component's public properties and setter methods.

Implementation itself is very straightforward: We are wrapping GD calls into comfortable API with `save`, `load`, and `resize` methods. To be able to chain API calls, `load` and `resize` are returning the component itself.

We can access our class by its component name using `Yii::app()`. In our case it will be `Yii::app()->image`.

There's more...

Besides creating your own components, you can do more.

Overriding existing application components

Most of the time there will be no need to create your own application components since other types of extensions such as widgets or behaviors are covering almost all types of reusable code. However, overriding core framework components is a common practice and can be used to customize the framework's behavior for your specific needs without hacking into the core.

For example, to be able to get the user's role from the database using `Yii::app()->user->role` you can extend the `CWebUser` component like the following:

```php
<?php
class WebUser extends CWebUser {
    private $_model = null;

    function getRole() {
        if ($user = $this->getModel()) {
            return $user->role;
        }
        else return 'guest';
    }

    private function getModel() {
        if ($this->_model === null) {
            if ($this->id === null) return null;
            $this->_model = User::model()->findByPk($this->id);
        }
        return $this->_model;
    }
}
```

To replace the standard user component `main.php` configuration should be customized:

```php
...
// application components
'components'=>array(
    'user'=>array(
        'class' => 'WebUser',
        // other properties
    ),
    ...
```

In the preceding code, we specified a new `class` for the `user` component.

Further reading

In order to learn more about components, refer to the following API pages:

▶ http://www.yiiframework.com/doc/api/CComponent/

▶ http://www.yiiframework.com/doc/api/CApplicationComponent/

See also

▶ The recipe named *Making extensions distribution-ready* in this chapter

Creating reusable controller actions

Common actions such as deleting the AR model by the primary key or getting data for AJAX autocomplete could be moved into reusable controller actions and later attached to controllers as needed.

In this recipe, we will create reusable `delete` action that will delete the specified AR model by its primary key.

Getting ready

▶ Create a fresh Yii application using `yiic webapp`.

▶ Create a new database and configure it.

▶ Execute the following SQL:

```
CREATE TABLE `post` (
  `id` int(11) NOT NULL auto_increment,
  `text` text,
  `title` varchar(255) default NULL,
  PRIMARY KEY  (`id`)
);

CREATE TABLE `comment` (
  `id` int(11) NOT NULL auto_increment,
  `text` text,
  PRIMARY KEY  (`id`)
);
```

▶ Generate models for `post` and `comment` using Gii.

How to do it...

Carry out the following steps:

1. Create `protected/extensions/actions/EDeleteAction.php`:

```php
<?php
class EDeleteAction extends CAction
{
  public $modelName;
  public $redirectTo = array('index');

  /**
   * Runs the action.
   * This method is invoked by the controller owning this action.
   */
  public function run($pk)
  {
    CActiveRecord::model($this->modelName)->deleteByPk($pk);
    if(Yii::app()->getRequest()->getIsAjaxRequest())
    {
      Yii::app()->end(200, true);
    }
    else
    {
      $this->getController()->redirect($this->redirectTo);
    }
  }
}
```

2. Now we need to attach it to the controller `protected/controllers/DeleteController.php`:

```php
<?php
class DeleteController extends CController
{
  public function actions()
  {
    return array(
      'deletePost' => array(
        'class' => 'ext.actions.EDeleteAction',
        'modelName' => 'Post',
        'redirectTo' => array('indexPosts'),
      ),
      'deleteComment' => array(
        'class' => 'ext.actions.EDeleteAction',
        'modelName' => 'Comment',
```

```
                    'redirectTo' => array('indexComments'),
              ),
          );
      }

      public function actionIndexPosts()
      {
        echo "I'm index action for Posts.";
      }

      public function actionIndexComments()
      {
        echo "I'm index action for Comments.";
      }
  }
```

3. That is it. Now you can delete a post by visiting `/delete/deletePost/pk/<pk>` and delete a comment by visiting `/delete/deleteComment/pk/<pk>`. After the deletion, you will be redirected to a corresponding index action.

How it works...

To create an external controller action you need to extend your class from `CAction`. The only mandatory method to implement is `run`. In our case, it accepts the parameter named `pk` from `$_GET` using the automatic parameter binding feature of Yii and tries to delete a corresponding model.

To make it customizable we've created two public properties configurable from the controller. These are `modelName` that holds a name of the model we are working with, and `redirectTo` that specifies a route the user will be redirected to.

Configuration itself is done by implementing the `actions` method in your controller. There, you can attach the action once or multiple times and configure its public properties.

There's more...

There are two usable methods implemented in `CAction`. First is `getController` that we can use to get an instance of the controller that the action is attached to. You will need it to redirect to another action or, for example, generate URL.

Another method is `getId` that returns action name specified in the controller's `actions` method.

Further reading

To learn more about external controller action refer to the following API pages:

- ▶ http://www.yiiframework.com/doc/api/CAction/
- ▶ http://www.yiiframework.com/doc/api/CController/#actions-detail

See also

- ▶ The recipe named *Creating reusable controllers* in this chapter
- ▶ The recipe named *Making extensions distribution-ready* in this chapter

Creating reusable controllers

In Yii, you can create reusable controllers. If you are creating a lot of applications or controllers that are of the same type, moving all common code into a reusable controller will save you a lot of time.

In this recipe, we will create a simple reusable `api` controller that will implement a simple JSON CRUD API for a model. It will take input data from POST and GET and will respond with JSON data and a corresponding HTTP response code.

Getting ready

- ▶ Create a fresh Yii application using `yiic webapp`.
- ▶ Generate a model using Gii. In our example we'll use the `Post` model but you can use any model you want.

How to do it...

Carry out the following steps:

1. Create `protected/extensions/json_api/JsonApiController.php`:

```php
<?php
class JsonApiController extends CController
{
  const RESPONSE_OK = 'OK';
  const RESPONSE_NO_DATA = 'No data';
  const RESPONSE_NOT_FOUND = 'Not found';
  const RESPONSE_VALIDATION_ERRORS = 'Validation errors';

  public $modelName;

  public function init()
  {
```

```
    parent::init();
    if(empty($this->modelName))
      throw new CException("You should set modelName before
        using JsonApiController.");
}

public function actionCreate()
{
  if(empty($_POST))
    $this->respond(400, self::RESPONSE_NO_DATA);

  $model = new $this->modelName;
  $model->setAttributes($_POST);

  if($model->save())
    $this->respond(200, self::RESPONSE_OK);
  else
    $this->respond(400, self::RESPONSE_VALIDATION_ERRORS,
      $model->getErrors());
}

public function actionGet($pk)
{
  $model = CActiveRecord::model
    ($this->modelName)->findByPk($pk);
  if(!$model)
    $this->respond(404, self::RESPONSE_NOT_FOUND);

  $this->respond(200, self::RESPONSE_OK,
    $model->getAttributes());
}

public function actionUpdate($pk)
{
  if(empty($_POST))
    $this->respond(400, self::RESPONSE_NO_DATA);

  $model = CActiveRecord::model
    ($this->modelName)->findByPk($pk);
  if(!$model)
    $this->respond(404, self::RESPONSE_NOT_FOUND);

  $model->setAttributes($_POST);
  if($model->save())
    $this->respond(200, self::RESPONSE_OK);
```

```
    else
      $this->respond(400, self::RESPONSE_VALIDATION_ERRORS,
        $model->getErrors());
  }

  public function actionDelete($pk)
  {
    if(CActiveRecord::model($this->modelName)->deleteByPk($pk))
    {
      $this->respond(200, self::RESPONSE_OK);
    }
    else {
      $this->respond(404, self::RESPONSE_NOT_FOUND);
    }
  }

  protected function respond($httpCode, $status, $data = array())
  {
    $response['status'] = $status;
    $response['data'] = $data;

    echo CJSON::encode($response);

    Yii::app()->end($httpCode, true);
  }
}
```

2. Now we need to connect it to our application via `protected/config/main.php`. It can be done by adding controller configuration to the `controllerMap` property of `CWebApplication` so we need to place the following right after the configuration array opening:

```
...
'controllerMap' => array(
  'api' => array(
    'class' => 'ext.json_api.JsonApiController',
    'modelName' => 'Post',
  ),
),
...
```

3. That is it. We have connected the controller and specified that it should work with the `Post` model.

You will need forms to post data but if you have some data already you can use get methods right from a URL like `/api/get/pk/1`. Applications should return data like the following:

```
{"status":"OK","data":{"id":"1","text":"post1",
    "title":"post1","is_deleted":"0"}}
```

How it works...

When you are running an application and passing a route such as `api/get`, prior to executing `ApiController::actionGet` Yii checks if there is `controllerMap` defined. Since we have an `api` controller defined there, Yii executes it instead of going the usual way.

In the controller itself we've defined the `modelName` property to be able to connect the controller multiple times and have an API for multiple models. We are setting it when attaching the controller.

The controller itself isn't that much different from a regular one with only a few tricks:

▶ When working with Active Record we are creating a new class like the following:

```
$model = new $this->modelName;
```

▶ And getting model finder like the following:

```
$model = CActiveRecord::model($this->modelName);
```

▶ This allows us not to be bound to a specific model but to specify a model name.

▶ We're using `CJSON` to encode arrays and models to JSON.

▶ `Yii::app()->end()` is used to end application execution with HTTP response code specified.

There's more...

In order to learn more about the controllers map, refer to the following API page:

```
http://www.yiiframework.com/doc/api/CWebApplication#controllerMap-
detail
```

See also

▶ The recipe named *Creating reusable controller actions* in this chapter
▶ The recipe named *Making extensions distribution-ready* in this chapter

Creating a widget

A widget is a reusable part of a view that not only renders some data but does it according to some logic. It can even get data from models and use its own views, so it is like a reduced reusable version of a module.

Let's create a widget that will draw a pie chart using Google APIs.

Getting ready

Create a fresh Yii application using `yiic`.

How to do it...

1. Create `protected/extensions/chart/EChartWidget.php`:

```php
<?php
class EChartWidget extends CWidget
{
  public $title;
  public $data=array();
  public $labels=array();

  public function run()
  {
    echo "<img
      src=\"http://chart.apis.google.com/chart?chtt=".urlencode
      ($this->title)."&cht=pc&chs=300x150&chd=".
      $this->encodeData($this->data)."&chl=".implode
      ('|', $this->labels)."\">";
  }

  protected function encodeData($data)
  {
    $maxValue=max($data);

    $chars='ABCDEFGHIJKLMNOPQRSTUVWXYZabcdefghijklmnopqrstuvwx
      yz0123456789';

    $chartData="s:";
    for($i=0;$i<count($data);$i++)
    {
      $currentValue=$data[$i];
```

```
    if($currentValue>-1)
      $chartData.=substr($chars,61*($currentValue/$maxValue),1);
    else
      $chartData.='_';
  }

  return $chartData."&chxt=y&chxl=0:|0|".$maxValue;
  }
}
```

2. Now create a controller `protected/controllers/ChartController.php`:

```php
<?php
class ChartController extends CController
{
  public function actionIndex()
  {
    $value = rand(10, 90);
    $this->widget('ext.chart.EChartWidget', array(
      'title' => 'Do you like it?',
      'data' => array(
        $value, 100-$value
      ),
      'labels' => array(
        'No',
        'Yes',
      ),
    ));
  }
}
```

3. Now try to run the index action of the controller. You should see a pie chart like the following:

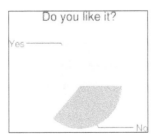

How it works...

Like in every other type of extension, we are creating some public properties we can configure when calling a widget using `CController::widget`. In this case, we are configuring title, data set, and data labels.

The main method of a widget is `run()`. In our widget, we are generating a URL pointing to the Google charting API, and then echoing `<img>` tag.

There's more...

To learn more about widgets refer to the following API pages:

- `http://www.yiiframework.com/doc/api/CWidget/`
- `http://www.yiiframework.com/doc/api/CCaptcha/`

See also

- The recipe named *Configuring components* in *Chapter 1, Under the Hood*
- The recipe named *Configuring widget defaults* in *Chapter 1*
- The recipe named *Creating custom input widget with CWidget* in *Chapter 4, Working with Forms*
- The recipe named *Making extensions distribution-ready* in this chapter

Creating CLI commands

Yii has a good command-line support and allows creating reusable console commands. Console commands are faster to create than web GUIs. If you need to create some kind of utility for your application that will be used by developers or administrators, console commands are the right tool. To show how to create a console command we'll create a simple command that will clean up various things such as cache, temp directories, and so on.

Getting ready

Create a fresh Yii application using `yiic webapp`.

How to do it...

Carry out the following steps:

1. Create `protected/extensions/clean_command/ECleanCommand.php`:

```php
<?php
class ECleanCommand extends CConsoleCommand
{
```

```php
public $webRoot;
public function actionCache()
{
  $cache=Yii::app()->getComponent('cache');
      if($cache!==null){
          $cache->flush();
          echo "Done.\n";
      }
      else {
          echo "Please configure cache component.\n";
      }
}

public function actionAssets()
{
  if(empty($this->webRoot))
  {
    echo "Please specify a path to webRoot in command
      properties.\n";
    Yii::app()->end();
  }

  $this->cleanDir($this->webRoot.'/assets');

      echo "Done.\n";
}

public function actionRuntime()
{
  $this->cleanDir(Yii::app()->getRuntimePath());
  echo "Done.\n";
}

private function cleanDir($dir)
{
  $di = new DirectoryIterator ($dir);
      foreach($di as $d)
      {
          if(!$d->isDot())
          {
              echo "Removed ".$d->getPathname()."\n";
              $this->removeDirRecursive($d->getPathname());
          }
      }
}
```

```
    private function removeDirRecursive($dir)
    {
        $files = glob($dir.'*', GLOB_MARK);
        foreach ($files as $file)
        {
            if (is_dir($file))
                    $this-
        >removeDirRecursive($file);
            else
                    unlink($file);
        }
        if (is_dir($dir))
                rmdir($dir);
    }
}
```

2. Now we need to attach a command to the console application. By default the console application uses a separate bootstrap file `yiic.php`:

```
<?php

// change the following paths if necessary
$yiic=dirname(__FILE__).'/../../framework/yiic.php';
$config=dirname(__FILE__).'/config/console.php';

require_once($yiic);
```

3. Therefore, the configuration is `protected/config/console.php`. Let's add our console command to the `commandMap` property:

```
// This is the configuration for yiic console application.
// Any writable CConsoleApplication properties can be configured
here.
return array(
  'basePath'=>dirname(__FILE__).DIRECTORY_SEPARATOR.'..',
  'name'=>'My Console Application',

  'commandMap' => array(
    'clean' => array(
      'class' => 'ext.clean_command.ECleanCommand',
      'webRoot' => 'path/to/your/application/webroot',
    ),
  ),
);
```

4. Don't forget to change `webRoot` to the actual path. That's it. Now go to protected directory and try running these commands:

```
yiic clean
yiic clean cache
yiic clean assets
yiic clean runtime
```

How it works...

All console commands should be extended from the `CConsoleCommand` class. Since all console commands are run in `CConsoleApplication` instead of `CWebApplication`, we don't have a way to determine the web application server root. For this purpose we are creating a configurable public property called `webRoot`.

The console command structure itself is like a typical controller. We are defining several actions we can run via `yiic <console command> <command action>`.

As you can see, there are no views used so we can focus on programming tasks instead of design, markup, and so on. Still, you need to provide some useful output so users will know what is going on. This is done through simple PHP echo statements.

There's more...

Custom help

If your command is relatively complex such as `message` or `migrate` bundled with Yii, it's a good decision to provide some extra description of the available options and actions. It can be done by overriding the `getHelp` method:

```php
public function getHelp()
{
    $out = "Clean command allows you to clean up various
        temporary data Yii and an application are generating.\n\n";
    return $out.parent::getHelp();
}
```

Running just `yiic clean` will output:

```
Clean command allows you to clean up various temporary data Yii and an applicati
on are generating.

Usage: W:\home\server.local\www\app\yiic.php clean <action>
Actions:
        cache
        assets
        runtime
```

Further reading

To learn more about creating console applications and commands refer to the following:

- ▶ The recipe named `http://www.yiiframework.com/doc/guide/topics.console`
- ▶ `http://www.yiiframework.com/doc/api/CConsoleCommand/`
- ▶ `http://www.yiiframework.com/doc/api/CConsoleApplication/`

See also

- ▶ The recipe named *Making extensions distribution-ready* in this chapter

Creating filters

A filter is a class that can run before/after an action is executed. It can be used to modify execution context or decorate output. In our example we'll implement a simple output filter that will compress HTML output removing all optional formatting.

 Don't use this filter in production: GZIP will do a better job in reducing bandwidth. Moreover, it is not safe to remove formatting for pre, textarea, among others.

Getting ready

Create a fresh Yii application using `yiic`.

How to do it...

Carry out the following steps:

1. Create `protected/extensions/compress_html/ECompressHtmlFilter.php`:

```php
<?php
class ECompressHtmlFilter extends CFilter
{
  protected function preFilter($filterChain)
  {
    ob_start();
    return parent::preFilter($filterChain);
  }

  protected function postFilter($filterChain)
  {
    $out = ob_get_clean();
```

```
        echo preg_replace("~>(\s+|\t+|\n+)<~", "><", $out);
        parent::postFilter($filterChain);
    }
}
```

2. That's it. Now we need to connect it to application. Since we already have `SiteController` let's add filter to it by overriding `filters` method:

```
public function filters()
{
  return array(
    array(
      'ext.compress_html.ECompressHtmlFilter'
    ),
  );
}
```

3. Now run application and check HTML source code. It should be a single line of text such as:

```
<!DOCTYPE html PUBLIC "-//W3C//DTD XHTML 1.0 Transitional//
EN" "http://www.w3.org/TR/xhtml1/DTD/xhtml1-transitional.
dtd"><html xmlns="http://www.w3.org/1999/xhtml" xml:lang="en"
lang="en"><head><meta http-equiv="Content-Type" content="text/
html; charset=utf-8" /><meta name="language" content="en" /><!--
blueprint CSS framework -->
...
```

How it works...

A filter should at minimum implement the `IFilter` interface but since we want to do post- and pre-filtering, we can directly extend `CFilter`. The plan is to somehow get all of the content generated by an action and do some processing prior to sending it to a browser. PHP's output buffering fits well for this task, so we override `preFilter` to start buffering by calling `ob_start` there and `postFilter` to get the buffer content with `ob_get_clean`, and do processing with a regular expression and echo result.

Note that we are calling parent methods when overriding `preFilter` and `postFilter`. It allows the developer to build a chain of filters when configuring controller.

There's more...

In order to learn more about filters, refer to the following API pages:

▶ http://www.yiiframework.com/doc/api/CFilter
▶ http://www.yiiframework.com/doc/api/IFilter

▶ The recipe named *Making extensions distribution-ready* in this chapter

Creating modules

If you have created a complex application part and want to use it with some degree of customization in your next project, most probably you need to create a module.

In this recipe, we will see how to create a wiki module. For simplicity, we will not focus on the user and permissions management and let everyone edit everything.

Getting ready

Carry out the following steps:

1. Create a fresh Yii application using `yiic webapp`.

2. Configure MySQL database and execute the following SQL:

```
CREATE TABLE `wiki` (
  `id` varchar(255) NOT NULL,
  `text` text NOT NULL,
  PRIMARY KEY  (`id`)
)
```

3. Generate `Wiki` model using Gii.

4. Generate `Wiki` module using Gii.

5. Move `protected/models/Wiki.php` to `protected/modules/wiki/models/`.

6. Add `wiki` to `modules` section of `protected/config/main.php`:

```
'modules'=>array(
  // uncomment the following to enable the Gii tool
  'gii'=>array(

    'class'=>'system.gii.GiiModule',
    'password'=>false,
  ),
  'wiki'
),
```

How to do it...

Let's do some planning first:

- ▶ A wiki is a set of pages where one page can link to another using its name
- ▶ Typically wiki uses simpler human-readable markup instead of HTML
- ▶ If a user goes to a page that doesn't yet exist he's prompted to create one
- ▶ To delete a page a user needs to save it with an empty body

Based on this planning we'll use markdown as markup language. We will add a way to link to another page by name. Let's say it will be [[page name]] or [[Custom title|page name]] if you need a custom titled link.

1. First, let's add wiki links to CMarkdownParser. Create protected/modules/ wiki/components/WikiMarkdownParser.php:

    ```php
    <?php
    class WikiMarkdownParser extends CMarkdownParser
    {
      public function transform($text)
      {
        $text = preg_replace_callback('~\[\[(.*?)(?:\|(.*?))?\]\]~',
          array($this, 'processWikiLinks'), $text);
        return parent::transform($text);
      }

      protected function processWikiLinks($matches)
      {
        $page = $matches[1];
        $title = isset($matches[2]) ? $matches[2] : $matches[1];
        return CHtml::link(CHtml::encode($title), array(
          'view', 'id' => $page,
        ));
      }
    }
    ```

2. Now let's use it by adding the getHtml method to protected/modules/wiki/ models/Wiki.php model:

    ```php
    public function getHtml()
    {
      $parser = new WikiMarkdownParser();
      return $parser->transform($this->text);
    }
    ```

We're moving to customizing the `protected/modules/wiki/controller/` `DefaultController.php` controller. We'll need just two actions there: `view` action and `edit` action. Additionally we'll create an `index` action that will just call view with `id` = index. Since we don't need a view for the `index` action it can be deleted safely.

1. Now edit `protected/modules/wiki/controller/DefaultController.php`:

```
class DefaultController extends Controller
{
  public function actionIndex()
  {
    $this->actionView('index');
  }

  public function actionView($id)
  {
    $model = Wiki::model()->findByPk($id);
    if(!$model)
    {
      $this->actionEdit($id);
      Yii::app()->end();
    }

    $this->render('view', array(
      'model' => $model,
    ));
  }

  public function actionEdit($id)
  {
    $model = Wiki::model()->findByPk($id);
    if(!$model)
    {
      $model = new Wiki();
      $model->id = $id;
    }

    if(!empty($_POST['Wiki']))
    {
      if(!empty($_POST['Wiki']['text']))
      {
        $model->text = $_POST['Wiki']['text'];
        if($model->save())
          $this->redirect(array('view', 'id' => $id));
      }
```

```
      else
      {
        Wiki::model()->deleteByPk($id);
      }
    }

    $this->render('edit', array(
      'model' => $model
    ));
  }
}
```

2. In addition, we will need two views. `protected/modules/wiki/views/default/view.php`:

```
<h2>
  <?php echo CHtml::encode($model->id)?>
  [<?php echo CHtml::link('edit', array('edit', 'id' =>
    $model->id))?>]
</h2>
<?php echo $model->html ?>
```

3. Another one `protected/modules/wiki/views/default/edit.php`:

```
<h2>Editing <?php echo CHtml::encode($model->id)?></h2>

<?php echo CHtml::beginForm()?>
  <?php echo CHtml::activeTextArea($model, 'text',
    array('cols' => 100, 'rows' => 20))?>
  <br /><br />
  <?php echo CHtml::submitButton('Done')?>
<?php echo CHtml::endForm()?>
```

4. That is it. Now run the wiki module and check it out entering some text. Don't forget to add internal links like `[[rules]]`:

5. The preceding page will look like the following when being edited:

6. Since we moved the `Wiki` model from application to module, the module doesn't have any dependencies on the application itself, so we can move it to an extension package like `protected/extensions/wiki/`, changing the module configuration `protected/config/main.php` to:

```
'modules'=>array(
  // uncomment the following to enable the Gii tool
  'gii'=>array(
    'class'=>'system.gii.GiiModule',
    'password'=>false,
  ),
  'wiki'=>array(
    'class' => 'ext.wiki.WikiModule'
  ),
),
```

How it works...

Each module created contains a main module class like `WikiModule` where we can define configurable properties, define imports, change paths, attach controllers, and so on. By default, a module generated with Gii runs `index` action of the `default` controller:

```
public function actionIndex()
{
  $this->actionView('index');
}
```

In our `wiki` module `index` we are just calling `view` action passing `id = index` to it:

```
$model = Wiki::model()->findByPk($id);
if(!$model)
{
  $this->actionEdit($id);
  Yii::app()->end();
}

$this->render('view', array(
  'model' => $model,
));
```

If there is a model with such an ID we are displaying it using a view.

If there is no page with such an ID, we are, again, delegating processing to another action. This time it's `edit`:

```
$model = Wiki::model()->findByPk($id);
if(!$model)
{
  $model = new Wiki();
  $model->id = $id;
}

if(!empty($_POST['Wiki']))
{
  if(!empty($_POST['Wiki']['text']))
  {
    $model->text = $_POST['Wiki']['text'];
    if($model->save())
      $this->redirect(array('view', 'id' => $id));
  }
  else
  {
    Wiki::model()->deleteByPk($id);
  }
}

$this->render('edit', array(
  'model' => $model
));
```

If there is no model with an ID passed we're creating new one; if there is a model, we are editing it. Edit form data comes from POST and if a text is empty we are deleting a model. If there is a text we are saving a model.

There's more...

To learn more about modules refer to the following:

- http://www.yiiframework.com/doc/guide/basics.module
- http://www.yiiframework.com/doc/api/CWebModule/
- http://www.yiiframework.com/doc/api/CModule/
- http://www.yiiframework.com/doc/api/GiiModule/

See also

- The recipe named *Making extensions distribution-ready* in this chapter

Creating a custom view renderer

There are many PHP template engines out there. Yii offers only two template types out of the box: native PHP and Prado-like templates. If you want to use one of the existing template engines or create your own one you have to implement it. Of course, if it's not yet implemented by the Yii community

In this recipe we'll implement Smarty templates support.

Getting ready

- Create a fresh Yii application using yiic webapp.
- Get the latest Smarty 3 release from http://www.smarty.net/.
- Extract contents of libs directory to protected/vendors/smarty/.

How to do it...

Carry out the following steps:

1. Create protected/extensions/smarty/ESmartyViewRenderer.php:

```php
<?php
class ESmartyViewRenderer extends CApplicationComponent
  implements IViewRenderer
{
    public $fileExtension='.tpl';
    public $filePermission=0755;

    private $smarty;
```

```
    function init()
{
    Yii::import('application.vendors.smarty.*');

    spl_autoload_unregister(array('YiiBase','autoload'));
    require_once('Smarty.class.php');
    spl_autoload_register(array('YiiBase','autoload'));

    $this->smarty = new Smarty();

    $this->smarty->template_dir = '';
    $compileDir = Yii::app()->getRuntimePath
        ().'/smarty/compiled/';

    if(!file_exists($compileDir)){
        mkdir($compileDir, $this->filePermission, true);
    }

    $this->smarty->compile_dir = $compileDir;
    $this->smarty->assign('Yii', Yii::app());
}

/**
 * Renders a view file.
 * This method is required by {@link IViewRenderer}.
 * @param CBaseController the controller or widget who is
 *     rendering the view file.
 * @param string the view file path
 * @param mixed the data to be passed to the view
 * @param boolean whether the rendering result should be
 *     returned
 * @return mixed the rendering result, or null if the rendering
 *     result is not needed.
 */
public function renderFile($context,$sourceFile,$data,$return) {
    // current controller properties will be accessible as
{this.property}
    $data['this'] = $context;

    if(!is_file($sourceFile) || ($file=realpath($sourceFile))=
        ==false)
        throw new CException(Yii::t('ext','View file
"$sourceFile" does not exist.', array('{file}'=>$sourceFile)));

    $this->smarty->assign($data);

    if($return)
        return $this->smarty->fetch($sourceFile);
```

```
      else
        $this->smarty->display($sourceFile);
    }
}
```

2. Now we need to connect view rendered to application. In `protected/config/`
    `main.php` we need to override the `viewRenderer` component:

    ```
    ...
    // application components
    'components'=>array(
      ...
      'viewRenderer'=>array(
        'class'=>'ext.smarty.ESmartyViewRenderer',
      ),
    ),
    ...
    ```

3. Now let's test it. Create `protected/controllers/SmartyController.php`:

    ```php
    <?php
    class SmartyController extends Controller
    {
      function actionNative()
      {
        $this->render('native', array(
          'username' => 'Alexander',
        ));
      }

      function actionSmarty()
      {
        $this->render('smarty', array(
          'username' => 'Alexander',
        ));
      }
    }
    ```

4. Now we need views. `protected/views/smarty/native.php`:

    ```
    Hello, <?php echo $username?>!
    ```
    `protected/views/smarty/smarty.tpl`:
    ```
    Hello, {$username}!
    ```

5. Now try running controller actions. In both cases you should get:

    Hello, Alexander!

How it works...

A view renderer is a child of `CApplicationComponent` that implements the `IViewRenderer` interface with only one method called `renderFile`:

```
/**
 * Renders a view file.
 * @param CBaseController $context the controller or widget who is
     rendering the view file.
 * @param string $file the view file path
 * @param mixed $data the data to be passed to the view
 * @param boolean $return whether the rendering result should be
returned
 * @return mixed the rendering result, or null if the rendering result
is
     not needed.
 */
public function renderFile($context,$file,$data,$return);
```

Therefore, we are getting context, template path, data, and return flag that determines if we need to echo the processing result immediately or return it. In our case processing itself is done by the Smarty template engine so we need to properly initialize it and call its processing methods.

Importing and initializing Smarty is a bit tricky:

```
Yii::import('application.vendors.smarty.*');

spl_autoload_unregister(array('YiiBase','autoload'));
require_once('Smarty.class.php');
spl_autoload_register(array('YiiBase','autoload'));

$this->smarty = new Smarty();

$this->smarty->template_dir = '';
$compileDir = Yii::app()->getRuntimePath().'/smarty/compiled/';

if(!file_exists($compileDir)){
  mkdir($compileDir, $this->filePermission, true);
}

$this->smarty->compile_dir = $compileDir;
$this->smarty->assign('Yii', Yii::app());
```

First we are using `Yii::import` to tell Yii we want to use classes from `protected/vendors/smarty/`. Since Yii autoloader conflicts with the one included in Smarty and we can't control how Smarty does it, we need to unregister Yii's one, require Smarty and then register Yii autoloader back. Since the Yii template directory can vary, we are resetting the Smarty default option to an empty string. It is a good practice to store Yii temporary files in the application runtime directory. That is why we are setting the compile directory, where Smarty stores its templates compiled into PHP, to `runtime/smarty/compiled`. Not to disturb developers too much we are creating this directory automatically if it does not exist. Also, we are creating a special Smarty template variable named Yii that points to `Yii::app()` and allows to get application properties inside of a template.

Rendering itself is a bit simpler:

```
// current controller properties will be accessible as {this.property}
$data['this'] = $context;

if(!is_file($sourceFile) || ($file=realpath($sourceFile))===false)
  throw new CException(Yii::t('ext','View file "$sourceFile" does not
exist.', array('{file}'=>$sourceFile)));

$this->smarty->assign($data);

if($return)
  return $this->smarty->fetch($sourceFile);
else
  $this->smarty->display($sourceFile);
```

We are assigning another Smarty variable called `this` that will allow getting controller properties such as page title.

To ease debugging, the template is checked for existence and if it doesn't exist an error message with the template name is displayed.

All data set via `$this->render` is passed to the Smarty template as is. Then we are either rendering templates or returning it depending on the `$return` argument.

There's more...

You can get ready to use Smarty view renderer with plugins and configuration support at `http://www.yiiframework.com/extension/smarty-view-renderer`.

 It's OK to use a custom template engine in your application. However, if you are creating a reusable extension try to avoid using template engines other than the native PHP.

Further reading

To learn more about Smarty and view renderers in general refer to the following:

- ▶ `http://www.smarty.net/`
- ▶ `http://www.yiiframework.com/doc/api/IViewRenderer/`
- ▶ `http://www.yiiframework.com/doc/api/CViewRenderer/`
- ▶ `http://www.yiiframework.com/doc/api/CPradoViewRenderer/`

See also

- ▶ The recipe named *Making extensions distribution-ready* in this chapter

Making extensions distribution-ready

In this chapter, you have learned how to create various types of Yii extensions. Now we'll talk about how to share your results with people and why it's important.

Getting ready

Let's form a checklist for a good extension first. A good programming product should follow these points:

- ▶ Consistent, easy to read and use API
- ▶ Good documentation
- ▶ People should be able to find it
- ▶ Extension should apply to the most common use cases
- ▶ Should be maintained
- ▶ Well-tested code; ideally with unit tests
- ▶ You need to provide support for it

Of course, having all these requires a lot of work but these are necessary to create a good product.

How to do it...

Let's review our list in more detail starting with API. API should be consistent, easy to read and use. Consistent means that overall style should not change so no different variable naming such as `camelCasedVariableNames` and `underscored_variable_names`, no inconsistent names such as `isFlag1()` and `isNotFlag2()`, and so on. Everything should obey the rules you've defined for your code. This allows less checking of documentation and focusing on coding.

Code without any documentation is almost useless. An exception is relatively simple code but even if it's only a few lines it doesn't feel right if there is not a single word about how to install and use it. What makes a good documentation?

The purpose of the code and its pros. It should be as visible as possible and should be written loud and clear. For example, if an extension is sending an e-mail, the description should be something like:

> *EMailer allows you to send an e-mail in an easy and convenient way. It handles non-English text and title properly. Moreover you can use Yii views as e-mail templates.*

Code is useless if developers don't know where to put it and what should be in application configuration. Don't expect that people know how to do framework-specific things. Installation guide should be verbose. Step-by-step form is preferred by a majority of developers. If code needs SQL schema to work, provide it.

Even if your API methods and properties are named properly you still need to document them with phpDoc comments specifying argument types and return types, providing a brief description for each method. Don't forget protected and private methods and properties since sometimes it's necessary to read these to understand the details of how code works. Also, consider listing public methods and properties in documentation so it can be used as a reference.

Provide use case examples with well-commented code. Try to cover most common ways of extension usage. In an example don't try to solve multiple problems at a time since it can be confusing.

Extension should have a version number and a change log. It will allow the community to check if they have the latest version and check what is changed before upgrading.

 It's important to make your code flexible so it will apply to many use cases. But, since it's not possible to create code for every possible use case, try to cover the most common ones.

It's important to make people feel comfortable. Providing a good documentation is a first step. The second is providing a proof your code works as expected and will work with further updates. The best way to do it is a set of unit tests.

Extension should be maintained. At least until it's stable and there are no more feature requests and bug reports. So expect questions, reports, and reserve some time to work on the code further. If you can't devote more time to maintain extensions, but it's very innovative and no one did it before, it's still worth sharing it. If the community likes it, someone will definitely offer his or her help.

Finally, you need to make extensions available. A common place for Yii extensions is `http://www.yiiframework.com/extensions/`. You need to be a registered forum member with a few posts before you will be allowed to upload your code. Try to find a good descriptive name, write descriptive summary, and specify relevant category and tags. Don't use archives other than ZIP or GZIP since these are the most common archive formats and you can be sure anyone can unpack it.

Even if your extension is relatively simple and documentation is good, there could be questions and, for the first time, the only man who can answer them is you. Typically, questions are asked at official forums, so it is better to create a topic where people can discuss your code and provide a link at the extension page.

How it works...

If you want to share an extension with the community and be sure it will be useful and popular, you need to do more than just write code. Making extensions distribution-ready is much more work to do. It can be even more than creating an extension itself. So why is it good to share extensions with the community in the first place?

Comparing to a code you use in your own projects open source has its pros. You are getting people, a lot more people than you can get to test your closed source project. People who are using your extension are testing it, giving valuable feedback, and reporting bugs. If your code is popular, there will be passionate developers who will try to improve your code, to make it more extensive, more stable, and reusable. Moreover, it just feels good because of doing a good thing.

There's more...

We have covered the most important things. Still there are more to check out. Try existing extensions before writing your own. If an extension almost fits try contacting the extension author and contribute ideas you have. Reviewing existing code helps to find out useful tricks, dos, and don'ts. Also check wiki articles and the official forum from time to time, there is a lot of useful information about creating extensions and developing using Yii in general.

9
Error handling, Debugging, and Logging

In this chapter, we will cover:

- ▶ Using different log routes
- ▶ Analyzing the Yii error stack trace
- ▶ Logging and using the context information
- ▶ Implementing your own smart 404 handler

Introduction

It is not possible to create a bug-free application if it is relatively complex, so developers have to detect errors and deal with them as fast as possible. Yii has a good set of utility classes to handle logging and handling errors. Moreover, in the debug mode, Yii gives you a stack trace if there is an error. Using it, you can fix errors faster.

In this chapter, we will review logging, analyzing the exception stack trace, and implementing our own error handler.

Using different log routes

Logging is the key to understanding what your application actually does when you have no chance to debug it. Believe or not, but even if you are 100% sure that the application will behave as expected, in production it can do many things you were not aware of. This is OK, as no one can be aware of everything. Therefore, if we are expecting an unusual behavior, we need to know about it as soon as possible and have enough details to reproduce it. This is where logging comes in handy.

Yii allows a developer not only to log messages but also to handle them differently depending on the message level and category. You can, for example, write a message to DB, send an e-mail, or just show it in the browser.

In this recipe, we will handle log messages in a wise manner: The most important message will be sent through an e-mail, less important messages will be saved in files A and B, and the profiling will be routed to Firebug. Additionally, in a development mode, all messages and profiling information will be displayed on the screen.

Getting ready

Set up a fresh Yii application by using `yiic webapp` as described in the official guide.

How to do it...

Carry out the following steps:

1. Configure logging using `protected/config/main.php`:

```
array(
    ...
    'preload'=>array('log'),
    'components'=>array(
        ...
        'log'=>array(
            'class'=>'CLogRouter',
            'routes'=>array(
                array(
                    'class' => 'CEmailLogRoute',
                    'categories' => 'example',
                    'levels' => CLogger::LEVEL_ERROR,
                    'emails' => array('admin@example.com'),
                    'sentFrom' => 'log@example.com',
                    'subject' => 'Error at example.com',
                ),
```

```
            array(
                'class' => 'CFileLogRoute',
                'levels' => CLogger::LEVEL_WARNING,
                'logFile' => 'A',
            ),
            array(
                'class' => 'CFileLogRoute',
                'levels' => CLogger::LEVEL_INFO,
                'logFile' => 'B',
            ),
            array(
                'class' => 'CWebLogRoute',
                'categories' => 'example',
                'levels' => CLogger::LEVEL_PROFILE,
                'showInFireBug' => true,
                'ignoreAjaxInFireBug' => true,
            ),
            array(
                'class' => 'CWebLogRoute',
                'categories' => 'example',
            ),
        ),
    ),
),
),
```

2. Now, we will produce a few log messages in `protected/controllers/`
   `LogController.php` as follows:

```php
<?php
class LogController extends CController
{
    public function actionIndex()
    {
      Yii::trace('example trace message', 'example');

      Yii::log('info', CLogger::LEVEL_INFO, 'example');
      Yii::log('error', CLogger::LEVEL_ERROR, 'example');
      Yii::log('trace', CLogger::LEVEL_TRACE, 'example');
      Yii::log('warning', CLogger::LEVEL_WARNING, 'example');

      Yii::beginProfile('preg_replace', 'example');
      for($i=0;$i<10000;$i++){
        preg_replace('~^[ a-z]+~', '', 'test it');
```

```
            }
            Yii::endProfile('preg_replace', 'example');

            echo 'done';
        }
    }
```

3. Now run the preceding action multiple times. On the screen, you should see a web log similar to the one shown in the following screenshot:

done

| Application Log | | | |
Timestamp	Level	Category	Message
00:34:21.960349	trace	example	example trace message in W:\home\yiicmf\www\protected\controllers\LogController.php (6) in W:\home\yiicmf\www\index.php (12)
00:34:21.960485	info	example	info in W:\home\yiicmf\www\protected\controllers\LogController.php (8) in W:\home\yiicmf\www\index.php (12)
00:34:21.960575	error	example	error in W:\home\yiicmf\www\protected\controllers\LogController.php (9) in W:\home\yiicmf\www\index.php (12)
00:34:21.960663	trace	example	trace in W:\home\yiicmf\www\protected\controllers\LogController.php (10) in W:\home\yiicmf\www\index.php (12)
00:34:21.960751	warning	example	warning in W:\home\yiicmf\www\protected\controllers\LogController.php (11) in W:\home\yiicmf\www\index.php (12)
00:34:21.960793	profile	example	begin:preg_replace
00:34:22.006820	profile	example	end:preg_replace

A web log contains all the messages we have logged along with stack traces, timestamps, levels, and categories.

4. Now open Firefox's Firebug console. You should see profiler messages as shown in the following screenshot:

```
Application Log
  [01:02:12.933] [profile] [example] begin:preg_replace
  [01:02:12.965] [profile] [example] end:preg_replace
Issues with trunk Firefox for Firebug: http://getfirebug.com/knownissues
```

Yii uses firebug-compatible API, so you can view these messages in Chrome as follows:

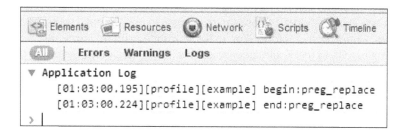

Alternatively, in Opera:

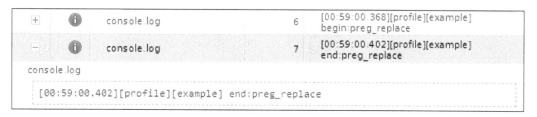

5. As we just changed the log file names and not paths, you should look in `protected/runtime/` to find log files named A and B. Inside, you will find messages as follows:

```
2011/04/17 00:58:53 [warning] [example] warning
in W:\home\yiicmf\www\protected\controllers\LogController.php (11)
in W:\home\yiicmf\www\index.php (12)
2011/04/17 00:59:00 [warning] [example] warning
in W:\home\yiicmf\www\protected\controllers\LogController.php (11)
in W:\home\yiicmf\www\index.php (12)
2011/04/17 00:59:56 [warning] [example] warning
in W:\home\yiicmf\www\protected\controllers\LogController.php (11)
in W:\home\yiicmf\www\index.php (12)
2011/04/17 01:02:07 [warning] [example] warning
in W:\home\yiicmf\www\protected\controllers\LogController.php (11)
in W:\home\yiicmf\www\index.php (12)
2011/04/17 01:02:12 [warning] [example] warning
in W:\home\yiicmf\www\protected\controllers\LogController.php (11)
in W:\home\yiicmf\www\index.php (12)
2011/04/17 01:03:00 [warning] [example] warning
in W:\home\yiicmf\www\protected\controllers\LogController.php (11)
in W:\home\yiicmf\www\index.php (12)
```

How it works...

When one logs a message using `Yii::log` or `Yii::trace`, Yii passes it to the log router. Depending on how it is configured, it passes messages to one or many routes. For example, e-mailing errors, writing debug information in file A, writing warning information in file B, and passing profiling results to the Firebug console. This is depicted in the following diagram:

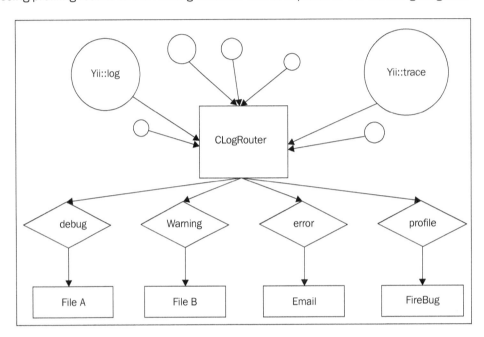

`CLogRouter` is typically attached to an application component named `log`. Therefore, in order to configure it, we should set its properties in the `protected/config/main.php`, `components` section. The only configurable property there is `routes` that contains an array of log route handlers and their configurations.

We have defined five log routes. Let's review them as follows:

```
array(
    'class' => 'CEmailLogRoute',
    'categories' => 'example',
    'levels' => CLogger::LEVEL_ERROR,
    'emails' => array('admin@example.com'),
    'sentFrom' => 'log@example.com',
    'subject' => 'Error at example.com',
),
```

`CEmailLogRoute` sends log messages through an e-mail. We limit category to `example` and level to `error`. An e-mail will be sent from `log@example.com` to `admin@example.com` and the subject will be `Error at example.com`.

```
array(
    'class' => 'CFileLogRoute',
    'levels' => CLogger::LEVEL_WARNING,
    'logFile' => 'A',
),
```

`CFileLogRoute` appends error messages to a file specified. We limit the message level to `warning` and use a file named `A`. We do the same for `info` level messages by using a file named `B`.

`CWebLogRoute` passes log messages to the browser as follows:

```
array(
    'class' => 'CWebLogRoute',
    'categories' => 'example',
),
```

The same log route can be used to pass log messages to Firebug or another console compatible with it.

```
array(
    'class' => 'CWebLogRoute',
    'categories' => 'example',
    'levels' => CLogger::LEVEL_PROFILE,
    'showInFireBug' => true,
    'ignoreAjaxInFireBug' => true,
),
```

In the preceding code, we limit category to `example`, log level to `profile`, and turn on the logging to Firebug. Additionally, we turn the logging off for AJAX-requests, as the JSON response can be spoiled by logging.

There's more...

There are more interesting things about Yii logging, which are covered in the following subsection:

Yii::trace vs Yii::log

`Yii::trace` is a simple wrapper around `Yii::log`:

```
if(YII_DEBUG)
        self::log($msg,CLogger::LEVEL_TRACE,$category);
```

Therefore, `Yii::trace` logs a message with a trace level, if Yii is in the debug mode.

Yii::beginProfile and Yii::endProfile

These methods are used to measure the execution time of some part of the application's code. In our `LogController`, we measured 10,000 executions of `preg_replace` as follows:

```
Yii::beginProfile('preg_replace', 'regex_test');
for($i=0;$i<10000;$i++){
    preg_replace('~^[ a-z]+~', '', 'test it');
}
Yii::endProfile('preg_replace', 'regex_test');
```

Log messages immediately

By default Yii keeps all log messages in memory until the application is properly terminated using `Yii::app()->end()`. That's done for performance reasons and generally works fine. However, if there is a PHP fatal error or `die()`/`exit()` in the code, some log messages will not be written at all. To make sure your messages will be logged you can flush them explicitly using `Yii::app()->log->flush(true)`.

Further reading

In order to learn more about logging, refer to the following URLs:

- ▶ `http://www.yiiframework.com/doc/guide/en/topics.logging`
- ▶ `http://www.yiiframework.com/doc/api/CLogRouter`
- ▶ `http://www.yiiframework.com/doc/api/CLogRoute`
- ▶ `http://www.yiiframework.com/doc/api/CDbLogRoute`
- ▶ `http://www.yiiframework.com/doc/api/CEmailLogRoute`
- ▶ `http://www.yiiframework.com/doc/api/CFileLogRoute`
- ▶ `http://www.yiiframework.com/doc/api/CWebLogRoute`
- ▶ `http://www.yiiframework.com/doc/api/CLogger`

See also

- ▶ The recipe named *Logging and using the context information* in this chapter

Analyzing the Yii error stack trace

When an error occurs, Yii can display the error stack trace along with the error. A stack trace is especially helpful when we need to know what really caused an error rather than just the fact that an error occurred.

Getting ready

▶ Set up a fresh Yii application by using `yiic webapp` as described in the official guide

▶ Configure a database and import the following SQL:

```
CREATE TABLE `article` (
  `alias` varchar(255) NOT NULL,
  `title` varchar(255) NOT NULL,
  `text` text NOT NULL,
  PRIMARY KEY (`alias`)
));
```

▶ Generate an `Article` model using Gii

How to do it...

Carry out the following steps:

1. Now we will need to create some code to work with. Create `protected/controllers/ErrorController.php` as follows:

```php
<?php
class ErrorController extends CController
{
    public function actionIndex()
    {
        $articles = $this->getModels('php');
        foreach($articles as $article)
        {
            echo $article->title;
            echo "<br />";
        }
    }

    private function getModels($alias)
    {
        $criteria = new CDbCriteria();
        $criteria->addSearchCondition('allas', $alias);
        return Article::model()->findAll($criteria);
    }
}
```

2. We will run the preceding action and we should get the following error:

```
CDbCommand failed to execute the SQL statement: SQLSTATE[42S22]:
Column not found: 1054 Unknown column 'allas' in 'where clause'.
The SQL statement executed was: SELECT * FROM `article` `t` WHERE
allas LIKE :ycp0
```

3. Moreover, the stack trace shows the following error:

```
Stack Trace

#0  □  W:\home\yiicmf\framework\db\CDbCommand.php(376): CDbCommand->queryInternal("fetchAll", array(2), array())

#1  □  W:\home\yiicmf\framework\db\ar\CActiveRecord.php(1288): CDbCommand->queryAll()

#2  □  W:\home\yiicmf\framework\db\ar\CActiveRecord.php(1412): CActiveRecord->query(CDbCriteria, true)

#3  □  W:\home\yiicmf\www\protected\controllers\ErrorController.php(18): CActiveRecord->findAll(CDbCriteria)

      13
      14      private function getModels($alias)
      15      {
      16          $criteria = new CDbCriteria();
      17          $criteria->addSearchCondition('allas', $alias);
      18          return Article::model()->findAll($criteria);
      19      }
      20  }


#4  □  W:\home\yiicmf\www\protected\controllers\ErrorController.php(6): ErrorController->getModels("php")

      01  <?php
      02  class ErrorController extends CController
      03  {
      04      public function actionIndex()
      05      {
      06          $articles = $this->getModels('php');
      07          foreach($articles as $article)
      08          {
      09              echo $article->title;
      10              echo "<br />";
      11          }


#5  □  W:\home\yiicmf\framework\web\actions\CInlineAction.php(50): ErrorController->actionIndex()

#6  □  W:\home\yiicmf\framework\web\CController.php(302): CInlineAction->runWithParams(array())

#7  □  W:\home\yiicmf\framework\web\CController.php(280): CController->runAction(CInlineAction)

#8  □  W:\home\yiicmf\framework\web\CController.php(258): CController->runActionWithFilters(CInlineAction, array())

#9  □  W:\home\yiicmf\framework\web\CWebApplication.php(329): CController->run("")

#10 □  W:\home\yiicmf\framework\web\CWebApplication.php(122): CWebApplication->runController("error")

#11 □  W:\home\yiicmf\framework\base\CApplication.php(155): CWebApplication->processRequest()

#12 □  W:\home\yiicmf\www\index.php(12): CApplication->run()

      07   defined('YII_DEBUG') or define('YII_DEBUG',true);
```

How it works...

From the error message, we know that we have no `allas` column in DB, but used it somewhere in the code. In our case, it is very simple to find it just by searching all the project files, but in a large project, a column can be stored in a variable. Moreover, we have everything to fix an error without leaving a screen where the stack trace is displayed. We just need to read it carefully.

The stack trace displays a chain of calls in the reversed order starting with the one that caused an error. In our case, it is `queryInternal`. Generally, we don't need to read the whole trace to get what is going on. The framework code itself is tested well, so the probability of error is less. That is why Yii displays the application trace entries expanded and the framework trace entries collapsed.

Therefore, we take the first expanded section and look for `allas`. After finding it, we can immediately tell it is used in `ErrorController.php` at line 17.

There's more...

In order to learn more about error handling, refer to the following URL:

`http://www.yiiframework.com/doc/guide/en/topics.error`

See also

- ▶ The recipe named *Logging and using the context information* in this chapter

Logging and using the context information

Sometimes a log message is not enough to fix an error. For example, if you are following best practices and developing and testing an application with all possible errors reported, you can get an error message. However, without the execution context, it is only telling you that there was an error and it is not clear what actually caused it.

For our example, we will use a very simple and poorly coded action that just echoes "Hello, <username>!" where the username is taken directly from `$_GET`.

Getting ready

- ▶ Configure PHP to use the most strict error reporting. In `php.ini`, replace the `error_reporting` value with "-1". This change requires restarting the server.
- ▶ Set up a fresh Yii application by using `yiic webapp` as described in the official guide.

How to do it...

Carry out the following steps:

1. First, we will need a controller to work with. Therefore, create `protected/controllers/LogController.php` as follows:

```php
<?php
class LogController extends CController
```

```
{
    public function actionIndex()
    {
        echo "Hello, ".$_GET['username'];
    }
}
```

2. Now, if we run the `index` action, we will get the error message "Undefined index: username". Let's configure the logger to write these kind of errors to a file. `protected/config/main.php`:

```
array(
    ...
    'preload'=>array('log'),
    'components'=>array(
        ...
        'log'=>array(
            'class'=>'CLogRouter',
            'routes'=>array(
                array(
                    'class'=>'CFileLogRoute',
                    'levels'=>'error',
                    'logFile' => 'errors',
                ),
                ...other log routes...
            ),
        ),
    ),
)
```

3. Run the `index` action again and check `protected/runtime/error`. There should be log information like the following:

```
2011/04/17 03:53:19 [error] [php] Undefined index: username (W:\
home\yiicmf\www\protected\controllers\LogController.php:30)
Stack trace:
#0 W:\home\yiicmf\framework\web\CController.php(280):
LogController->runAction()
#1 W:\home\yiicmf\framework\web\CController.php(258):
LogController->runActionWithFilters()
#2 W:\home\yiicmf\framework\web\CWebApplication.php(329):
LogController->run()
#3 W:\home\yiicmf\framework\web\CWebApplication.php(122):
CWebApplication->runController()
#4 W:\home\yiicmf\framework\base\CApplication.php(155):
CWebApplication->processRequest()
```

```
#5 W:\home\yiicmf\www\index.php(12): CWebApplication->run()
REQUEST_URI=/log/environment
in W:\home\yiicmf\www\protected\controllers\LogController.php (30)
in W:\home\yiicmf\www\index.php (12)
```

4. Now we can give our application to a testing team and check the errors log from time to time. We will know there are errors, but we will need to reproduce them somehow. In order to do this, we need to reconstruct the environment. Let's add it to the log as follows:

```
array(
    'class' => 'CFileLogRoute',
    'levels' => CLogger::LEVEL_ERROR,
    'logFile' => 'errors',
    'filter'=>'CLogFilter',
),
```

5. Now run action again. This time, you should get enough to reproduce the environment in detail:

```
2011/04/17 04:01:16 [info] [application] $_SERVER=array (
  'REDIRECT_STATUS' => '200',
  'HTTP_USER_AGENT' => 'Opera/9.80 (Windows NT 6.1; U; ru)
     Presto/2.8.131 Version/11.10',
  'HTTP_HOST' => 'yiicmf',
  'HTTP_ACCEPT' => 'text/html, application/xml;q=0.9, application/
     xhtml+xml, image/png, image/webp, image/jpeg, image/gif,
     image/x-xbitmap, */*;q=0.1',
  'HTTP_ACCEPT_LANGUAGE' => 'ru-RU,ru;q=0.9,en;q=0.8',
  'HTTP_ACCEPT_ENCODING' => 'gzip, deflate',
  'HTTP_PRAGMA' => 'no-cache',
  'HTTP_CACHE_CONTROL' => 'no-cache',
  'HTTP_CONNECTION' => 'Keep-Alive',

  …

  'SERVER_NAME' => 'yiicmf',
  'SERVER_ADDR' => '127.0.0.1',
  'SERVER_PORT' => '80',
  'REMOTE_ADDR' => '127.0.0.1',
  'DOCUMENT_ROOT' => 'W:/home/yiicmf/www',
  'SERVER_ADMIN' => 'admin@localhost',
  'SCRIPT_FILENAME' => 'W:/home/yiicmf/www/index.php',
  'REMOTE_PORT' => '55190',
  'REDIRECT_URL' => '/log/environment',
  'GATEWAY_INTERFACE' => 'CGI/1.1',
```

```
        'SERVER_PROTOCOL' => 'HTTP/1.1',
        'REQUEST_METHOD' => 'GET',
        'QUERY_STRING' => '',
        'REQUEST_URI' => '/log/environment',
        'SCRIPT_NAME' => '/index.php',
        'PHP_SELF' => '/index.php',
        'REQUEST_TIME' => 1302998476,
        'argv' =>
        array (
        ),
        'argc' => 0,
    )
2011/04/17 04:01:16 [error] [php] Undefined index: username (W:\
home\yiicmf\www\protected\controllers\LogController.php:30)
Stack trace:
#0 W:\home\yiicmf\framework\web\CController.php(280):
LogController->runAction()
#1 W:\home\yiicmf\framework\web\CController.php(258):
LogController->runActionWithFilters()
#2 W:\home\yiicmf\framework\web\CWebApplication.php(329):
LogController->run()
#3 W:\home\yiicmf\framework\web\CWebApplication.php(122):
CWebApplication->runController()
#4 W:\home\yiicmf\framework\base\CApplication.php(155):
CWebApplication->processRequest()
#5 W:\home\yiicmf\www\index.php(12): CWebApplication->run()
REQUEST_URI=/log/environment
in W:\home\yiicmf\www\protected\controllers\LogController.php (30)
in W:\home\yiicmf\www\index.php (12)
2011/04/17 04:01:16 [info] [application] User: Guest (ID: )
```

How it works...

In order to get more from the error logging, we use the `CLogFilter` class that preprocesses the logged messages before they are handled by a log route. It is the only log filter that is included in the Yii core and can be used to add more information about the execution context and environment. If we are logging a message manually, then we probably know what information we need, so we can set some `CLogFilter` options to write only what we really need:

```
array(
    'class' => 'CFileLogRoute',
    'levels' => CLogger::LEVEL_ERROR,
    'logFile' => 'errors',
    'filter'=> array(
```

```
        'class' => 'CLogFilter',
        'logUser' => false,
        'logVars' => array('_GET'),
    ),
),
```

The preceding code will log errors to a file named `errors`. Additionally to a message itself, it will log contents of `$_GET` if it is not empty.

There's more...

In order to learn more about log filters and context information, refer to the following URLs:

- ▶ `http://www.yiiframework.com/doc/api/CLogFilter`
- ▶ `http://www.yiiframework.com/doc/guide/en/topics.
  logging#logging-context-informations`

See also

- ▶ The recipe named *Using different log routes* in this chapter

Implementing your own smart 404 handler

In Yii, the error handling is very flexible, so you can create your own error handler for errors of specific type. In this recipe, we will handle a 404 not found error in a smart way: We will show a custom 404 page that will suggest the content based on what was entered in the address bar.

Getting ready

- ▶ Set up a fresh Yii application by using `yiic webapp` as described in the official guide
- ▶ Configure a database and import the following SQL:

```
CREATE TABLE `article` (
  `alias` varchar(255) NOT NULL,
  `title` varchar(255) NOT NULL,
  `text` text NOT NULL,
  PRIMARY KEY (`alias`)
));
```

- ▶ Generate an `Article` model using Gii
- ▶ Generate an `Article` crud using Gii

▶ Create the following articles:

Title	Alias	Text
Yii framework	yii-framework	Yii framework is good.
Why Yii	why-yii	Why should I use Yii?
PHP is a good tool	php-is-a-good-tool	PHP is nice!
Yii as a tool for apps	yii-as-a-tool-for-apps	Yii is a good tool for apps.

How to do it...

Carry out the following steps:

1. Try to run `http://your.application/yii`. You should get a standard 404-error page. Now we need to somehow change this page, but leave it as it is for other error types. In order to achieve this, we will use the application's `onException` event. Let's configure it to be handled by the `handle` static method of the `NotFoundHandler` class. We will do it by using `protected/config/main.php` as follows:

```
// events
'onException' => array('NotFoundHandler', 'handle'),
```

2. Now we need to implement the error handling itself. Create `protected/components/NotFoundHandler.php` as follows:

```php
<?php
class NotFoundHandler
{
  public static function handle(CExceptionEvent $event)
  {
    $exception = $event->exception;

    if(get_class($exception)=="CHttpException" &&
      $exception->statusCode===404)
    {
      $pathParts = explode('/', Yii::app()->
        getRequest()->getRequestUri());
      $pathPart = array_pop($pathParts);

      $criteria = new CDbCriteria();
      $criteria->addSearchCondition('alias', $pathPart);
      $criteria->limit = 5;

      $models = Article::model()->findAll($criteria);
```

```
        $controller = new CController(null);
        $controller->renderPartial('//error/404', array(
          'models' => $models,
        ));
        $event->handled = true;
      }
    }
  }
```

3. Also, we will need a view named `protected/views/error/404.php`:

```
<!doctype html>
<html>
  <head>
    <meta charset="utf-8" />
    <title>404</title>
  </head>
  <body>
    <h1>404</h1>

    <?php if(!empty($models)):?>
    <p>Probably you've searched for:</p>
    <ul>
      <?php foreach($models as $model):?>
      <li><a href="<?php echo $this->createUrl('article/view',
        array('id' => $model->alias))?>"><?php echo
        $model->title?></a></li>
      <?php endforeach?>
    </ul>
    <?php endif?>
  </body>
</html>
```

4. That is it. Now try the following URLs:

   ❑ `http://your.application/yii`
   ❑ `http://your.application/tool`

Each time, you will get several links to related articles.

How it works...

By using the configuration file, we attach an event handler to the `onException` event as follows:

```
'onException' => array('NotFoundHandler', 'handle'),
```

This means that we will use `NotFoundHandler::handle()`. Every event handler method accepts a single parameter named `$event` with event data inside. The exception handler parameter accepts the `CExceptionEvent` instance. As it contains the original exception, we can check for its type and error code as follows:

```
if(get_class($exception)=="CHttpException" &&
  $exception->statusCode===404)
```

If the exception doesn't match, the Yii works as before and if it does match, Yii executes our custom code:

```
$pathParts = explode('/', Yii::app()->getRequest()->getRequestUri());
$pathPart = array_pop($pathParts);
```

We get the last URL segment as it will most probably contain the article alias if the URL is in path format. Then, form DB criteria and get models as follows:

```
$criteria = new CDbCriteria();
$criteria->addSearchCondition('alias', $pathPart);
$criteria->limit = 5;
$models = Article::model()->findAll($criteria);
```

Then, we render a view in the following way:

```
$controller = new CController(null);
$controller->renderPartial('//error/404', array(
    'models' => $models,
));
```

Note that we are creating a new `CController` instance because 404 can be reached before the application will initialize a controller.

```
$event->handled = true;
```

Finally, we instruct Yii that the event is handled and there is no need to handle it further.

There's more...

The preceding method is not the only method for handling errors in a customized way. Other options are as follows:

- Extend `CErrorHandler` application component
- Use a controller action to handle errors by setting `CErrorHandler:: errorAction`

Further reading

In order to learn more about handling errors in Yii, refer to the following API pages:

- http://www.yiiframework.com/doc/api/CErrorHandler/
- http://www.yiiframework.com/doc/api/CApplication#onException-detail
- http://www.yiiframework.com/doc/api/CApplication#onError-detail

See also

- The recipe named *Using Yii events* in *Chapter 1, Under the Hood*

10
Security

In this chapter, we will cover:

- ► Using controller filters
- ► Using CHtml and CHtmlPurifier to prevent XSS
- ► Preventing SQL injections
- ► Preventing CSRF
- ► Using RBAC

Introduction

From this chapter, you will learn how to keep your application secure according to the general web application security principle "filter input escape output". We will cover topics such as creating your own controller filters, preventing XSS, CSRF, and SQL injections, escaping output, and using role-based access control.

Using controller filters

In many cases, we need to filter the incoming data or perform some actions based on this data. For example, with custom filters, we can filter visitors by IP, force users to use HTTPS, or redirect the user to an important setting page prior to using the application. Yii has two built-in usable filters. First is `CInlineFilter` which allows using the controller method as a filter, and the second (the one we will focus on) is `CAccessControlFilter` which allows controlling access to various controller actions.

In this recipe, we will implement the following:

- ▶ Limiting access to the controller action to authorized users only
- ▶ Limiting access to the controller action to specified IPs
- ▶ Limiting access to specific users
- ▶ Limiting access for users of a browser specified; in this case, we will also show the custom message

Getting ready

- ▶ Create a fresh application by using `yiic webapp`
- ▶ Create `protected/controllers/AccessController.php` as follows:

```php
<?php
class AccessController extends CController
{

  public function actionAuthOnly()
  {
    echo "Looks like you are authorized to run me.";
  }

  public function actionIp()
  {
    echo "Your IP is in our list. Lucky you!";
  }

  public function actionUser()
  {
    echo "You're the right man. Welcome!";
  }
}
```

How to do it...

Carry out the following steps:

1. Applying an access filter consists of two steps. First, we need to include a filter in the controller `filters` method. We do this as follows:

```php
public function filters()
{
  return array(
    'accessControl',
  );
}
```

2. Then, we can describe filtering rules in the `accessRules` method that is used by the access control filter as follows:

```
public function accessRules()
{
  return array(
    array(
      'deny',
      'expression' => 'strpos($_SERVER[\'HTTP_USER_AGENT\'],
        \'MSIE\') !== FALSE',
      'message' => "You're using the wrong browser, sorry.",
    ),
    array(
      'allow',
      'actions' => array('authOnly'),
      'users' => array('@'),
    ),
    array(
      'allow',
      'actions' => array('ip'),
      'ips' => array('127.0.0.1'),
    ),
    array(
      'allow',
      'actions' => array('user'),
      'users' => array('admin'),
    ),
    array('deny'),
  );
}
```

3. Now try to run controller actions using Internet Explorer and other browsers, using both `admin` and `demo` usernames.

How it works...

We will start with limiting access to the controller action to authorized users only. Add the following code in the `accessRules` method:

```
array(
    'allow',
    'actions' => array('authOnly'),
    'users' => array('@'),
),
array('deny'),
```

Each array here is an access rule. You can either use *allow rules* or *deny rules*. For each rule, there are several parameters.

 By default, Yii does not deny everything, so consider adding `array('deny')` to the end of your rules list if you need maximum security.

In our rule, we use two parameters. The first is `actions` parameter which takes an array of actions to which the rule will be applied. The second is the `users` parameter which takes an array of user IDs (ones returned by `Yii::app()->user->id`) to determine the users this rule applies to. In our case, we used one of the following special characters: @ means "all authenticated users", while * and ? stand for "all users" and "guest users" respectively.

 Rules are executed one by one starting from the top until one matches. If nothing matches, then the action is treated as allowed.

The next task is to limit access to specific IPs. In this case, the following two access rules are involved:

```
array(
    'allow',
    'actions' => array('ip'),
    'ips' => array('127.0.0.1'),
),
array('deny'),
```

The first rule allows access to the `ip` action from a list of IPs specified. In our case, we are using a loopback address which always points to our own computer. Try changing it to, for example, `127.0.0.2` to see how it works when the address does not match. The second rule denies everything including all other IPs.

Next, we limit access to one specific user as follows:

```
array(
  'allow',
  'actions' => array('user'),
  'users' => array('admin'),
),
array('deny'),
```

The preceding rule allows a user with an ID equal to `admin` to run the `user` action. Therefore, if you log in as `admin`, it will let you in, but if you log in as `demo`, it will not. This is the same type of rule that we used to limit access to authorized users. The only difference is that we are using an ID instead of a wildcard. Again, the second rule involved denies everything including all other users.

Finally, we need to deny access to a specific browser. For this recipe, we are denying all versions of Internet Explorer and, in fact, some other browsers with the same user agent strings. The rule itself is put on top, so it executes first as follows:

```
array(
  'deny',
  'expression' => 'strpos($_SERVER[\'HTTP_USER_AGENT\'], \'MSIE\')
    !== FALSE',
  'message' => "You're using the wrong browser, sorry.",
),
array('deny'),
```

> The detection technique which we are using is not very reliable, as "MSIE" is contained in many other user agent strings. For a list of possible user agent strings, you can refer to the following URL:
>
> `http://www.useragentstring.com/`

In the preceding code, we use another filter rule property named `expression`. It takes a PHP expression as a string, as an anonymous function (in PHP 5.3), or as a valid callback. In our case, we use a string.

Using PHP 5.3, the anonymous function will look like the following:

```
array(
  'deny',
  'expression' => function(){
    return strpos($_SERVER['HTTP_USER_AGENT'], 'MSIE') !== FALSE;
  },
  'message' => "You're using the wrong browser, sorry.",
),
```

The preceding expression checks if the user agent string contains MSIE. Depending on your requirements, you can specify any PHP code. The second parameter named `message` is used to change a message shown to the user when the access is denied.

There's more...

In order to learn more about the access control and filters, refer to the following URLs:

- ▶ `http://www.yiiframework.com/doc/guide/en/topics.auth#access-control-filter`
- ▶ `http://www.yiiframework.com/doc/guide/en/basics.controller#filter`
- ▶ `http://www.yiiframework.com/doc/api/CAccessControlFilter`

See also

- ▶ The recipe named *Using RBAC* in this chapter

Using CHtml and CHtmlPurifier to prevent XSS

XSS stands for **cross-site scripting** and is a type of vulnerability which allows one to inject a client-side script (typically, JavaScript) in the page viewed by other users. Considering the power of the client-side scripting this can lead to very serious consequences such as bypassing security checks, getting another user credentials, or data leaks.

In this recipe, we will see how to prevent XSS by escaping the output with both `CHtml` and `CHtmlPurifier`.

Getting ready

- ▶ Generate a fresh web application by using `yiic webapp`
- ▶ Create `protected/controllers/XssController.php` as follows:

```php
<?php
class XssController extends CController
{
  public function actionSimple()
  {
    echo 'Hello, '.$_GET['username'].'!';
  }
}
```

Normally, it will be used as /xss/simple?username=Alexander. However, as the main security principle "filter input, escape output" was not taken into account, malicious users will be able to use it in the following way:

```
/xss/simple?username=<script>alert('XSS');</script>
```

The preceding will result in a script execution which is shown in the following screenshot:

Note that instead of just alerting XSS, it is possible, for example, to steal page contents or perform some website-specific things such as deleting all users' data.

How to do it...

Carry out the following steps:

1. In order to prevent the XSS alert shown in the preceding screenshot, we need to escape the data before passing it onto the browser. We do this as follows:

    ```
    class XssController extends CController
    {
      public function actionSimple()
      {
        echo 'Hello, '.CHtml::encode($_GET['username']).'!';
      }
    }
    ```

2. Now instead of an alert, we will get properly escaped HTML as shown in the following screenshot:

3. Therefore, the basic rule is to always escape all dynamic data. For example, we should do the same for a link name:

```
echo CHtml::link(CHtml::encode($_GET['username']), array());
```

4. That is it. You have a page that is free from XSS. Now what if we want to allow some HTML to pass? We cannot use `CHtml::encode` anymore because it will render HTML as just a code and we need the actual representation. Fortunately, there is a tool bundled with Yii that allows filtering out the malicious HTML. It is named as HTML Purifier and can be used in the following way:

```
public function actionHtml()
{
  $this->beginWidget('CHtmlPurifier');
  echo $_GET['html'];
  $this->endWidget();
}
```

Alternatively, you can use it in the following way:

```
public function actionHtml()
{
  $purifier=new CHtmlPurifier();
  echo $purifier->purify($_GET['html']);
}
```

5. Now if we access the `html` action using a URL such as `/xss/html?html=Hello, <strong>username</strong>!<script>alert('XSS')</script>` the HTML purifier will remove the malicious part and we will get the following result:

How it works...

Internally, CHtml::encode looks like the following:

```
public static function encode($text)
{
    return htmlspecialchars($text,ENT_QUOTES,Yii::app()->charset);
}
```

So basically, we use the PHP's internal htmlspecialchars function which is pretty secure if one does not forget to pass the correct charset in the third argument.

CHtmlPurifier uses the HTML Purifier library which is the most advanced solution out there to prevent XSS inside of HTML. We have used its default configuration which is OK for most of the user-entered content. In order to learn more about how to configure it, refer to links mentioned in the *Further reading* subsection of this recipe.

There's more...

There are more things to know about XSS and HTML purifier, which are discussed in the following section:

XSS types

There are two main types of XSS injections, which are as follows:

1. Non-persistent
2. Persistent

The first type is exactly the one that we have used in the recipe and is the most common XSS type that can be found in most insecure web applications. Data passed by the user or through a URL is not stored anywhere, so the injected script will be executed only once and only for the user who entered it. Still, it is not as secure as it looks. Malicious users can include XSS in a link to another website and their core will be executed when another user will follow the link.

The second type is much more serious as the data entered by a malicious user is stored in the database and is shown to many, if not all, website users. Using this type of XSS, one can literally destroy your website by "commanding" all users to delete all data to which they have access.

Configuring the HTML purifier

The HTML purifier can be configured as follows:

```
$p = new CHtmlPurifier();
$p->options = array('URI.AllowedSchemes'=>array(
    'http' => true,
```

```
    'https' => true,
));
$text = $p->purify($text);
```

For a list of all possible keys which you can use in the `options` array, refer to the following URL:

```
http://htmlpurifier.org/live/configdoc/plain.html
```

HTML purifier performance

As the HTML purifier performs a lot of processing and analysis, its performance is not so good. Therefore, it is a good idea not to process text every time you are outputting it. Instead, it can be saved in a separate database field as discussed in *Chapter 6, Database, Active Record, and Model Tricks*, in the *Applying markdown and HTML* or cached.

Further reading

In order to learn more about XSS and how to deal with it, refer to the following resources:

- `http://htmlpurifier.org/docs`
- `http://ha.ckers.org/xss.html`
- `http://shiflett.org/blog/2007/may/character-encoding-and-xss`

See also

- The recipe named *Applying markdown and HTML* in *Chapter 6*

Preventing SQL injections

SQL injection is a type of code injection that uses vulnerability at the database level and allows executing arbitrary SQL allowing malicious users to carry out such actions as deleting data or raising their privileges.

In this recipe, we will see examples of vulnerable code and fix it.

Getting ready

- Create a fresh application by using `yiic webapp`
- Create and configure a new database
- Execute the following SQL:
```
CREATE TABLE `user` (
  `id` int(11) unsigned NOT NULL AUTO_INCREMENT,
  `username` varchar(100) NOT NULL,
```

```
`password` varchar(32) NOT NULL,
  PRIMARY KEY (`id`)
);
INSERT INTO `user`(`id`,`username`,`password`) VALUES ( '1','Alex'
,'202cb962ac59075b964b07152d234b70');
INSERT INTO `user`(`id`,`username`,`password`) VALUES ( '2','Qiang
','202cb962ac59075b964b07152d234b70');
```

▶ Generate a User model using Gii

How to do it...

1. First, we will implement a simple action that checks if the username and password that came from a URL are correct. Create protected/controllers/ SqlController.php:

```php
<?php
class SqlController extends CController
{
  public function actionSimple()
  {
    $userName = $_GET['username'];
    $password = md5($_GET['password']);
    $sql = "SELECT * FROM user WHERE username = '$userName'
      AND password = '$password' LIMIT 1;";
    $user = Yii::app()->db->createCommand($sql)->queryRow();
    if($user)
    {
      echo "Success";
    }
    else
    {
      echo "Failure";
    }
  }
}
```

2. Let's try to access it using the /sql/simple?username=test&password=test URL. As we are aware of neither the username nor password, it will—as expected— print "Failure".

3. Now try another URL: `/sql/simple?username=%27+or+%271%27%3D%271%2`
   `7%3B+--&password=whatever`. This time, it lets us in though we still don't know
   anything about actual credentials. The decoded part of the username value looks
   like the following:

```
' or '1'='1'; --
```

Close the quote, so that the syntax will stay correct.

Add `OR '1'='1'` that makes the condition always true.

Use `; --` to end the query and comment the rest.

4. As no escaping was done, the whole query executed was:

```
SELECT * FROM user WHERE username = '' or
'1'='1'; --' AND password = '008c5926ca861023c1d2a36653fd88e2'
LIMIT 1;
```

The best way to fix it is to use a prepared statement as follows:

```
public function actionPrepared()
{
  $userName = $_GET['username'];
  $password = md5($_GET['password']);
  $sql = "SELECT * FROM user WHERE username = :username
    AND password = :password LIMIT 1;";
  $command = Yii::app()->db->createCommand($sql);
  $command->bindValue('username', $userName);
  $command->bindValue('password', $password);
  $user = $command->queryRow();
  if ($user)
  {
    echo "Success";
  }
  else
  {
    echo "Failure";
  }
}
```

5. Now check `/sql/prepared` with the same malicious parameters. This time
   everything went fine and we have the "Failure" message. The same principle
   applies to Active Record. The only difference is that AR uses other syntax:

```
public function actionAr()
{
  $userName = $_GET['username'];
  $password = md5($_GET['password']);
```

```
$result = User::model()->exists("username = :username
  AND password = :password", array(
  'username' => $userName,
  'password' => $password,
));
if($result)
{
  echo "Success";
}
else
{
  echo "Failure";
}
}
```

In the preceding code, we used the `:username` and `:password` parameters and passed parameter values as a second argument. If we had written the preceding code by just using the first argument, it would be vulnerable:

```
public function actionWrongAr()
{
  $userName = $_GET['username'];
  $password = md5($_GET['password']);

  $result = User::model()->exists("username = $userName
    AND password = $password");
  if($result)
  {
    echo "Success";
  }
  else
  {
    echo "Failure";
  }
}
```

If used properly, prepared statements can save you from all types of SQL injections. Still there are some common problems:

▶ You can bind only one value to a single parameter, so if you want to query `WHERE IN(1, 2, 3, 4)`, you will have to create and bind four parameters.

▶ Prepared statement cannot be used for table names, column names, and other keywords.

When using Active Record, the first problem can be solved by using the criteria `addInCondition` method as follows:

```
public function actionIn()
{
  $criteria = new CDbCriteria();
  $criteria->addInCondition('username', array('Qiang', 'Alex'));
  $users = User::model()->findAll($criteria);
  foreach($users as $user)
  {
    echo $user->username."<br />";
  }
}
```

The second problem can be solved in multiple ways. First is to rely on Active Record and PDO quoting:

```
public function actionColumn()
{
  $attr = $_GET['attr'];
  $value = $_GET['value'];

  $users = User::model()->findAllByAttributes(array
    ($attr => $value));
  foreach($users as $user)
  {
    echo $user->username."<br />";
  }
}
```

The second and the most secure way is using the whitelist approach as follows:

```
public function actionWhitelist()
{
  $attr = $_GET['attr'];
  $value = $_GET['value'];

  $allowedAttr = array('username', 'id');

  if(!in_array($attr, $allowedAttr))
    throw new CException("Attribute specified is not allowed.");

  $users = User::model()->findAllByAttributes(array
    ($attr => $value));
  foreach($users as $user)
  {
    echo $user->username."<br />";
  }
}
```

How it works...

The main goal when preventing the SQL injection is to properly filter the input. In all cases except table names, we have used prepared statements—a feature supported by most relational database servers. It allows you to build statements once and then use them multiple times and provides a safe way to bind parameter values.

In Yii, you can use prepared statements for both Active Record and DAO. When using DAO, it can be achieved by using either `bindValue` or `bindParam`. The latter is useful when we want to execute multiple queries of the same type while varying parameter values:

```
$command = Yii::app()->db->createCommand($sql);
$username, $password;
$command->bindParam('username', $username);
foreach($records as $record)
{
    $username = $record['username'];
    $command->execute();
}
```

Most Active Record methods accept either criteria or parameters. To be safe, you should use these instead of just passing the raw data in.

As for quoting table names, columns, and other keywords, you can either rely on Active Record or use the whitelist approach.

There's more...

In order to learn more about SQL injections and working with database through Yii, refer to the following URLs:

▶ http://www.slideshare.net/billkarwin/sql-injection-myths-and-fallacies

▶ http://www.yiiframework.com/doc/api/CDbConnection

▶ http://www.yiiframework.com/doc/api/CDbCommand

See also

▶ The recipe named *Getting data from a database* in *Chapter 6*

▶ The recipe named *Using CDbCriteria* in *Chapter 6*

Preventing CSRF

CSRF or **XSRF** stands for **cross-site request forgery**, where a malicious user tricks the user's browser to silently perform an HTTP-request to the website when the user is logged in. An example of such an attack is inserting an invisible image tag with `src` pointing to `http://example.com/site/logout`. Even if the image tag is inserted in another website, you will be immediately logged out from example.com. Consequences of CSRF could be very serious: destroying website data, preventing all website users from logging in, exposing private data, and so on.

In this recipe, we will see how to make sure our application is CSRF-resistant.

Getting ready

Create a fresh application by using `yiic webapp`.

How to do it...

Let's start with some facts about CSRF:

▶ As CSRF should be performed by the victim user's browser, the attacker cannot normally change HTTP headers sent. However, there were both browser and Flash plugin vulnerabilities found that were allowing to spoof headers, so we should not rely on these.

▶ The attacker should pass the same parameters and values as the user would normally do.

Considering these, a good method of dealing with CSRF is passing and checking the unique token during form submissions and additionally using GET according to the HTTP specification.

Yii includes a built-in token generation and token checking. Additionally, it can automate inserting a token in HTML forms.

1. In order to turn the anti-CSRF protection on, we should add the following to `protected/config/main.php` as follows:

```
'components'=>array(
  ...
  'request'=>array(
    'enableCsrfValidation'=>true,
  ),
  ...
),
```

2. After configuring the application, you should use `CHtml::beginForm` and `CHtml::endForm` instead of HTML form tags:

```
public function actionCreate()
{
    echo CHtml::beginForm();
    echo CHtml::submitButton();
    echo CHtml::endForm();
}
```

3. Yii will automatically add a hidden token field as follows:

```
<form action="/csrf/create" method="post">
<div style="display:none"><input type="hidden" value="e4d1021e79ac
269e8d6289043a7a8bc154d7115a" name="YII_CSRF_TOKEN" />
```

4. If you save this form as HTML and try submitting it, you will get a message like the one shown in the following screenshot instead of the regular data processing:

How it works...

Internally, a part of `CHtml::beginForm()` looks like this:

```
if($request->enableCsrfValidation && !strcasecmp($method,'post'))
    $hiddens[]=self::hiddenField($request->csrfTokenName,
    $request->getCsrfToken(),array('id'=>false));
if($hiddens!==array())
    $form.="\n".self::tag('div',array('style'=>'display:none'),
    implode("\n",$hiddens));
```

In the preceding code `getCsrfToken()` generates a unique token value and writes it to a cookie. Then, on next requests, both the cookie and POST values are compared. If they don't match, an error message is shown instead of the usual data processing.

If you need to perform a POST request but not build a form using `CHtml`, then you can pass a parameter with a name from `Yii::app()->request->csrfTokenName` and a value from `Yii::app()->request->getCsrfToken()`.

![There's more...]

There are more ways to improve your application security, which are discussed in the following subsections:

Extra measures

If your application requires a very high security level, such as a bank account management system, extra measures could be taken.

First, you can turn off the "remember me" feature using `protected/config/main.php` as follows:

```
'components' => array(
    ...
'user'=>array(
        // enable cookie-based authentication
        'allowAutoLogin'=>false,
),
    ...
),
```

Then, you can lower the session timeout as follows:

```
'components' => array(
    ...
    'session' => array(
        'timeout' => 200,
    ),
    ...
),
```

Of course, these measures will make the user experience worse, but they will add an additional level of security.

Using GET and POST properly

HTTP insists on not using GET for operations that change data or state. Sticking to this rule is a good practice. It will not prevent all types of CSRF, but at least will make some injections such as `<img src=` pointless.

Further reading

In order to learn more about the security in Yii, refer to the following URL:

`http://www.yiiframework.com/doc/guide/en/topics.security`

▶ The recipe named *Using CHtml and CHtmlPurifier to prevent XSS* in this chapter

Using RBAC

RBAC is the most powerful access control method available in Yii. It is described in the guide, but since it is rather complex and powerful, it is not so easy to understand how it actually works without getting under the hood a little.

In this recipe, we will take roles hierarchy from the definitive guide, import it, and explain what is happening internally.

Getting ready

▶ Create a fresh web application by using `yiic webapp`

▶ Create a MySQL database and configure it

▶ Import SQL from `framework/web/auth/schema-mysql.sql`

▶ Configure the `authManager` component in your `protected/config/main.php` as follows:

```
return array(
  'components'=>array(
    ...
    'authManager'=>array(
      'class'=>'CDbAuthManager',
      'connectionID'=>'db',
    ),
  ),
  ...
);
```

▶ Add additional roles to `protected/components/UserIdentity.php`. The `users` array should look like the following:

```
$users=array(
  // username => password
  'demo'=>'demo',
  'admin'=>'admin',
  'readerA'=>'123',
  'authorB'=>'123',
  'editorC'=>'123',
  'adminD'=>'123',
);
```

How to do it...

Carry out the following steps:

1. Create `protected/controllers/RbacController.php` as follows:

```php
<?php
class RbacController extends CController
{
  public function filters()
  {
    return array(
      'accessControl',
    );
  }

  public function accessRules()
  {
    return array(
      array(
        'allow',
        'actions' => array('deletePost'),
        'roles' => array('deletePost'),
      ),
      array(
        'allow',
        'actions' => array('init', 'test'),
      ),
      array('deny'),
    );
  }


  public function actionInit()
  {
    $auth=Yii::app()->authManager;

    $auth->createOperation('createPost','create a post');
    $auth->createOperation('readPost','read a post');
    $auth->createOperation('updatePost','update a post');
    $auth->createOperation('deletePost','delete a post');

    $bizRule='return Yii::app()->user->id==$params
      ["post"]->authID;';
```

```
$task=$auth->createTask('updateOwnPost','update a
  post by author himself',$bizRule);
$task->addChild('updatePost');

$role=$auth->createRole('reader');
$role->addChild('readPost');

$role=$auth->createRole('author');
$role->addChild('reader');
$role->addChild('createPost');
$role->addChild('updateOwnPost');

$role=$auth->createRole('editor');
$role->addChild('reader');
$role->addChild('updatePost');

$role=$auth->createRole('admin');
$role->addChild('editor');
$role->addChild('author');
$role->addChild('deletePost');

$auth->assign('reader','readerA');
$auth->assign('author','authorB');
$auth->assign('editor','editorC');
$auth->assign('admin','adminD');

echo "Done.";
}

public function actionDeletePost()
{
  echo "Post deleted.";
}

public function actionTest()
{
  $post = new stdClass();
  $post->authID = 'authorB';

  echo "Current permissions:<br />";
  echo "<ul>";
    echo "<li>Create post: ".Yii::app()->user->checkAccess
      ('createPost')."</li>";
```

```
        echo "<li>Read post: ".Yii::app()->user->checkAccess
          ('readPost')."</li>";
        echo "<li>Update post: ".Yii::app()->user->checkAccess
          ('updatePost', array('post' => $post))."</li>";
        echo "<li>Delete post: ".Yii::app()->user->checkAccess
          ('deletePost')."</li>";
      echo "</ul>";
    }
  }
```

2. Now run `init` once to create the RBAC hierarchy. Then, try to log in as `readerA`, `authorB`, `editorC`, and `adminD` (password is "123") and visit `test` and `deletePost`.

Current permissions:

- Create post:
- Read post: 1
- Update post: 1
- Delete post:

How it works...

The RBAC hierarchy is a directed acyclic graph, that is, a set of nodes (authorization items) and their directed connections or edges. There are three types of nodes available: roles, tasks, and operations:

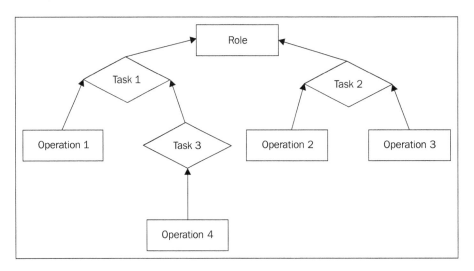

A role is the authorization item attached to the user (that is, a moderator or an admin). Operation determines if an action can be performed (that is, deleting post, editing post, and so on). A task is a group of operations (that is, manage task, and so on).

There are two ways to assign a role to a user, which are as follows:

▶ By using `Yii::app()->authManager->assign()`

▶ By configuring `defaultRoles` in the application configuration for the `authManager` component

Default roles are typically used when we need to assign a role to a huge part of the users based on some PHP expression such as `Yii::app()->user->isGuest`.

According to rules described in the definitive guide, it is forbidden to connect higher-level nodes to lower-level nodes. For example, connect a role to a task. The opposite is permitted, so we can connect a task to a role.

When checking access, we typically pass the name of an operation and, optionally, some parameters. Internally, Yii tries to find a way from an operation specified to the current user's role using reversed breadth-first search (`http://en.wikipedia.org/wiki/Breadth-first_search`). Therefore, when we want to find out if a user with Role has an access to perform Operation 4, Yii will go the following way:

Operation4 – Task3 – Task1 – Role

Each node can contain a business rule or `bizRule`. This business rule is a string containing some PHP code that returns either true or false. The returned value determines if we can go through the node or not.

In the end, we have either reached a role that means access is granted, or tried every possible path and failed which means access is denied.

There are two ways we can check if user can perform an operation specified:

1. Using controller's `accessRules` specifying an operation, a task, or a role in the `roles` parameter of an access rule.

2. Using `Yii::app()->user->checkAccess()`.

By using the second way, we can pass some data which makes its way through the authorization hierarchy and passes to every `bizRule` encountered.

Now, we will get back to our example. The code of the `init` action uses the `authManager` component to create the following hierarchy:

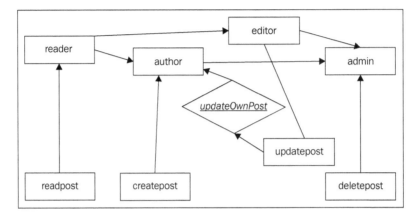

For testing permissions, we have created two actions: `test` which lists CRUD permissions and `deletePost` which is limited through the access filter. The rule for the access filter contains the following code:

```
array(
  'allow',
  'actions' => array('deletePost'),
  'roles' => array('deletePost'),
),
```

This means that we are allowing all users who have the `deletePost` permission to run the `deletePost` action. Yii starts checking with the `deletePost` operation and the only way it can go is `admin`. This means only users with the `admin` role will be able to delete a post.

 Besides the fact the access rule element is named `roles`, you can specify an RBAC hierarchy node, be it a role, task, or an operation.

When we check for the `readPost` permission for a user logged in as `authorB`, Yii checks `readPost`, `reader`, and then `editor`. Checking for `updatePost` is complex:

```
Yii::app()->user->checkAccess('updatePost', array('post' => $post))
```

We use a second parameter to pass a post (in our case, we have simulated it with `stdClass`). If a user is logged in as `authorB`, then to get access we need to go from `updatePost` to `author`. In the lucky case, we have to go through only `updatePost`, `updateOwnPost`, and `author`. As `updateOwnPost` has a `bizRule` defined, it will be run with a parameter passed to `checkAccess`. If the result is true, then access will be granted. As Yii does not know what the shortest way is, it tries to check all possibilities until either there is success or no possible ways left.

There's more...

There are some useful tricks that will help you to use RBAC efficiently, which are discussed in the following subsections:

Naming RBAC nodes

A complex hierarchy becomes difficult to understand without using some kind of a naming convention. One possible convention that helps not to get us confused is as follows:

```
[group_][own_]entity_action
```

Where `own` is used when the rule determines an ability to modify an element only if the current user is the owner of the element and `group` is just a namespace. Entity is a name of the entity we are working with and action is the action that we are performing.

For example, if we need to create a rule that determines if the user can delete a blog post, we will name it as `blog_post_delete`. If the rule determines if a user can edit the `own` blog comment, the name will be `blog_own_comment_edit`.

A way to keep the hierarchy simple and efficient

Follow these recommendations when possible to maximize the performance and reduce hierarchy complexity:

- ▶ Avoid attaching multiple roles to a single user.
- ▶ Don't connect nodes of the same type. So, for example, avoid connecting one task to another one.

Avoiding RBAC

In order to keep the hierarchy even simpler, we can avoid creating and using additional nodes in some cases by replacing them with additional conditions. A good example is the editing of Post. We can create a `blog_own_post_edit` node with `bizRule` as follows:

```
return Yii::app()->user->id==$params["post"]->author_id;
```

Alternatively, we can add the same logic to the post selection routine as follows:

```
$post = Post::model()->findByAttributes(array(
  'id' => $id,
  'author_id' => Yii::app()->user->id,
));
If(!$post)
  throw new CHttpException(404);
```

By using the second way, we will avoid getting an RBAC hierarchy node from storage and traversing it.

Further reading

In order to learn more about role-based access control, refer to the following resources:

- ▶ http://www.yiiframework.com/doc/guide/en/topics.auth#role-based-access-control
- ▶ http://en.wikipedia.org/wiki/Role-based_access_control
- ▶ http://en.wikipedia.org/wiki/Directed_acyclic_graph

See also

- ▶ The recipe named *Using controller filters* in this chapter

11
Performance Tuning

In this chapter, we will cover:

- ▶ Following best practices
- ▶ Speeding up sessions handling
- ▶ Using cache dependencies and chains
- ▶ Profiling an application with Yii

Introduction

Yii is one of the fastest frameworks out there. Still, when developing and deploying an application, it is good to have some extra performance for free, as well as following best practices for the application itself. In this chapter, we will see how to configure Yii to gain extra performance. In addition, we will learn some best practices of developing an application that will run smoothly until we have very high loads.

Following best practices

In this recipe, we will see how to configure Yii for best performances and will see some additional principles of building responsive applications. These principles are both general and Yii-related. Therefore, we will be able to apply some of these even without using Yii.

Getting ready

- ▶ Install APC (`http://www.php.net/manual/en/apc.installation.php`)
- ▶ Generate a fresh Yii application using `yiic webapp`

How to do it...

Carry out the following steps:

1. First, we need to turn off the debug mode. This can be done by editing `index.php` as follows:

    ```
    defined('YII_DEBUG') or define('YII_DEBUG',false);
    ```

2. The next step is to use `yiilite.php`. Again, we need to edit `index.php` and change

    ```
    $yii=dirname(__FILE__).'/../framework/yii.php';
    ```

    to the following:

    ```
    $yii=dirname(__FILE__).'/../framework/yiilite.php';
    ```

3. Now we will move on to `protected/config/main.php` and replace it with the following:

    ```php
    <?php

    // uncomment the following to define a path alias
    // Yii::setPathOfAlias('local','path/to/local-folder');

    // This is the main Web application configuration. Any writable
    // CWebApplication properties can be configured here.
    return array(
      'basePath'=>dirname(__FILE__).DIRECTORY_SEPARATOR.'..',
      'name'=>'My Web Application',

      // preloading 'log' component
      'preload'=>array('log'),

      // autoloading model and component classes
      'import'=>array(
        'application.models.*',
        'application.components.*',
      ),

      'modules'=>array(
        // uncomment the following to enable the Gii tool
        /*
        'gii'=>array(
          'class'=>'system.gii.GiiModule',
          'password'=>'Enter Your Password Here',
    ```

```
      // If removed, Gii defaults to localhost only.
        Edit carefully to taste.
      'ipFilters'=>array('127.0.0.1','::1'),
    ),
  */
),

// application components
'components'=>array(
  'user'=>array(
    // enable cookie-based authentication
    'allowAutoLogin'=>true,
  ),
  'urlManager'=>array(
    'urlFormat'=>'path',
    'rules'=>array(
      '<controller:\w+>/<id:\d+>'=>'<controller>/view',
      '<controller:\w+>/<action:\w+>/<id:\d+>'=>
        '<controller>/<action>',
      '<controller:\w+>/<action:\w+>'=>'<controller>/<action>',
    ),
  ),
  'db'=>array(
    'connectionString' => 'mysql:host=localhost;dbname=test',
    'username' => 'root',
    'password' => '',
    'charset' => 'utf8',

    'schemaCachingDuration' => 180,
  ),
  'errorHandler'=>array(
    // use 'site/error' action to display errors
        'errorAction'=>'site/error',
      ),
  'log'=>array(
    'class'=>'CLogRouter',
    'routes'=>array(
      array(
        'class'=>'CFileLogRoute',
        'levels'=>'error, warning',
      ),
      // uncomment the following to show log messages on
       web pages
      /*
```

```
            array(
              'class'=>'CWebLogRoute',
            ),
            */
          ),
        ),
        'session' => array(
          'class' => 'CCacheHttpSession',
        ),
        'cache' => array(
          'class' => 'CApcCache',
        ),
      ),

      // application-level parameters that can be accessed
      // using Yii::app()->params['paramName']
      'params'=>array(
        // this is used in contact page
        'adminEmail'=>'webmaster@example.com',
      ),
    );
```

4. That is it. Now we don't have to worry about the overhead of Yii itself and can focus on our application.

How it works...

When YII_DEBUG is set to false, Yii turns off all the trace level logging, uses less error handling code, stops checking the code (for example, Yii checks for invalid regular expressions in router rules), and uses minified JavaScript libraries.

yiilite.php contains the most commonly executed Yii parts. By using it, we can avoid including the extra script and use less memory for APC cache.

> Note that the benefit of using yiilite.php varies according to the server setup and sometimes, it is slower when using it. It is a good idea to measure the performance and choose what works faster for you.

Now we will review the additional component configuration which we performed:

```
'db'=>array(
  'connectionString' => 'mysql:host=localhost;dbname=test',
  'username' => 'root',
```

```
    'password' => '',
    'charset' => 'utf8',

    'schemaCachingDuration' => 180,
),
```

Setting `schemaCachingDuration` to a number of seconds allows caching the database schema used by Yii's Active Record. This is highly recommended for production servers and it significantly improves the Active Record performance. In order for it to work, you need to properly configure the cache component as follows:

```
'cache' => array(
  'class' => 'CApcCache',
),
```

The APC cache is one of the fastest cache solutions if you are using a single server. Enabling cache also has a positive effect on other Yii components. For example, Yii router or `urlManager` starts to cache routes in this case.

Finally, we configure the `session` component as follows:

```
'session' => array(
  'class' => 'CCacheHttpSession',
),
```

The preceding code enables storing sessions in APC which is significantly faster than the default file-based session handling.

There's more...

Of course, you can get into a situation where the preceding settings will not help to achieve sufficient performance level. In most cases, it means either that the application itself is a bottleneck or you need more hardware.

Server-side performance is just a part of the big picture

Server-side performance is only one of the things that affect the overall performance. By optimizing the client side such as serving CSS, images, and JavaScript files proper caching and minimizing the amount of HTTP-requests can give a good visual performance gain even without optimizing the PHP code.

Things to be done without using Yii

Some things are better to be done without Yii. For example, image resizing on the fly is better to be done in a separate PHP script in order to avoid the extra overhead.

Active record versus query builder and SQL

Use query builder or SQL in performance critical application parts. Generally, AR is most useful when adding and editing records, as it adds a convenient validation layer and is less useful when selecting records.

Always check for slow queries first

Database can become a bottleneck in a second if a developer accidentally forgets to add an index to a table that is being read often or vice versa, or adds too many indexes to a table we are writing to very often. The same goes for selecting unnecessary data and unneeded JOINs.

Cache or save results of "heavy" processes

If you can avoid running a "heavy" process in every page load, it is better to do so. For example, it is good practice to save or cache results of parsing the markdown text, purifying it (this is a very resource intensive process) once, and then using the ready to display HTML.

Handling too much processing

Sometimes there is too much processing to handle it immediately. It can be building of complex reports or just simple sending e-mails (if your project is heavily loaded). In this case, it is better to put it into a queue and process later by using cron or other specialized tools.

Further reading

For further information, refer to the following URL:

`http://www.yiiframework.com/doc/guide/en/topics.performance`

See also

- ▶ The recipe named *Speeding up sessions handling* in this chapter
- ▶ The recipe named *Using cache dependencies and chains* in this chapter
- ▶ The recipe named *Profiling an application with* Yii in this chapter

Speeding up sessions handling

Native session handling in PHP is fine in most cases. There are at least two possible reasons why you will want to change the way sessions are handled:

- ▶ When using multiple servers, you need to have a common session storage for both servers
- ▶ Default PHP sessions use files, so the maximum performance possible is limited by disk I/O

In this recipe, we will see how to use an efficient storage for Yii sessions.

Getting ready

▶ Generate a fresh Yii application using `yiic webapp`
▶ You should have `php_apc` and `php_memcache` extensions installed, as well as `memcached` itself to follow this recipe

How to do it...

We will stress test the website by using the Apache **ab** tool. It is being distributed with Apache binaries, so if you are using Apache, you will find it inside the `bin` directory. Run the following command replacing `your.website` with the actual hostname you are using:

`ab -n 1000 -c 5 http://your.website/index.php?r=site/contact`

This will send 1,000 requests, five at a time, and will output stats as follows:

```
Z:\web\usr\local\apache\bin>ab -n 1000 -c 5 http://perf/index.php?r=site/
contact
This is ApacheBench, Version 2.0.40-dev <$Revision: 1.146 $> apache-2.0
Copyright 1996 Adam Twiss, Zeus Technology Ltd, http://www.zeustech.net/
Copyright 2006 The Apache Software Foundation, http://www.apache.org/


Benchmarking perf (be patient)



Server Software:        Apache/2.2.4
Server Hostname:        perf
Server Port:            80

Document Path:          /index.php?r=site/contact
Document Length:        6671 bytes

Concurrency Level:      5
Time taken for tests:   11.889185 seconds
Complete requests:      1000
Failed requests:        0
Write errors:           0
Total transferred:      7103000 bytes
HTML transferred:       6671000 bytes
```

```
Requests per second:      84.11 [#/sec] (mean)
Time per request:         59.446 [ms] (mean)
Time per request:         11.889 [ms] (mean, across all concurrent
requests)
Transfer rate:            583.39 [Kbytes/sec] received


Connection Times (ms)
              min   mean[+/-sd] median    max
Connect:       0     0    1.5       0       15
Processing:   28    58   58.6      47      830
Waiting:      27    57   58.5      47      827
Total:        30    58   58.7      47      830


Percentage of the requests served within a certain time (ms)
   50%      47
   66%      52
   75%      57
   80%      60
   90%      70
   95%     100
   98%     205
   99%     457
  100%     830 (longest request)
```

We are interested in requests per second metric. The number means that the website can process 84.11 requests per second if there are five requests at a time.

 Note that the debug is not turned off since we are interested in changes to session handling speed.

Now add the following to the `protected/config/main.php`, `components` section:

```
'session' => array(
                'class' =>
'CCacheHttpSession',
                'cacheID' =>
'sessionCache',
),
'sessionCache' => array(
                'class' => 'CApcCache',
),
```

Run ab again with the same settings. This time, you should get better results. In my case, it was 131.33 requests per second. This means APC, as a session handler, performed 56% better than the default file-based session handler.

Now let's try another cache backend—memcached. Change `CApcCache` in config to `CMemCache` and make sure that `memcached` is started. Then, run ab again. In my case, `memcached` performed a bit better than the file cache serving 92.04 requests per second.

 Don't rely on exact results provided here. It all depends on software versions, settings, and hardware used. Always try to run all tests yourself in an environment where you are going to deploy your application.

You can get a significant performance gain by choosing a right session handling backend. Yii supports more caching backends out of the box, including eAccelerator, WinCache, XCache, and Zend data cache that comes with the Zend Server. Moreover, you can implement your own cache backend to use fast noSQL storages, such as Redis.

How it works...

By default, Yii uses native PHP sessions. This means, in most cases, that the filesystem is used. A filesystem cannot deal with high concurrency efficiently. For example, when changing the concurrency setting for the ab test to 10—while using the default session settings—ab is unable to finish tests with only 326 requests of 1,000 succeeded. Both APC and memcached perform fine in this situation:

```
'session' => array(
                'class' =>
'CCacheHttpSession',
                'cacheID' =>
'sessionCache',
),
'sessionCache' => array(
                'class' => 'CApcCache',
),
```

In the preceding config section, we instruct Yii to use `CCacheHttpSession` as a session handler. With this component, we can delegate session handling to the cache component specified in `cacheID`. This time we are using `CApcCache`.

 When using APC or memcached backend, you should take into account the fact that when using these solutions, the application user can possibly lose session if the maximum cache capacity is reached.

Note that when using a cache backend for a session, you cannot rely on a session as temporary data storage, since then there will be no memory to store more data in either APC or memcached. In such a case, these will just purge all data or delete some of it.

In the preceding tests, APC was the fastest backend but if you are using multiple servers, you cannot use it as there will be no way to share the session data between servers. In case of memcached, it is easy because it can be easily accessed from as many servers as you want.

 Various cache backends provide different levels of stability. For example, it is a known fact that APC becomes unstable when it is filled up or when you try writing to a single key from multiple processes.

There's more...

In order to learn more about caching and sessions, refer to the following resources:

- `http://www.yiiframework.com/doc/api/CCache`
- `http://www.yiiframework.com/doc/api/CHttpSession/`
- `http://php.net/manual/en/book.apc.php`
- `http://memcached.org/`
- `http://stackoverflow.com/questions/930877/apc-vs-eaccelerator-vs-xcache`

See also

- The recipe named *Following best practices* in this chapter

Using cache dependencies and chains

Yii supports many cache backends, but what really makes Yii cache flexible is the dependency and dependency chaining support. There are situations when you cannot just simply cache data for an hour because the information cached can be changed at any time.

In this recipe, we will see how to cache a whole page and still always get fresh data when it is updated. The page will be dashboard-type and will show five latest articles added and a total calculated for an account. Note that an operation cannot be edited as it was added, but an article can.

Getting ready

- ▶ Install APC (http://www.php.net/manual/en/apc.installation.php)
- ▶ Generate a fresh Yii application by using `yiic webapp`
- ▶ Set up a cache in the `components` section of `protected/config/main.php` as follows:

```
'cache' => array(
  'class' => 'CApcCache',
),
```

- ▶ Set up and configure a fresh database
- ▶ Execute the following SQL:

```
CREATE TABLE `account` (
  `id` int(11) unsigned NOT NULL AUTO_INCREMENT,
  `amount` decimal(10,2) NOT NULL,
  PRIMARY KEY (`id`)
);
CREATE TABLE `article` (
  `id` int(11) unsigned NOT NULL AUTO_INCREMENT,
  `title` varchar(255) NOT NULL,
  `text` text NOT NULL,
  PRIMARY KEY (`id`)
);
```

- ▶ Generate models for the `account` and `article` tables using Gii
- ▶ Configure the `db` and `log` application components through `protected/config/main.php`, so we can see actual DB queries. In the end, the config for these components should look like the following:

```
'db'=>array(
  'connectionString' => 'mysql:host=localhost;dbname=test',
  'username' => 'root',
  'password' => '',
  'charset' => 'utf8',

  'schemaCachingDuration' => 180,

  'enableProfiling'=>true,
  'enableParamLogging' => true,
),
'log'=>array(
  'class'=>'CLogRouter',
  'routes'=>array(
```

```
        array(
          'class'=>'CProfileLogRoute',
        ),
      ),
    ),
```

▶ Create `protected/controllers/DashboardController.php` as follows:

```php
<?php
class DashboardController extends CController
{
  public function actionIndex()
  {
    $db = Account::model()->getDbConnection();
    $total = $db->createCommand("SELECT SUM(amount)
      FROM account")->queryScalar();

    $criteria = new CDbCriteria();
    $criteria->order = "id DESC";
    $criteria->limit = 5;
    $articles = Article::model()->findAll($criteria);

    $this->render('index', array(
      'total' => $total,
      'articles' => $articles,
    ));
  }

  public function actionRandomOperation()
  {
    $rec = new Account();
    $rec->amount = rand(-1000, 1000);
    $rec->save();

    echo "OK";
  }

  public function actionRandomArticle()
  {
    $n = rand(0, 1000);

    $article = new Article();
    $article->title = "Title #".$n;
    $article->text = "Text #".$n;
    $article->save();

    echo "OK";
  }
}
```

► Create `protected/views/dashboard/index.php` as follows:

```
<h2>Total: <?php echo $total?></h2>
<h2>5 latest articles:</h2>
<?php foreach($articles as $article):?>
  <h3><?php echo $article->title?></h3>
  <div><?php echo $article->text?></div>
<?php endforeach ?>
```

► Run `dashboard/randomOperation` and `dashboard/randomArticle` several times. Then, run `dashboard/index` and you should see a screen similar to the one shown in the following screenshot:

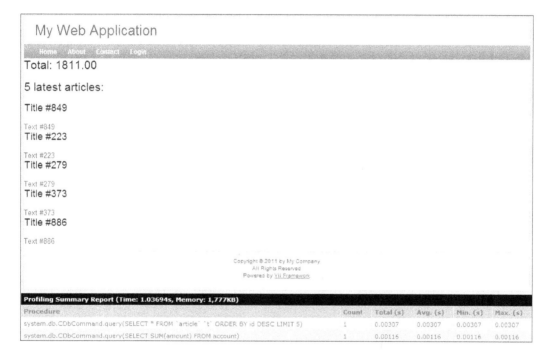

How to do it...

Carry out the following steps:

1. We need to modify the controller code as follows:

```
class DashboardController extends CController
{
  public function filters()
  {
    return array(
      array(
```

```
          'COutputCache +index',
          // will expire in a year
          'duration'=>24*3600*365,
          'dependency'=>array(
            'class'=>'CChainedCacheDependency',
            'dependencies'=>array(
              new CGlobalStateCacheDependency('article'),
              new CDbCacheDependency('SELECT id FROM account
                ORDER BY id DESC LIMIT 1'),
            ),
          ),
        ),
      );
  }

  public function actionIndex()
  {
    $db = Account::model()->getDbConnection();
    $total = $db->createCommand("SELECT SUM(amount) FROM
      account")->queryScalar();

    $criteria = new CDbCriteria();
    $criteria->order = "id DESC";
    $criteria->limit = 5;
    $articles = Article::model()->findAll($criteria);

    $this->render('index', array(
      'total' => $total,
      'articles' => $articles,
    ));
  }

  public function actionRandomOperation()
  {
    $rec = new Account();
    $rec->amount = rand(-1000, 1000);
    $rec->save();

    echo "OK";
  }

  public function actionRandomArticle()
  {
    $n = rand(0, 1000);

    $article = new Article();
    $article->title = "Title #".$n;
```

```
        $article->text = "Text #".$n;
        $article->save();

        Yii::app()->setGlobalState('article', $article->id);

        echo "OK";
    }
}
```

2. That is it. Now, after loading `dashboard/index` several times, you will get only one simple query, as shown in the following screenshot:

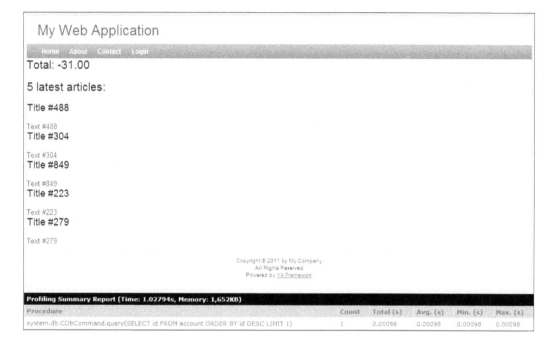

Also, try to run either `dashboard/randomOperation` or `dashboard/randomArticle` and refresh `dashboard/index` after that. The data should change.

How it works...

In order to achieve maximum performance while doing minimal code modification, we use a full-page cache by using a filter as follows:

```
public function filters()
{
    return array(
        array(
            'COutputCache +index',
```

```
      // will expire in a year
      'duration'=>24*3600*365,
      'dependency'=>array(
        'class'=>'CChainedCacheDependency',
        'dependencies'=>array(
          new CGlobalStateCacheDependency('article'),
          new CDbCacheDependency('SELECT id FROM account ORDER
            BY id DESC LIMIT 1'),
        ),
      ),
    ),
  );
}
```

The preceding code means that we apply full-page cache to the `index` action. Page will be cached for a year and the cache will refresh if one of the dependency data changes. Therefore, in general, the dependency works as follows:

▶ First run: Gets the fresh data as described in the dependency, saves for future reference, and updates cache.

▶ Gets the fresh data as described in dependency, gets the saved data, and then compares the two.

▶ If they are equal, uses the cached data.

▶ If not, updates cache, uses the fresh data, and saves the fresh dependency data for future reference.

In our case, two dependency types are used: global state and DB. Global state dependency uses data from `Yii::app()->getGlobalState()` to decide if we need to invalidate cache while DB dependency uses the SQL query result for the same purpose.

The question that you have now is probably, "why have we used DB for one case and global state for another?" That is a good question!

The goal of using the DB dependency is to replace heavy calculations and select the light query that gets as little data as possible. The best thing about this type of dependency is that we don't need to embed any additional logic in the existing code. In our case, we can use this type of dependency for account operations, but cannot use it for articles as the article content can be changed. Therefore, for articles, we set a global state named `article` to the added article's ID which basically means that we are scheduling cache invalidation:

```
Yii::app()->setGlobalState('article', $article->id);
```

Note that if we edit the article 100 times in a row and view it only after that, the cache will be invalidated and updated only once.

There's more...

In order to learn more about caching and using cache dependencies, refer to the following URLs:

- `http://www.yiiframework.com/doc/guide/en/caching.data#cache-dependency`
- `http://www.yiiframework.com/doc/guide/en/caching.page`

See also

- The recipe named *Creating filters* in *Chapter 8, Extending Yii*
- The recipe named *Using controller filters* in *Chapter 10, Security*

Profiling an application with Yii

If all of the best practices for deploying a Yii application are applied and you still do not have the performance you want, then most probably, there are some bottlenecks with the application itself. The main principle while dealing with these bottlenecks is that you should never assume anything and always test and profile the code before trying to optimize it.

In this recipe, we will try to find bottlenecks in the Yii blog demo application.

Getting ready

- Download the latest Yii 1.1.x version from the following URL:

  `http://www.yiiframework.com/download/`

- Unpack `demos/blog` in your webroot and `framework`, one level above it:

  ```
  framework
  www
      ...
      index.php
      ...
  ```

- In `index.php`, correct the path to `yii.php`. It should be as follows:

  `$yii=dirname(__FILE__).'/../framework/yii.php';`

- In `protected/yiic.php`, correct the path to `yiic.php`. It should be:

  `$yiic=dirname(__FILE__).'/../../framework/yiic.php';`

▶ Change `protected/config/console.php` with the following:

```
return array(
    'basePath'=>dirname(__FILE__).DIRECTORY_SEPARATOR.'..',
    'name'=>'My Console Application',

    'import'=>array(
        'application.models.*',
        'application.components.*',
    ),

    'components'=>array(
        'db'=>array(
            'connectionString' => 'mysql:host=localhost;dbname=blog',
            'emulatePrepare' => true,
            'username' => 'root',
            'password' => '',
            'charset' => 'utf8',
            'tablePrefix' => 'tbl_',
        ),
    ),
);
```

▶ In `protected/config/main.php`, comment the SQLite db settings and use MySQL:

```
/*'db'=>array(
    'connectionString' => 'sqlite:protected/data/blog.db',
    'tablePrefix' => 'tbl_',
),*/
// uncomment the following to use a MySQL database
'db'=>array(
    'connectionString' => 'mysql:host=localhost;dbname=blog',
    'emulatePrepare' => true,
    'username' => 'root',
    'password' => '',
    'charset' => 'utf8',
    'tablePrefix' => 'tbl_',
),
```

▶ Create a new database in MySQL and import `protected/data/schema.mysql.sql`.

▶ As there is not that much data, we need to generate more. Create `protected/commands/DataCommand.php` as follows:

```
<?php
class DataCommand extends CConsoleCommand
```

```
{
  public function actionIndex()
  {
    $db = Yii::app()->db;

    echo "Creating tags.\n";
    for($t=1; $t<=50; $t++)
    {
      $db->createCommand()->insert('tbl_tag', array(
        'name' => "tag $t",
        'frequency' => rand(1, 20),
      ));
    }
    echo "Done.\n";

    for($i=1; $i<=1000; $i++)
    {
      $tags = array();
      for($rt=1; $rt<=10; $rt++)
      {
        $tags[] = "tag ".rand(1, 100);
      }

      $db->createCommand()->insert('tbl_post', array(
        'title' => "Post #$i",
        'content' => "<strong>Hello!</strong> This is
          the content #$i",
        'tags' => implode(", ", $tags),
        'status' => Post::STATUS_PUBLISHED,
        'create_time' => time(),
        'update_time' => time(),
        'author_id' => 1,
      ));

      $postId = $db->getLastInsertID();

      for($j=1; $j<=10; $j++)
      {
        $db->createCommand()->insert('tbl_comment', array(
          'content' => "Comment text $j.",
          'status' => Comment::STATUS_APPROVED,
          'create_time' => time(),
          'author' => "Commenter $j",
          'email' => "commenter$j@example.com",
```

```
            'url' => "http://example.com/",
            'post_id' => $postId,
          ));
        }

      if($i%50==0)
        echo "\nAdded $i posts.\n";
    }

    echo "All done.\n";
  }
}
```

▶ Run it by entering `yiic data` in console and have a cup of coffee.

How to do it...

We have a blog with lots of posts and comments and it works somehow but not fast enough. We want to check it page-by-page and get the bottlenecks for each one.

1. We will start with using proper configuration for caching and turn on the SQL profiler. Your `protected/config/main.php` should look like the following:

```
...
return array(
...
  'components'=>array(
    ...
    'db'=>array(
      'connectionString' => 'mysql:host=localhost;dbname=blog',
      'username' => 'root',
      'password' => '',
      'charset' => 'utf8',
      'tablePrefix' => 'tbl_',

      'schemaCachingDuration' => 180,

      'enableProfiling'=>true,
      'enableParamLogging' => true,
    ),
    ...
    'log'=>array(
      'class'=>'CLogRouter',
      'routes'=>array(
        array(
          'class' => 'CProfileLogRoute',
```

```
        ),
      ),
    ),

    'session' => array(
      'class' => 'CCacheHttpSession',
    ),
    'cache' => array(
      'class' => 'CApcCache',
    ),
  ),
  …
);
```

2. Now run the front page of the blog several times and check what the profiler screen shows us:

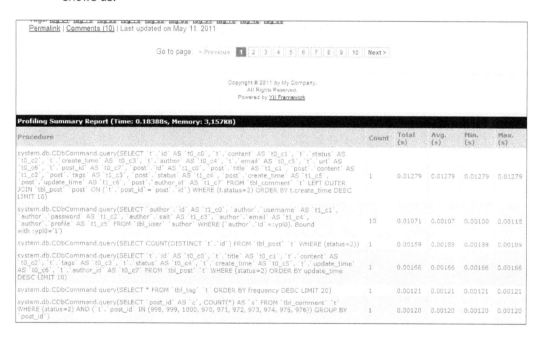

3. The slowest query is the following:

```
SELECT `t`.`id` AS `t0_c0`, `t`.`content` AS `t0_c1`, `t`.`status`
AS `t0_c2`, `t`.`create_time` AS `t0_c3`, `t`.`author` AS `t0_
c4`, `t`.`email` AS `t0_c5`, `t`.`url` AS `t0_c6`, `t`.`post_
id` AS `t0_c7`, `post`.`id` AS `t1_c0`, `post`.`title` AS `t1_
c1`, `post`.`content` AS `t1_c2`, `post`.`tags` AS `t1_c3`,
`post`.`status` AS `t1_c4`, `post`.`create_time` AS `t1_c5`,
`post`.`update_time` AS `t1_c6`, `post`.`author_id` AS `t1_c7`
FROM `tbl_comment` `t`
```

```
LEFT OUTER JOIN `tbl_post` `post` ON (`t`.`post_id`=`post`.`id`)
WHERE (t.status=2)
ORDER BY t.create_time DESC
LIMIT 10
```

4. Now we can add `EXPLAIN` in front of it and run it through the SQL console or any other SQL management tool. It will show us that there are no indexes used when filtering and sorting records. Therefore, if we add indexes for `tbl_post.status` and `tbl_post.create_time`, it will improve `SELECT` performance, as shown in the following screenshot:

Procedure	Count	Total (s)	Avg. (s)	Min. (s)	Max. (s)
Profiling Summary Report (Time: 0.16588s, Memory: 3,157KB)					
system.db.CDbCommand.query(SELECT `author`.`id` AS `t1_c0`, `author`.`username` AS `t1_c1`, `author`.`password` AS `t1_c2`, `author`.`salt` AS `t1_c3`, `author`.`email` AS `t1_c4`, `author`.`profile` AS `t1_c5` FROM `tbl_user` `author` WHERE (`author`.`id`=:ypl0). Bound with :ypl0='1')	10	0.01077	0.00108	0.00098	0.00119
system.db.CDbCommand.query(SELECT COUNT(DISTINCT `t`.`id`) FROM `tbl_post` `t` WHERE (status=2))	1	0.00206	0.00206	0.00206	0.00206
system.db.CDbCommand.query(SELECT `t`.`id` AS `t0_c0`, `t`.`title` AS `t0_c1`, `t`.`content` AS `t0_c2`, `t`.`tags` AS `t0_c3`, `t`.`status` AS `t0_c4`, `t`.`create_time` AS `t0_c5`, `t`.`update_time` AS `t0_c6`, `t`.`author_id` AS `t0_c7` FROM `tbl_post` `t` WHERE (status=2) ORDER BY update_time DESC LIMIT 10)	1	0.00153	0.00153	0.00153	0.00153
system.db.CDbCommand.query(SELECT `t`.`id` AS `t0_c0`, `t`.`content` AS `t0_c1`, `t`.`status` AS `t0_c2`, `t`.`create_time` AS `t0_c3`, `t`.`author` AS `t0_c4`, `t`.`email` AS `t0_c5`, `t`.`url` AS `t0_c6`, `t`.`post_id` AS `t1_c0`, `post`.`title` AS `t1_c1`, `post`.`content` AS `t1_c2`, `post`.`tags` AS `t1_c3`, `post`.`status` AS `t1_c4`, `post`.`create_time` AS `t1_c5`, `post`.`update_time` AS `t1_c6`, `post`.`author_id` AS `t1_c7` FROM `tbl_comment` `t` LEFT OUTER JOIN `tbl_post` `post` ON (`t`.`post_id` = `post`.`id`) WHERE (t.status=2) ORDER BY t.create_time DESC LIMIT 10)	1	0.00140	0.00140	0.00140	0.00140
system.db.CDbCommand.query(SELECT * FROM `tbl_tag` `t` ORDER BY frequency DESC LIMIT 20)	1	0.00119	0.00119	0.00119	0.00119
system.db.CDbCommand.query(SELECT `post_id` AS `c`, COUNT(*) AS `s` FROM `tbl_comment` `t` WHERE (status=2) AND (`t`.`post_id` IN (998, 999, 1000, 970, 971, 972, 973, 974, 975, 976)) GROUP BY `post_id`)	1	0.00115	0.00115	0.00115	0.00115

5. Next, we have 10 queries used to get the author of each post. Most probably, there is a way to combine these into a single one. As we are running `post/index`, we will check the `PostController`, `actionIndex` methods:

```
$criteria=new CDbCriteria(array(
    'condition'=>'status='.Post::STATUS_PUBLISHED,
    'order'=>'update_time DESC',
    'with'=>'commentCount',
));
if(isset($_GET['tag']))
    $criteria->addSearchCondition('tags',$_GET['tag']);

$dataProvider=new CActiveDataProvider('Post', array(
    'pagination'=>array(
        'pageSize'=>Yii::app()->params['postsPerPage'],
    ),
    'criteria'=>$criteria,
));

$this->render('index',array(
    'dataProvider'=>$dataProvider,
));
```

6. When the data provider is getting posts, it uses criteria defined earlier. As we can see, a criterion allows us to get the count of comments by using the most efficient query possible. `commentCount` is a relation defined in the `Post` model and if we check its `relations` method, we will find that there is an `author` relation as well. By changing the `with` part of the criterion to

```
'with'=> array('commentCount', 'author'),
```

we have got rid of 10 additional queries. Instead, we have a single query that is performing very well:

Profiling Summary Report (Time: 0.15162s, Memory: 3,173KB)

Procedure	Count	Total (s)	Avg. (s)	Min. (s)	Max. (s)
system.db.CDbCommand.query(SELECT COUNT(DISTINCT `t`.`id`) FROM `tbl_post` `t` LEFT OUTER JOIN `tbl_user` `author` ON (`t`.`author_id` = `author`.`id`) WHERE (status=2))	1	0.00262	0.00262	0.00262	0.00262
system.db.CDbCommand.query(SELECT `t`.`id` AS `t0_c0`, `t`.`title` AS `t0_c1`, `t`.`content` AS `t0_c2`, `t`.`tags` AS `t0_c3`, `t`.`status` AS `t0_c4`, `t`.`create_time` AS `t0_c5`, `t`.`update_time` AS `t0_c6`, `t`.`author_id` AS `t0_c7`, `author`.`id` AS `t1_c0`, `author`.`username` AS `t1_c1`, `author`.`password` AS `t1_c2`, `author`.`salt` AS `t1_c3`, `author`.`email` AS `t1_c4`, `author`.`profile` AS `t1_c5` FROM `tbl_post` `t` LEFT OUTER JOIN `tbl_user` `author` ON (`t`.`author_id` = `author`.`id`) WHERE (status=2) ORDER BY update_time DESC LIMIT 10)	1	0.00256	0.00256	0.00256	0.00256
system.db.CDbCommand.query(SELECT `t`.`id` AS `t0_c0`, `t`.`content` AS `t0_c1`, `t`.`status` AS `t0_c2`, `t`.`create_time` AS `t0_c3`, `t`.`author` AS `t0_c4`, `t`.`email` AS `t0_c5`, `t`.`url` AS `t0_c6`, `t`.`post_id` AS `t0_c7`, `post`.`id` AS `t1_c0`, `post`.`title` AS `t1_c1`, `post`.`content` AS `t1_c2`, `post`.`tags` AS `t1_c3`, `post`.`status` AS `t1_c4`, `post`.`create_time` AS `t1_c5`, `post`.`update_time` AS `t1_c6`, `post`.`author_id` AS `t1_c7` FROM `tbl_comment` `t` LEFT OUTER JOIN `tbl_post` `post` ON (`t`.`post_id` = `post`.`id`) WHERE (t.status=2) ORDER BY t.create_time DESC LIMIT 10)	1	0.00157	0.00157	0.00157	0.00157
system.db.CDbCommand.query(SELECT * FROM `tbl_tag` `t` ORDER BY frequency DESC LIMIT 20)	1	0.00134	0.00134	0.00134	0.00134
system.db.CDbCommand.query(SELECT `post_id` AS `c`, COUNT(*) AS `s` FROM `tbl_comment` `t` WHERE (status=2) AND (`t`.`post_id` IN (998, 999, 1000, 970, 971, 972, 973, 974, 975, 976)) GROUP BY `post_id`)	1	0.00115	0.00115	0.00115	0.00115

7. Now the SQL part works better. We can improve it further, but you have an idea and can do it as homework. Overall, it is still not perfect. We will add profiling markers to the controller code as follows:

```
Yii::beginProfile('preparing_data');
$criteria=new CDbCriteria(array(
    'condition'=>'status='.Post::STATUS_PUBLISHED,
    'order'=>'update_time DESC',
    'with'=> array('commentCount', 'author'),
));
if(isset($_GET['tag']))
    $criteria->addSearchCondition('tags',$_GET['tag']);

$dataProvider=new CActiveDataProvider('Post', array(
    'pagination'=>array(
        'pageSize'=>Yii::app()->params['postsPerPage'],
    ),
    'criteria'=>$criteria,
));
Yii::endProfile('preparing_data');
```

```
Yii::beginProfile('rendering_data');
$this->render('index',array(
  'dataProvider'=>$dataProvider,
));
Yii::endProfile('rendering_data');
```

8. Now run the front page again and check the profiler:

Profiling Summary Report (Time: 0.14753s, Memory: 3,142KB)

Procedure	Count	Total (s)	Avg. (s)	Min. (s)	Max. (s)
rendering_data	1	0.11444	0.11444	0.11444	0.11444
preparing_data	1	0.01111	0.01111	0.01111	0.01111
system.db.CDbCommand.query(SELECT COUNT(DISTINCT `t`.`id`) FROM `tbl_post` `t` LEFT OUTER JOIN `tbl_user` `author` ON (`t`.`author_id`=`author`.`id`) WHERE (status=2))	1	0.00278	0.00278	0.00278	0.00278
system.db.CDbCommand.query(SELECT `t`.`id` AS `t0_c0`, `t`.`title` AS `t0_c1`, `t`.`content` AS `t0_c2`, `t`.`tags` AS `t0_c3`, `t`.`status` AS `t0_c4`, `t`.`create_time` AS `t0_c5`, `t`.`update_time` AS `t0_c6`, `t`.`author_id` AS `t0_c7`, `author`.`id` AS `t1_c0`, `author`.`username` AS `t1_c1`, `author`.`password` AS `t1_c2`, `author`.`salt` AS `t1_c3`, `author`.`email` AS `t1_c4`, `author`.`profile` AS `t1_c5` FROM `tbl_post` `t` LEFT OUTER JOIN `tbl_user` `author` ON (`t`.`author_id`=`author`.`id`) WHERE (status=2) ORDER BY update_time DESC LIMIT 10)	1	0.00227	0.00227	0.00227	0.00227
system.db.CDbCommand.query(SELECT `t`.`id` AS `t0_c0`, `t`.`content` AS `t0_c1`, `t`.`status` AS `t0_c2`, `t`.`create_time` AS `t0_c3`, `t`.`author` AS `t0_c4`, `t`.`email` AS `t0_c5`, `t`.`url` AS `t0_c6`, `t`.`post_id` AS `t0_c7`, `post`.`id` AS `t1_c0`, `post`.`title` AS `t1_c1`, `post`.`content` AS `t1_c2`, `post`.`tags` AS `t1_c3`, `post`.`status` AS `t1_c4`, `post`.`create_time` AS `t1_c5`, `post`.`update_time` AS `t1_c6`, `post`.`author_id` AS `t1_c7` FROM `tbl_comment` `t` LEFT OUTER JOIN `tbl_post` `post` ON (`t`.`post_id`=`post`.`id`) WHERE (t.status=2) ORDER BY t.create_time DESC LIMIT 10)	1	0.00142	0.00142	0.00142	0.00142
system.db.CDbCommand.query(SELECT * FROM `tbl_tag` `t` ORDER BY frequency DESC LIMIT 20)	1	0.00122	0.00122	0.00122	0.00122
system.db.CDbCommand.query(SELECT `post_id` AS `c`, COUNT(*) AS `s` FROM `tbl_comment` `t` WHERE (status=2) AND (`t`.`post_id` IN (998, 999, 1000, 970, 971, 972, 973, 974, 975, 976)) GROUP BY `post_id`)	1	0.00118	0.00118	0.00118	0.00118

9. It looks like the `rendering data` part took most of the time. As rendering takes part in a view, let's check `protected/views/post/index.php`:

```php
<?php if(!empty($_GET['tag'])): ?>
<h1>Posts Tagged with <i><?php echo CHtml::encode($_GET['tag']); ?></i></h1>
<?php endif; ?>

<?php $this->widget('zii.widgets.CListView', array(
  'dataProvider'=>$dataProvider,
  'itemView'=>'_view',
  'template'=>"{items}\n{pager}",
)); ?>
```

10. `CListView` uses `_view` to render each record. Let's add two more profiling markers to it as follows:

```php
<?php Yii::beginProfile('_view')?>
<div class="post">
  ...
</div>
<?php Yii::endProfile('_view')?>
```

11. Now run the application again and check the profiler:

Profiling Summary Report (Time: 0.13788s, Memory: 3,156KB)

Procedure	Count	Total (s)	Avg. (s)	Min. (s)	Max. (s)
rendering_data	1	0.11014	0.11014	0.11014	0.11014
_view	10	0.07646	0.00765	0.00619	0.01765
preparing_data	1	0.01735	0.01735	0.01735	0.01735
system.db.CDbCommand.query(SELECT `t`.`id` AS `t0_c0`, `t`.`title` AS `t0_c1`, `t`.`content` AS `t0_c2`, `t`.`tags` AS `t0_c3`, `t`.`status` AS `t0_c4`, `t`.`create_time` AS `t0_c5`, `t`.`update_time` AS `t0_c6`, `t`.`author_id` AS `t0_c7`, `author`.`id` AS `t1_c0`, `author`.`username` AS `t1_c1`, `author`.`password` AS `t1_c2`, `author`.`salt` AS `t1_c3`, `author`.`email` AS `t1_c4`, `author`.`profile` AS `t1_c5` FROM `tbl_post` `t` LEFT OUTER JOIN `tbl_user` `author` ON	1	0.00240	0.00240	0.00240	0.00240

12. Something is obviously wrong with this view file. In order to determine what exactly, we are moving `<?php Yii::beginProfile('_view')?>` down while `<?php Yii::endProfile('_view')?>` goes up. Finally, we should stop around

```php
<?php
    $this->beginWidget('CMarkdown', array('purifyOutput'=>true));
    echo $data->content;
    $this->endWidget();
?>
```

If you are the only author of the blog and don't care about someone entering malicious code, then you can just leave `echo $data->content`.

 Other options will be caching the purified output or pre-processing it on saving a post.

13. Let's assume it is our case. Remove the widget code and run the profiler one more time:

Profiling Summary Report (Time: 0.07810s, Memory: 2,259KB)

Procedure	Count	Total (s)	Avg. (s)	Min. (s)	Max. (s)
rendering_data	1	0.04011	0.04011	0.04011	0.04011
preparing_data	1	0.01937	0.01937	0.01937	0.01937
system.db.CDbCommand.query(SELECT COUNT(DISTINCT `t`.`id`) FROM `tbl_post` `t` LEFT OUTER JOIN `tbl_user` `author` ON (`t`.`author_id` = `author`.`id`) WHERE (status=2))	1	0.00262	0.00262	0.00262	0.00262
system.db.CDbCommand.query(SELECT `t`.`id` AS `t0_c0`, `t`.`title` AS `t0_c1`, `t`.`content` AS `t0_c2`, `t`.`tags` AS `t0_c3`, `t`.`status` AS `t0_c4`, `t`.`create_time` AS `t0_c5`, `t`.`update_time` AS `t0_c6`, `t`.`author_id` AS `t0_c7`, `author`.`id` AS `t1_c0`, `author`.`username` AS `t1_c1`, `author`.`password` AS `t1_c2`, `author`.`salt` AS `t1_c3`, `author`.`email` AS `t1_c4`,	1	0.00198	0.00198	0.00198	0.00198

14. A lot better. Finally, we have gotten down from 0.184 second to 0.078 second. That is about 42% less than the initial processing time.

We can achieve more by performing more profiling and fixing. Probably, you will say these values were acceptable from the beginning. That is true, until you will get more readers and the server will not be able to generate pages for all these people in parallel. What this performance gain really means is that if you have, for example, 10,000 readers in the beginning and performance is starting to drop, after optimizing the code, you can handle an additional 4,200 readers without buying new hardware.

How it works...

First, we configured the application cache and cached the DB schema to exclude these possible bottlenecks from profiling results. In a production environment, these will be cached for sure. Then, we turn on the profiling DB queries and run the application multiple times; in the first run, Yii will cache the schema and routes, and the second run will be clean.

As the typical web application bottleneck is a database, we start to look at the SQL query anomalies—the most time-consuming queries and same type queries repeating multiple times.

Long running queries are typically a bad DB design (wrong index placement or no indexes, too much normalization, and so on). Therefore, we can feed a query to MySQL adding EXPLAIN in front of the query and it will give back a query profile that tells us what to do.

When a same type query is executed multiple times, most probably it is something we are getting for each entity we are displaying. In our case, it was the author for each blog post. In most cases, we can get these in a single query or even in the same query, which selects entities themselves.

As for the non-SQL part, we divided the controller 50/50, then took the slowest part, and divided it again. We repeated that until a bottleneck was identified. Of course, we used some assumptions to do less the routine job of adding profiler marks, but sometimes it is better not to assume anything since a bottleneck can be hidden in a very innocent looking code.

There's more...

In order to learn more about profiling, refer to the following resources:

- ▶ http://www.yiiframework.com/doc/guide/en/topics. logging#performance-profiling
- ▶ http://www.yiiframework.com/doc/guide/en/topics. logging#profiling-sql-executions
- ▶ http://www.xdebug.org/docs/profiler
- ▶ http://pecl.php.net/package/xhprof

See also

- ▶ The recipe named *Using different log routes* in *Chapter 9, Error Handling, Debugging, and Logging*
- ▶ The recipe named *Following best practices* in this chapter
- ▶ The recipe named *Speeding up sessions handling* in this chapter

12
Using External Code

In this chapter, we will cover:

- ▶ Using Zend Framework from Yii
- ▶ Customizing the Yii autoloader
- ▶ Using Kohana inside Yii
- ▶ Using PEAR inside Yii

Introduction

Typically, an application requires more than any framework can give. Sometimes, you need a full-featured library to send an e-mail and sometimes, it is just about implementation of the specific API. No framework can cover every possible task that a developer has. That is why Yii covers the most common ones and leaves the rest to the developer and external libraries.

In this chapter, we will try to use a non-Yii code with Yii, including Zend Framework, Kohana, and Pear.

Using Zend Framework from Yii

Yii provides many excellent solutions with which you can build an application. Still, you probably will need more. One of the best places to look at is Zend Framework classes. These are of high quality and solve many tasks, such as using Google APIs or working with e-mails.

In this recipe, we will see how to use the Zend_Mail package to send e-mails from Yii application. We will use both a simple approach of using the whole framework and will also implement a custom autoloader that will allow us to use only Zend_Mail and its dependencies.

- ▶ Create a fresh application by using `yiic webapp`
- ▶ Download the Zend Framework code from the following URL:

  `http://framework.zend.com/download/current/`

  In this recipe, we have used Version 1.11.6
- ▶ Extract `library/Zend` from the downloaded archive to `protected/vendors/Zend`

Carry out the following steps:

1. We will create a simple controller that will send an e-mail. Create `protected/controllers/MailtestController.php` as follows:

```php
<?php
class MailtestController extends CController
{
  public function actionIndex()
  {
    $mail = new Zend_Mail('utf-8');
    $mail->setHeaderEncoding(Zend_Mime::ENCODING_QUOTEDPRINTABLE);
    $mail->addTo("alexander@example.com", "Alexander Makarov");
    $mail->setFrom("robot@example.com", "Robot");
    $mail->setSubject("Test email");
    $mail->setBodyText("Hello, world!");
    $mail->setBodyHtml("Hello, <strong>world</strong>!");
    $mail->send();

    echo "OK";
  }
}
```

2. Now try to run `mailtest/index` and you will get the following result:

```
PHP Error

include(Zend_Mail.php): failed to open stream: No such file or directory

W:\home\ext\framework\YiiBase.php(398)

386        * @return boolean whether the class has been loaded successfully
387        */
388       public static function autoload($className)
389       {
390           // use include so that the error PHP file may appear
391           if(isset(self::$_coreClasses[$className]))
392               include(YII_PATH.self::$_coreClasses[$className]);
393           else if(isset(self::$classMap[$className]))
394               include(self::$classMap[$className]);
395           else
396           {
397               if(strpos($className,'\\')===false)
398                   include($className.'.php');
399               else  // class name with namespace in PHP 5.3
400               {
401                   $namespace=str_replace('\\','.',ltrim($className,'\\'));
402                   if(($path=self::getPathOfAlias($namespace))!==false)
403                       include($path.'.php');
404                   else
405                       return false;
406               }
407               return class_exists($className,false) || interface_exists($className,false);
408           }
409           return true;
410       }
```

Stack Trace

```
#0  ⊞ W:\home\ext\framework\YiiBase.php(398): YiiBase::autoload()

#1  unknown(0): YiiBase::autoload("Zend_Mail")

#2  ⊟ W:\home\ext\www\protected\controllers\MailtestController.php(8): spl_autoload_call("Zend_Mail")

     03 {
     04       public function actionIndex()
```

3. This means that the Yii autoloader failed to include the `Zend_Mail` class. This is expected because it knows nothing about the Zend Framework naming convention. So logically, we have the following two solutions to this:

  ❏ Include classes explicitly
  ❏ Create our own autoloader

4. We will now start with including classes. All Zend Framework classes do have `require_once` statements for all dependencies. These statements rely on adding an additional PHP include path and look like the following:

```
require_once 'Zend/Mail/Transport/Abstract.php';
```

5. When using `Yii::import` to import a directory, it works like adding a directory into the PHP include path, so we can solve our problem as follows:

```php
class MailtestController extends CController
{
  public function actionIndex()
  {
    Yii::import('application.vendors.*');
    require "Zend/Mail.php";

    $mail = new Zend_Mail('utf-8');
    $mail->setHeaderEncoding(Zend_Mime::ENCODING_QUOTEDPRINTABLE);
    $mail->addTo("alexander@example.com", "Alexander Makarov");
    $mail->setFrom("robot@example.com", "Robot");
    $mail->setSubject("Test email");
    $mail->setBodyText("Hello, world!");
    $mail->setBodyHtml("Hello, <strong>world</strong>!");
    $mail->send();

    echo "OK";
  }
}
```

6. Now it will send an e-mail properly without any error. This method will work if you don't have too many Zend Framework classes used. If you are using it heavily, then you will have to include a lot that will add unnecessary complexity. Now, let's use `Zend_Loader_Autoloader` to achieve this.

7. The best place to add another autoloader is in the `index.php` bootstrap. This way, you will be able to autoload classes during the whole execution flow:

```php
// change the following paths if necessary
$yii=dirname(__FILE__).'/../framework/yii.php';
$config=dirname(__FILE__).'/protected/config/main.php';

// remove the following lines when in production mode
defined('YII_DEBUG') or define('YII_DEBUG',true);
// specify how many levels of call stack should be shown
  in each log message
defined('YII_TRACE_LEVEL') or define('YII_TRACE_LEVEL',3);
```

```
require_once($yii);
$app = Yii::createWebApplication($config);

// adding Zend Framework autoloader
Yii::import('application.vendors.*');
require "Zend/Loader/Autoloader.php";
Yii::registerAutoloader(array('Zend_Loader_Autoloader',
  'autoload'), true);

$app->run();
```

8. Now we can remove

```
Yii::import('application.vendors.*');
require "Zend/Mail.php";
```

from `MailtestController` and it will still work fine without any errors meaning that Zend Framework autoloading now works.

How it works...

Let's review what is going on behind the scenes and how it works starting with the first way. We have used `Yii::import` that, when used like `Yii::import('path.alias.*')`, behaves like adding another PHP include path. As there was no autoloader in Zend Framework originally, it has all the necessary `require_once` calls. So, if you use a single component, such as `Zend_Mail`, you don't need more than one `require_once`.

The second method doesn't force you to use a single `require` statement. As Yii allows using multiple autoloaders and in latest versions, Zend Framework has its own autoloader, we can use it in our application. The best time to do this is right after the application bootstrap was loaded, but application was not run. To achieve this, we break `Yii::createWebApplication($config)->run()` into two separate statements in `index.php` and insert an autoloader initialization between these:

```
Yii::import('application.vendors.*');
require "Zend/Loader/Autoloader.php";
Yii::registerAutoloader(array('Zend_Loader_Autoloader',
  'autoload'), true);
```

We still need `Yii::import('application.vendors.*')` because Zend Framework classes will continue to use `require_once`. Then, we require an autoloader class and add it to the end of the PHP autoloading stack by using `Yii::registerAutoloader` with the second argument set to `true`.

In order to learn more about the Yii import, autoloading, and Zend Framework usage, refer to the following URLs:

- `http://www.yiiframework.com/doc/api/YiiBase/#import-detail`
- `http://www.yiiframework.com/doc/api/YiiBase/#registerAutoloader-detail`
- `http://framework.zend.com/`
- `http://www.yiiframework.com/doc/guide/en/extension.integration`
- `http://framework.zend.com/manual/en/zend.loader.autoloader.html`

See also

- The recipe named *Customizing the Yii* autoloader in this chapter

Customizing the Yii autoloader

Yii uses a naming convention and an autoloader to load only classes which are really needed and to avoid including files explicitly. As other frameworks and libraries could use a different naming convention, Yii provides an ability to customize rules of autoloading classes. In the *Using Zend Framework from Yii* recipe in this chapter, we used `Zend_Loader_Autoloader` to be able to use Zend Framework classes without including them explicitly. If we are using only Zend Framework core classes, then its complex autoloader is a bit too much. Moreover, there are still `require_once` calls in each Zend Framework class, so it still loads tons of unused files. In this recipe, we will create a very simple and fast autoloader that will allow us to do the same, but faster.

Getting ready

- Create a fresh application by using `yiic webapp`
- Download Zend Framework code from the following URL:

    `http://framework.zend.com/download/current/`

    In this recipe, we have used Version 1.11.6
- Extract `library/Zend` from the downloaded archive to `protected/vendors/Zend`

▶ Create `protected/controllers/MailtestController.php` as follows:

```php
<?php
class MailtestController extends CController
{
  public function actionIndex()
  {
    $mail = new Zend_Mail('utf-8');
    $mail->setHeaderEncoding(Zend_Mime::ENCODING_QUOTEDPRINTABLE);
    $mail->addTo("alexander@example.com", "Alexander Makarov");
    $mail->setFrom("robot@example.com", "Robot");
    $mail->setSubject("Test email");
    $mail->setBodyText("Hello, world!");
    $mail->setBodyHtml("Hello, <strong>world</strong>!");
    $mail->send();

    echo "OK";
  }
}
```

How to do it...

Carry out the following steps:

1. Create `protected/components/EZendAutoloader.php` as follows:

```php
<?php
class EZendAutoloader
{
  /**
   * @var array class prefixes.
   */
  static $prefixes = array(
    'Zend'
  );

  /**
   * @var string path to where Zend classes root is located
   */
  static $basePath = null;

  /**
   * Class autoload loader.
   *
   * @static
```

```
 * @param string $className
 * @return boolean
 */
static function loadClass($className)
{
  foreach(self::$prefixes as $prefix)
  {
    if(strpos($className, $prefix.'_')!==false)
    {
      if(!self::$basePath) self::$basePath =
        Yii::getPathOfAlias("application.vendors").'/';
      include self::$basePath.str_replace
        ('_','/',$className).'.php';
      return class_exists($className, false) ||
        interface_exists($className, false);
    }
  }
  return false;
}
```

Now modify `index.php`. Replace

```
Yii::createWebApplication($config)->run();
```
with

```
$app = Yii::createWebApplication($config);


// adding custom Zend Framework autoloader
Yii::import("application.vendors.*");
Yii::import("application.components.EZendAutoloader", true);
Yii::registerAutoloader(array('EZendAutoloader','loadClass'), true);


$app->run();
```

Try running `mailtest/index`. It should send an e-mail and output "OK" which means autoloading works correctly. Still, we are importing the `vendors` directory to satisfy Zend Framework `require_once` calls by loading all possible classes explicitly. The only way to fix it is to remove all occurrences of **require_once** from Zend Framework. If you're under Linux you can use:

```
% cd path/to/ZendFramework/library
% find . -name '*.php' -not -wholename '*/Loader/Autoloader.php' \
  -not -wholename '*/Application.php' -print0 | \
  xargs -0 sed --regexp-extended --in-place 's/(require_once)/\/\/ \1/g'
```

In addition, on MacOSX:

```
% cd path/to/ZendFramework/library
% find . -name '*.php' | grep -v './Loader/Autoloader.php' | \
xargs sed -E -i~ 's/(require_once)/\/\/ \1/g'
% find . -name '*.php~' | xargs rm -f
```

Or you can simply use IDE or other tools to replace require_once with //require_once.

After doing it you can remove Yii::import("application.vendors.*") from index.php and try loading mailtest/index again. It should send another e-mail and output "OK". That means Zend Framework classes are now working without require_once.

How it works...

Frameworks and libraries that use autoloading rely on PHP SPL autoload. It is triggered when you use a class that is not included yet and PHP is going to fail. Using spl_autoload_register, you can register multiple autoload callbacks. Therefore, if the first one fails, then another one will take initiative and will try to load a class. Yii is not an exception. By default, it uses its own autoloader implementation YiiBase::autoload. We have used Yii::registerAutoloader in index.php to add an additional autoloader. The method implementation is as follows:

```
public static function registerAutoloader($callback, $append=false)
{
  if($append)
  {
    self::$enableIncludePath=false;
    spl_autoload_register($callback);
  }
  else
  {
    spl_autoload_unregister(array('YiiBase','autoload'));
    spl_autoload_register($callback);
    spl_autoload_register(array('YiiBase','autoload'));
  }
}
```

So internally, this is the same SPL autoloader, and the registerAutoloader method just adds another callback and by default makes sure it is registered before Yii's own autoloader. If we pass true as the second parameter value then the custom autoloader is registered after the Yii internal one. It does not allow triggering of the custom autoloader for Yii classes.

Now, we will move on to our custom autoloader. All SPL autoload callbacks accept a single argument containing the name of the class that needs to be loaded. Given this name, it should try to include a file containing a class with the specified name. In order to get more flexibility, we defined the following two properties:

1. The `prefixes` property defines a list of prefixes a class should begin with to be autoloaded with our custom autoloader. By default, it is `Zend`.

2. The `basePath` defines a path to a directory where the `Zend` directory is. By default, it equals to `protected/vendors`.

For each prefix, we check if the class we are trying to load begins with it and if we need to use an autoloader. If it matches, then we replace "_" with "/" in the class name and use it as a complete path to the file we are including.

In the final step, we get rid of `require_once` that prevents us from loading only classes that are absolutely required.

There's more...

As the class loading happens all the time, we use an external library; it should perform as fast as it can. This means that autoloading method should be simple and efficient. Other things to note are as follows:

▶ `require_once` is slower than just `require`

▶ Using `file_exists` or `is_file` will slow down the loading

▶ You should use absolute paths instead of relative ones to ensure that APC performs efficiently when `apc.stat = 0` (it allows not to check if the file was changed and gain more performance on the production server)

Further reading

In order to learn more about Yii autoloading and APC, refer to the following URLs:

▶ http://www.yiiframework.com/doc/api/YiiBase/#import-detail

▶ http://www.yiiframework.com/doc/api/
YiiBase/#registerAutoloader-detail

▶ http://php.net/manual/en/function.spl-autoload.php

▶ http://www.php.net/manual/en/apc.configuration.php#ini.apc.stat

See also

▶ The recipe named *Using Zend Framework from Yii* in this chapter

Using Kohana inside Yii

Sometimes to write a custom autoloader, you need to dig into another framework source code. An example of it is the Kohana framework. In this recipe, we will handle the image resizing by using one of the Kohana classes.

Getting ready

- Create a fresh application using `yiic webapp`
- Download the Kohana framework archive from the following URL:

  `http://kohanaframework.org/download`

  In this recipe, we have used Version 3.1.

- Extract the `system` and `modules` directories to `protected/vendors/Kohana`.

How to do it...

Carry out the following steps:

1. First, we will need the actual code which performs the image resizing and displays an image. Create `protected/controllers/ImageController.php` as follows:

```php
<?php
class ImageController extends CController
{
  public function actionIndex()
  {
    $image = new Image_GD(Yii::getPathOfAlias
      ("system")."/yii-powered.png");
    $image->resize(80, 80);
    Yii::app()->request->sendFile("image.png", $image->render());
  }
}
```

2. Try to run `image/index` and you will get the following error:

```
PHP Error

include(Image_GD.php): failed to open stream: No such file or directory

W:\home\ext\framework\YiiBase.php(398)

386        * @return boolean whether the class has been loaded successfully
387        */
388      public static function autoload($className)
389      {
390          // use include so that the error PHP file may appear
391          if(isset(self::$_coreClasses[$className]))
392              include(YII_PATH.self::$_coreClasses[$className]);
393          else if(isset(self::$classMap[$className]))
394              include(self::$classMap[$className]);
395          else
396          {
397              if(strpos($className,'\\')===false)
398                  include($className.'.php');
399              else  // class name with namespace in PHP 5.3
400              {
401                  $namespace=str_replace('\\','.',ltrim($className,'\\'));
402                  if(($path=self::getPathOfAlias($namespace))!==false)
403                      include($path.'.php');
404                  else
405                      return false;
406              }
407              return class_exists($className,false) || interface_exists($className,false);
408          }
409          return true;
410      }
```

```
Stack Trace

#0   +   W:\home\ext\framework\YiiBase.php(398): YiiBase::autoload()

#1   unknown(0): YiiBase::autoload("Image_GD")

#2   -   W:\home\ext\www\protected\controllers\ImageController.php(9): spl_autoload_call("Image_GD")

         public function actionIndex()
```

3. This means that Yii cannot find Kohana classes. In order to help it, we will need a custom autoloader. So, create `protected/components/EKohanaAutoloader.php` as follows:

```php
<?php
class EKohanaAutoloader
{
  /**
   * @var list of paths to search for classes.
   * Add full paths to modules here.
   */
  static $paths = array();
```

```
/**
 * Class autoload loader.
 *
 * @static
 * @param string $className
 * @return boolean
 */
static function loadClass($className)
{
if(!defined("SYSPATH"))
  define("SYSPATH", Yii::getPathOfAlias
    ("application.vendors.Kohana.system"));

if(empty(self::$paths))
  self::$paths = array(Yii::getPathOfAlias
    ("application.vendors.Kohana.system"));

$path = 'classes/'.str_replace
    ('_', '/', strtolower($className)).'.php';

foreach (self::$paths as $dir)
{
  if (is_file($dir."/".$path))
    require $dir."/".$path;
}

return false;
}
}
```

4. In order to use it, we need to modify `index.php`. Replace

    ```
    Yii::createWebApplication($config)->run();
    ```
    with the following:

    ```
    $app = Yii::createWebApplication($config);

    // adding custom Kohana autoloader
    Yii::import("application.components.EKohanaAutoloader", true);
    EKohanaAutoloader::$paths = array(Yii::getPathOfAlias
      ("application.vendors.Kohana.modules.image"));
    Yii::registerAutoloader(array
      ('EKohanaAutoloader','loadClass'), true);

    $app->run();
    ```

5. Now run `image/index` again and you should see a screen similar to one shown in the following screenshot instead of an error:

That means Kohana classes were loaded successfully.

> Note that the Kohana class loader provided was not optimized in terms of performance and is not intended for intensive production use.

How it works...

Kohana 3 relies on autoloading and has a very special naming convention. As a result, calling its classes directly is too much work and creating an autoloader is the only reasonable way to implement it if we are not modifying Kohana classes.

We will take a look at the Kohana autoloader which is present at the following location:

`protected/vendors/Kohana/system/classes/kohana/core.php`

The method name is `auto_load`:

```
public static function auto_load($class)
{
  try
  {
    // Transform the class name into a path
    $file = str_replace('_', '/', strtolower($class));

    if ($path = Kohana::find_file('classes', $file))
    {
      // Load the class file
      require $path;
```

```
      // Class has been found
      return TRUE;
    }

    // Class is not in the filesystem
    return FALSE;
  }
  catch (Exception $e)
  {
    Kohana_Exception::handler($e);
    die;
  }
}
```

From this part, we can say that it uses a class to form a relative path which is then used to find a file inside of the `classes` directory:

```
$file = str_replace('_', '/', strtolower($class));
```

Now let's go deeper inside `find_file`:

```
public static function find_file
  ($dir, $file, $ext = NULL, $array = FALSE)
{
  if ($ext === NULL)
  {
    // Use the default extension
    $ext = EXT;
  }
  elseif ($ext)
  {
    // Prefix the extension with a period
    $ext = ".{$ext}";
  }
  else
  {
    // Use no extension
    $ext = '';
  }

  // Create a partial path of the filename
  $path = $dir.DIRECTORY_SEPARATOR.$file.$ext;

  if (Kohana::$caching === TRUE AND isset
    (Kohana::$_files[$path.($array ? '_array' : '_path')]))
  {
```

```
    // This path has been cached
    return Kohana::$_files[$path.($array ? '_array' : '_path')];
  }

  if (Kohana::$profiling === TRUE AND class_exists
    ('Profiler', FALSE))
  {
    // Start a new benchmark
    $benchmark = Profiler::start('Kohana', __FUNCTION__);
  }

  if ($array OR $dir === 'config' OR $dir === 'i18n'
    OR $dir === 'messages')
  {
    // Include paths must be searched in reverse
    $paths = array_reverse(Kohana::$_paths);

    // Array of files that have been found
    $found = array();

    foreach ($paths as $dir)
    {
      if (is_file($dir.$path))
      {
        // This path has a file, add it to the list
        $found[] = $dir.$path;
      }
    }
  }
  else
  {
    // The file has not been found yet
    $found = FALSE;

    foreach (Kohana::$_paths as $dir)
    {
      if (is_file($dir.$path))
      {
        // A path has been found
        $found = $dir.$path;

        // Stop searching
        break;
      }
```

```
        }
    }

    if (Kohana::$caching === TRUE)
    {
        // Add the path to the cache
        Kohana::$_files[$path.($array ? '_array' : '_path')] = $found;

        // Files have been changed
        Kohana::$_files_changed = TRUE;
    }

    if (isset($benchmark))
    {
        // Stop the benchmark
        Profiler::stop($benchmark);
    }

    return $found;
}
```

As we know that our file extension is always `.php`, the directory is always `classes`, and as we don't care about the caching or profiling right now, the useful part is as follows:

```
$path = $dir.DIRECTORY_SEPARATOR.$file.$ext;
foreach (Kohana::$_paths as $dir)
{
    if (is_file($dir.$path))
    {
        // A path has been found
        $found = $dir.$path;

        // Stop searching
        break;
    }
}
```

We are pretty close. The only thing left is `Kohana::$_paths`:

```
/**
 * @var   array   Include paths that are used to find files
 */
protected static $_paths = array(APPPATH, SYSPATH);
```

We don't care about the application, so we can omit the APPPATH part. Moreover, SYSPATH is a path to the system directory. As most of the Kohana classes are there, it is reasonable to make this a default.

When the autoloader class is ready, we use Yii::registerAutoloader in index.php to register it. It is important to register the autoloader after the default one built in Yii, so we pass true as the Yii::registerAutoloader second parameter value. Our image class is not in the core and is located in the image module, so we set paths to the image module path in the following way:

```
EKohanaAutoloader::$paths = array(Yii::getPathOfAlias
    ("application.vendors.Kohana.modules.image"));
```

There's more...

As image resizing is a common task, it is better from both reusability and performance perspectives to separate this task from the rest of the application and create a separate PHP script that will handle the image resizing. For example, it will allow using the following code:

```
<img src="/image.php?src=avatar.png&size=s" />
```

This means, take avatar.png as the source image and resize it to 100×100 pixels. Possible steps the image.php script will take are as follows:

▶ If an already processed image exists, serve it

▶ If there is no image yet, read the source image, resize it, and write it as the processed one

In order to achieve better performance, you can configure the web server to serve existing images directly, avoid serving with a PHP script, and redirecting the non-existing ones to the processing script.

Further reading

In order to learn more about Yii autoloading and Kohana, refer to the following URLs:

▶ http://www.yiiframework.com/doc/api/
    YiiBase/#registerAutoloader-detail

▶ http://kohanaframework.org/

See also

▶ The recipe named *Customizing the Yii autoloader* in this chapter

Using PEAR inside Yii

Another traditional place to look for PHP libraries is PEAR. There is a very special naming convention, so in order to use the PEAR code, we can either implement another autoloader or include files directly. In this recipe, we will use the PEAR `Text_Password` class to generate a random password.

Getting ready

▶ Create a fresh application by using `yiic webapp`

▶ Make sure that PEAR is installed and configured properly (`http://pear.php.net/manual/en/installation.php`)

How to do it...

The page of the PEAR package that we want to use is `http://pear.php.net/package/Text_Password`. Important things: there are "Easy Install" and documentation.

1. We will install the package first. Open the console and type what is suggested in "Easy Install section":

   ```
   pear install Text_Password
   ```

2. It should respond with the following:

   ```
   downloading Text_Password-1.1.1.tgz ...

   Starting to download Text_Password-1.1.1.tgz (4,357 bytes)
   .....      done: 4,357 bytes

   install ok: channel://pear.php.net/Text_Password-1.1.1
   ```

3. Now we can try using it. We will generate 10 random passwords, the length of which equals to 8. Create `protected/controllers/PasswordController.php` as follows:

   ```php
   class PasswordController extends CController
   {
     public function actionIndex()
     {
       require "Text/Password.php";
       $textPassword = new Text_Password();
       $passwords = $textPassword->createMultiple(10, 8);
       echo "<ul>";
       foreach($passwords as $password)
       {
   ```

```
        echo "<li>".$password."</li>";
      }
      echo "</ul>";
    }
  }
```

How it works...

Using PEAR packages in Yii is easy. You don't need to configure Yii or write any additional code to the one provided in the PEAR package's guide.

There's more...

In order to learn more about PEAR, refer to the following URLs:

- ▶ http://pear.php.net/manual/en/installation.php
- ▶ http://pear.php.net/package/Text_Password
- ▶ http://pear.php.net/

See also

- ▶ The recipe named *Using Zend Framework from Yii* in this chapter

13
Deployment

In this chapter, we will cover:

- ▶ Changing the Yii directories layout
- ▶ Moving an application out of webroot
- ▶ Sharing the framework directory
- ▶ Moving configuration parts into separate files
- ▶ Using multiple configurations to simplify the deployment
- ▶ Implementing and executing cron jobs
- ▶ Maintenance mode

Introduction

In this chapter, we will cover various tips which are especially useful on application deployment and when developing an application in a team, or when you just want to make your development environment more comfortable.

Changing the Yii directories layout

Yii has a pre-defined convention for directories layout. It allows us to significantly lower the learning curve but sometimes, the custom directory structure fits the project better.

In this recipe, we will rename a few directories and share common libraries around separate projects.

The plan is to:

- Rename `protected` to `app`
- Create a `shared` directory where we can store components shared across multiple applications
- Move `runtime` out of `app`

Getting ready

- Get a framework copy from the Yii website
- Set up the following directory structure:

```
/var/www/example/
    framework/
www/
```

- Unpack the `framework` directory contents to `/var/www/example/framework/`

How to do it...

Carry out the following steps:

1. Go to the `framework` directory.
2. Run `yiic webapp /var/www/example/www/`.
3. Go to `/var/www/example/www` and rename `protected` to `app`.
4. Replace all occurrences of `protected` with `app` in `index.php` and `index-test.php`.

    Now, we have a custom directory named `protected`.

5. Create `/var/www/shared`.
6. In your `main.php` config add:

```
// uncomment the following to define a path alias
Yii::setPathOfAlias('shared','/var/www/shared');
…
// This is the main Web application configuration. Any writable
// CWebApplication properties can be configured here.
return array(
    …

    // autoloading model and component classes
    'import'=>array(
        …
        'shared.*',
    ),
```

That is it. Now you can place your own components under `/var/www/shared` and the application will be aware of them. In addition, if you add the same settings to another application config, another application will be able to use these components as well.

1. Move `runtime` from the `/var/www/example/www/app` directory to `/var/www/example/runtime`.

2. Modify your `main.php` config as follows:

```
return array(
    ...
    'runtimePath' => Yii::getPathOfAlias('system').'/../runtime/',
```

3. That is it. Now the `runtime` directory is outside of the application directory.

How it works...

The application directory name and path are determined only at two places: `index.php` and `index-test.php`, so it is relatively easy to change these. We just need to update two bootstrap files after renaming the application directory.

When creating a shared directory, we define a custom path alias. It is a very convenient way of using additional directories if you are referring to them often:

```
Yii::setPathOfAlias('shared','/var/www/shared');
```

`setPathOfAlias` accepts two arguments. First is the name that we will use when setting options accepting paths, `Yii::getPathOfAlias` and `Yii::import`. Second is the actual path to the directory. As we want to use components transparently, we are adding `shared.*` to the list of application imports. This allows classes from the `/var/www/shared` directory to be loaded automatically.

The last path we change is a path to the `runtime` directory. For this case, Yii defines an application property named `runtimePath`. We can set it to change the path used as follows:

```
    'runtimePath' => Yii::getPathOfAlias('system').'/../runtime/',
```

As we want to place `runtime` in the same file structure level where the `framework` directory is, we get the `framework` directory path by using `getPathOfAlias` and then append the relative path to our `runtime` directory.

An application defines some other properties allowing you to change the extensions path, translations path, and modules path. Other paths such as views path or cache files path could be configured by changing another component's properties. For a view, it is `CController::viewPath` and for cache (in case of using file cache), it is `CFileCache::cachePath`.

There's more...

In order to learn more about Yii directory paths, refer to the following URLs:

- `http://www.yiiframework.com/doc/api/YiiBase#getPathOfAlias-detail`
- `http://www.yiiframework.com/doc/api/YiiBase#setPathOfAlias-detail`
- `http://www.yiiframework.com/doc/api/YiiBase#import-detail`
- `http://www.yiiframework.com/doc/api/CApplication#setExtensionPath-detail`
- `http://www.yiiframework.com/doc/api/CApplication#setRuntimePath-detail`
- `http://www.yiiframework.com/doc/api/CApplication#setLocaleDataPath-detail`
- `http://www.yiiframework.com/doc/api/CModule#setModulePath-detail`
- `http://www.yiiframework.com/doc/api/CController#viewPath-detail`

See also

- The recipe named *Moving an application out of webroot* in this chapter

Moving an application out of webroot

By default, when generating web application by using `yiic webapp` command, Yii puts both the `index.php` and `protected` directory in a single place that is typically the server's webroot. It allows running Yii in very restricted environments, but for security purposes and ease of development, it is better to keep your code out of webroot if it can be kept out of it.

In this recipe, we will see how to move a Yii application out of the server's webroot located at `/var/www/website/www/`.

Getting ready

- Copy the `framework` directory to `/var/www/website/`
- Go to `/var/www/website/framework/` and run `yiic webapp /var/www/website/www/`
- You should get the default web application files under `/var/www/website/www/`

How to do it...

Carry out the following steps:

1. First, we need to move `/var/www/website/www/protected/` to `/var/www/website/protected/`. As the path was changed, the application will fail to run now. Both `index.php` and `index-test.php` need some fixing. The `index.php` file has the following content:

```
// change the following paths if necessary
$yii=dirname(__FILE__).'/../framework/yii.php';
$config=dirname(__FILE__).'/protected/config/main.php';

// remove the following lines when in production mode
defined('YII_DEBUG') or define('YII_DEBUG',true);
// specify how many levels of call stack should be shown
   in each log message
defined('YII_TRACE_LEVEL') or define('YII_TRACE_LEVEL',3);

require_once($yii);
Yii::createWebApplication($config)->run();
```

2. There are two paths defined: path to the `framework` directory that was not changed and path to `config` that was changed. Let's update the latter as follows:

```
$config=dirname(__FILE__).'/../protected/config/main.php';
```

3. We need to do the same in `index-test.php`:

```
$config=dirname(__FILE__).'/../protected/config/test.php';
```

4. That is it. Now try to run the application and it should show a standard welcome screen, as shown in the following screenshot:

5. Now, we need to fix one more path in `protected/yiic.php`. We do this as follows:

```
// change the following paths if necessary
$yiic=dirname(__FILE__).'/../framework/yiic.php';
$config=dirname(__FILE__).'/config/console.php';

require_once($yiic);
```

How it works...

A Yii application can be moved to any place in a filesystem where we want it to be. The only thing you should correct is paths in `index.php` and `index-test.php`. This simple move gives you slightly better security as no application code will be executed directly, and there will be no leaks in the source code through version control meta files, and so on. Therefore, if your production environment allows moving the application code out of webroot, you certainly should consider doing it.

There's more...

The following article will give you an idea why it is better to have as little code as possible under webroot:

```
http://www.smashingmagazine.com/2009/09/25/svn-strikes-back-a-
serious-vulnerability-found/
```

See also

► The recipe named *Sharing the framework directory* in this chapter

Sharing the framework directory

If you run multiple Yii projects on a single web server, then you can consider sharing the framework code between the projects. This will save some disk space and will require less work when you upgrade your applications to a new framework version.

Getting ready

Copy the `framework` directory contents to `/var/www/common/yii/latest`.

How to do it...

Carry out the following steps:

1. Go to `/var/www/common/yii/latest` and run `yiic webapp /var/www/website1/www/`.

2. Go to `/var/www/common/yii/latest` and run `yiic webapp /var/www/website2/www/`.

3. You should get the default web application files under `/var/www/website1/www/` and `/var/www/website2/www/`.

4. That is it. Try to run applications to make sure that everything works.

How it works...

Using `yiic webapp` from the single framework copy will create applications referencing to this framework instance. We have two applications using the same framework copy, so when upgrading framework, we should only replace a single directory's contents.

If you have existing applications, then you can do the same by editing their `index.php` and `index-test.php` files, so `$yii` values will be as follows:

```
$yii='/var/www/common/yii/latest/yii.php';
```

There's more...

As the new Yii version can possibly introduce some backwards incompatible changes (typically, there are no such changes in minor releases), it is good to have a way to quickly roll everything back. For this purpose, you have to keep several framework versions under `/var/www/common/yii/` (for example: 1.1.8 and 1.1.7). When upgrading an application to 1.1.8, you are changing path to `yii.php` in `index.php` and `index-test.php` for a single application and testing for regressions. If there are any, you can either fix them or roll everything back by quickly changing a path back to 1.1.7. If everything is fine, then you can safely move on to test the next application.

See also

▶ The recipe named *Moving application out of webroot* in this chapter

Moving configuration parts into separate files

By default, a Yii application stores the entire web application configuration in a single file named `protected/config/main.php`. The same goes for the console application. It is good for both learning and small web applications where keeping everything inside of a single config file gives a developer the ability to quickly overview the whole application's settings. When we develop something bigger, we may face some inconvenience, such as the following:

► The configuration file becomes too bloated if there are many things to configure. Moreover, in a big application, there are typically many components used.

► If we need to adjust some settings, then we most probably end up repeating changes in both the web application config and console application config.

Getting ready

Create a fresh application by using `yiic webapp`.

How to do it...

Carry out the following steps:

1. We will review the default config first to identify parts we will reuse, as well as parts that will most probably be too large to have in a single file:

    ```php
    <?php

    // uncomment the following to define a path alias
    // Yii::setPathOfAlias('local','path/to/local-folder');

    // This is the main Web application configuration. Any writable
    // CWebApplication properties can be configured here.
    return array(
        'basePath'=>dirname(__FILE__).DIRECTORY_SEPARATOR.'..',
        'name'=>'My Web Application',

        // preloading 'log' component
        'preload'=>array('log'),

        // autoloading model and component classes
        'import'=>array(
            'application.models.*',
            'application.components.*',
        ),
    ```

```
'modules'=>array(
   // uncomment the following to enable the Gii tool
   /*
   'gii'=>array(
      'class'=>'system.gii.GiiModule',
      'password'=>'Enter Your Password Here',
       //If removed, Gii defaults to localhost only.
          Edit carefully to taste.
      'ipFilters'=>array('127.0.0.1','::1'),
   ),
   */
),

// application components
'components'=>array(
   'user'=>array(
      // enable cookie-based authentication
      'allowAutoLogin'=>true,
   ),
   // uncomment the following to enable URLs in path-format
   /*
   'urlManager'=>array(
      'urlFormat'=>'path',
      'rules'=>array(
         '<controller:\w+>/<id:\d+>'=>'<controller>/view',
         '<controller:\w+>/<action:\w+>/<id:\d+>'=>'
            <controller>/<action>',
         '<controller:\w+>/<action:\w+>'=>'
            <controller>/<action>',
      ),
   ),
   */
   'db'=>array(
      'connectionString' =>
        'sqlite:'.dirname(__FILE__).'/../data/testdrive.db',
   ),
   // uncomment the following to use a MySQL database
   /*
   'db'=>array(
      'connectionString' =>
        'mysql:host=localhost;dbname=testdrive',
      'emulatePrepare' => true,
      'username' => 'root',
      'password' => '',
      'charset' => 'utf8',
```

```
        ),
        */
        'errorHandler'=>array(
            // use 'site/error' action to display errors
                'errorAction'=>'site/error',
            ),
        'log'=>array(
            'class'=>'CLogRouter',
            'routes'=>array(
                array(
                    'class'=>'CFileLogRoute',
                    'levels'=>'error, warning',
                ),
                // uncomment the following to show log messages
                  on web pages
                /*
                array(
                    'class'=>'CWebLogRoute',
                ),
                */
            ),
        ),
    ),

    // application-level parameters that can be accessed
    // using Yii::app()->params['paramName']
    'params'=>array(
        // this is used in contact page
        'adminEmail'=>'webmaster@example.com',
    ),
);
```

The imports list and module configuration are typically not too large. The same goes for the most components configuration. What can grow with the application complexity are the `urlManager` component routes and application-level parameters. As for reusing, we will probably need the same imports, database connection, and application-level parameters for both the web application and console application.

1. Now, we will create the following config files under `protected/configs`:
    - ❑ `routes.php`
    - ❑ `params.php`
    - ❑ `import.php`
    - ❑ `db.php`

2. Now we need to move the corresponding sections of the `main.php` into separate files. We do this as follows:

```php
// uncomment the following to define a path alias
// Yii::setPathOfAlias('local','path/to/local-folder');

// This is the main Web application configuration. Any writable
// CWebApplication properties can be configured here.
return array(
    'basePath'=>dirname(__FILE__).DIRECTORY_SEPARATOR.'..',
    'name'=>'My Web Application',

    // preloading 'log' component
    'preload'=>array('log'),

    // autoloading model and component classes
    'import'=>require(dirname(__FILE__).'/import.php'),

    'modules'=>array(
        // uncomment the following to enable the Gii tool
        /*
        'gii'=>array(
            'class'=>'system.gii.GiiModule',
            'password'=>'Enter Your Password Here',
            // If removed, Gii defaults to localhost only.
               Edit carefully to taste.
            'ipFilters'=>array('127.0.0.1','::1'),
        ),
        */
    ),

    // application components
    'components'=>array(
        'user'=>array(
            // enable cookie-based authentication
            'allowAutoLogin'=>true,
        ),
        // uncomment the following to enable URLs in path-format
        'urlManager'=>array(
            'urlFormat'=>'path',
            'rules'=>require(dirname(__FILE__).'/routes.php'),
        ),
        'db'=>require(dirname(__FILE__).'/db.php'),
        'errorHandler'=>array(
```

```
            // use 'site/error' action to display errors
                'errorAction'=>'site/error',
           ),
        'log'=>array(
            'class'=>'CLogRouter',
            'routes'=>array(
                array(
                    'class'=>'CFileLogRoute',
                    'levels'=>'error, warning',
                ),
                // uncomment the following to show log messages
                  on web pages
                /*
                array(
                    'class'=>'CWebLogRoute',
                ),
                */
            ),
        ),
    ),

    // application-level parameters that can be accessed
    // using Yii::app()->params['paramName']
    'params'=>require(dirname(__FILE__).'/params.php'),
);
```

3. Each new config will contain the same values that were there in the main config. For example, `protected/configs/params.php` will contain the following:

```
<?php
return array(
    // this is used in contact page
    'adminEmail'=>'webmaster@example.com',
);
```

4. Now we need to change the console application `protected/configs/console.php`. We do this as follows:

```
// This is the configuration for yiic console application.
// Any writable CConsoleApplication properties can be
   configured here.
return array(
    'basePath'=>dirname(__FILE__).DIRECTORY_SEPARATOR.'..',
    'name'=>'My Console Application',
```

```
// autoloading model and component classes
'import'=>require(dirname(__FILE__).'/import.php'),

// application components
'components'=>array(
    'db'=>require(dirname(__FILE__).'/db.php'),
),

// application-level parameters that can be accessed
// using Yii::app()->params['paramName']
'params'=>require(dirname(__FILE__).'/params.php'),
);
```

5. That is it. Now we have separate configuration files for imports, database configuration, application routes, and application parameters.

How it works...

The preceding technique relies on the fact that Yii configuration files are native PHP files with arrays:

```
<?php
return array(…);
```

When we use the `require` construct:

```
'db'=>require(dirname(__FILE__).'/db.php')
```

It reads the file specified, and, if there is a `return` statement inside this file, it returns a value. Therefore, moving a part out of the main configuration file into a separate file requires creating a separate file, moving the configuration part into it right after the `return` statement, and using `require` in the main configuration file.

If separate applications (in our example, these are web applications and console applications) require some common configuration parts, then we can use `require` to move these into a separate file.

There's more...

In order to learn more about PHP **require** and **include** statements, refer to the following URLs:

▶ http://php.net/manual/en/function.require.php
▶ http://php.net/manual/en/function.include.php

See also

▶ The recipe named *Using multiple configurations to simplify the deployment* in this chapter

Using multiple configurations to simplify the deployment

In some cases, it is handy to use different configuration files for different cases. For example, we can use different configuration files for the development environment and production environment.

In this recipe, we will see how to choose a configuration file automatically and how to implement the configuration inheritance.

Getting ready

Create a fresh application by using `yiic webapp`.

How to do it...

Carry out the following steps:

1. We will assume that we are using `http://example.com/` as a production URL and `http://example.local/` as a development URL. Given this fact, we can choose the appropriate config from `index.php` as follows:

```
// change the following paths if necessary
$yii=dirname(__FILE__).'/../framework/yii.php';

if($_SERVER['HTTP_HOST']=='example.com')
{
  $config=dirname(__FILE__).'/../protected/config/production.php';
}
else
{
 // remove the following lines when in production mode
 defined('YII_DEBUG') or define('YII_DEBUG',true);
 // specify how many levels of call stack should be
   shown in each log message
 defined('YII_TRACE_LEVEL') or define('YII_TRACE_LEVEL',3);
```

```
  $config=dirname(__FILE__).'/../protected/config/development.php';
}

require_once($yii);
Yii::createWebApplication($config)->run();
```

2. The plan ahead is to leave all common configurations in main.php and override the environment-specific settings in development.php and production. php. Therefore, main.php stays the same. We put the following in protected/ configs/development.php as follows:

```php
<?php
return CMap::mergeArray(
  require(dirname(__FILE__).'/main.php'),
  array(
    'modules'=>array(
      'gii'=>array(
        'class'=>'system.gii.GiiModule',
        'password'=>false,
      ),
    ),
    'components'=>array(
      'db'=>array(
        'class'=>'system.db.CDbConnection',
        'connectionString'=>'mysql:host=localhost;
          dbname=example',
        'username'=>'root',
        'password'=>'',

        'charset'=>'utf8',
        'enableProfiling'=>true,
        'enableParamLogging'=>true,
      ),
      'log'=>array(
        'class'=>'CLogRouter',
        'routes'=>array(
          array(
            'class'=>'CProfileLogRoute',
          ),
        ),
      ),
    ),
  )
);
```

3. In addition, put the following in `protected/configs/production.php` as follows:

```php
<?php
return CMap::mergeArray(
  require(dirname(__FILE__).'/main.php'),
  array(
    'components'=>array(
      'db'=>array(
        'class'=>'system.db.CDbConnection',

        'connectionString'=>'mysql:host=localhost;dbname=example',
        'username'=>'example',
        'password'=>'2WXyVNb4dBSEK3HW',

        'charset'=>'utf8',

        'schemaCachingDuration'=>60*60,
      ),
      'cache'=>array(
        'class'=>'CFileCache',
      ),
    ),
  )
);
```

4. That is it. Now we can just upload files to the production server that runs `http://example.com/` and the application will use the `production.php` config that inherits all settings from `main.php`, overrides some of them, and adds some more settings.

How it works...

When we create a web application instance inside of `index.php`, it is possible to pass a single argument to `Yii::createWebApplication`. This argument is a path to the application configuration file. Given this fact, we can vary the path to this file based on some kind of criteria. In our case, it is the name of the host where the application is running:

```php
if($_SERVER['HTTP_HOST']=='example.com')
{
    $config=dirname(__FILE__).'/../protected/config/production.php';
}
else if($_SERVER['HTTP_HOST']=='example.local')
{
```

```
    // remove the following lines when in production mode
    defined('YII_DEBUG') or define('YII_DEBUG',true);
    // specify how many levels of call stack should be shown
      in each log message
    defined('YII_TRACE_LEVEL') or define('YII_TRACE_LEVEL',3);
    $config=dirname(__FILE__).'/../protected/config/development.php';
}
```

If host equals `example.com`, then we use the production config. Else, we use the development config and additionally, turn on the debugging.

 You can use virtually anything to choose the config file. For example, you can run the application in a debug mode at the production server if there is a cookie with a specific name and value.

As most of the development and production settings, such as application parameters and routes, will stay the same, we leave these in `main.php`. Moreover, as Yii configuration files are PHP arrays, we can use `CMap::mergeArray` to implement the configuration inheritance as follows:

```
return CMap::mergeArray(
    require(dirname(__FILE__).'/main.php'),
    array(…)
);
```

There's more...

In order to learn more about how exactly config files are merged, refer to the following URL:

`http://www.yiiframework.com/doc/api/CMap#mergeArray`

See also

▶ The recipe named *Moving configuration parts into separate files* in this chapter

Implementing and executing cron jobs

Sometimes, an application requires some background tasks such as re-generating a sitemap or refreshing statistics. A common way to implement this is by using cron jobs. When using Yii, there are two ways to do it which are as follows:

1. Emulate the browser to call the web application controller action.
2. Use the command line command to run as a job.

In this recipe, we will see how to implement both. For our recipe, we will implement writing the current timestamp into a `timestamp.txt` file under the `protected` directory.

Getting ready

Create a fresh application by using `yiic webapp`.

How to do it...

Carry out the following steps:

1. Create `protected/controllers/CronController.php` as follows:

```php
<?php
class CronController extends CController
{
  public function actionIndex()
  {
    $filename = Yii::getPathOfAlias
      ("application")."/timestamp.txt";
    file_put_contents($filename, time());
  }
}
```

2. Now we need a way to call it. As it is a web application controller, we need to somehow emulate a browser. In Linux, you can use one of the following commands in your crontab:

```
GET http://example.com/index.php?r=cron
wget -O - http://example.com/index.php?r=cron
lynx --dump http://example.com/index.php?r=cron >/dev/null
```

When we use a controller in this way, we need to make sure that it is used only as a cron job. For example, we can check for a value of a specific $_GET variable.

3. Create `protected/commands/CronCommand.php` as follows:

```php
<?php
class CronCommand extends CConsoleCommand
{
  public function run($args)
  {
    $filename = Yii::getPathOfAlias
      ("application")."/timestamp.txt";
```

```
        file_put_contents($filename, time());
    }
}
```

4. We can use the following in the crontab to execute it:

    ```
    /path/to/./yiic cron
    ```

Note that the full path is required to be specified in cron.

How it works...

GET, wget, and lynx fetch a page through HTTP, so we can use these to trigger the normal web application execution. This method has its pros and cons. The main pro is that we are executing a web application, so the environment is the same as in all other application parts. The main con is that it is not completely secure. Even if we use $_GET variable as a password, there is no guarantee that it will remain undisclosed forever.

The second method is much more secure because the console command can be executed only if one has an SSH access to the server. The con is that the environment is different from the web application.

There's more...

Another way to solve a problem is to use a message queue. Most implementations will deal with concurrency issues for you and will allow you to do the processing almost immediately if there are not too many requests. Implementations to check are:

- ▶   http://www.rabbitmq.com/
- ▶   http://kr.github.com/beanstalkd/
- ▶   http://activemq.apache.org/
- ▶   http://gearman.org/
- ▶   https://github.com/s0enke/dropr/
- ▶   http://www.zeromq.org/

Further reading

In order to learn more about Yii console applications, refer to the following URL:

```
http://www.yiiframework.com/doc/guide/en/topics.console
```

See also

- ▶   The recipe named *Creating CLI commands* in *Chapter 8, Extending Yii*

Maintenance mode

Sometimes, there is a need to fine tune some application settings or restore a database from a backup. When working on tasks such as these, it is not desirable to allow everyone to use the application because it can lead to losing the recent user messages or showing the application implementation details.

In this recipe, we will see how to show everyone except the developer a maintenance message.

Getting ready

Create a fresh application by using `yiic webapp`.

How to do it...

Carry out the following steps:

1. First, we need to create `protected/controllers/MaintenanceController. php`. We do this as follows:

    ```php
    <?php
    class MaintenanceController extends CController
    {
        public function actionIndex()
        {
            $this->renderPartial("index");
        }
    }
    ```

2. Then, we create a view named `protected/views/maintenance/index.php` as follows:

    ```html
    <!doctype html>
    <head>
        <meta charset="utf-8" />
        <title><?php echo CHtml::encode(Yii::app()->name)?>
            is under maintenance</title>
    </head>
    <body>
        <h1><?php echo CHtml::encode(Yii::app()->name)?>
            is under maintenance</h1>
        <p>We'll be back soon. If we aren't back for too long,
            please drop a message to <?php echo Yii::app()->params
            ['adminEmail']?>.</p>
    ```

```
        <p>Meanwhile, it's a good time to get a cup of coffee,
           to read a book or to check email.</p>
    </body>
```

3. Now we need to add a single line of code to `protected/config/main.php`
    as follows:

```
return array(
    'catchAllRequest'=>file_exists(dirname(__FILE__).'/.
      maintenance')
    && !(isset($_COOKIE['secret']) &&
    $_COOKIE['secret']=="password") ?
    array('maintenance/index') : null,
    ...
```

4. That is it. Now in order to go into the maintenance mode, you need to create a file
    named `.maintenance` in `protected/config/`.

My Web Application is under maintenance

We'll be back soon. If we aren't back for too long, please drop a message to webmaster@example.com.

Meanwhile, it's a good time to get a cup of coffee, to read a book or to check email.

In order to get it back to normal, you just need to delete it. To view the website in the
maintenance mode, you can create a cookie named `secret` with value equal to password.

How it works...

A Yii web application offers a way to intercept all possible requests and route these to a single
controller action. You can do this by setting `CWebApplication::catchAllRequests` to an
array containing application route as follows:

```
'catchAllRequest'=>array('maintenance/index'),
```

The maintenance controller itself is nothing special; it just renders a view with a text.

We need an easy way to turn the maintenance mode on and off. As the application config is a
regular PHP file, we can achieve it with a simple check for the file existence as follows:

```
file_exists(dirname(__FILE__).'/.maintenance')
```

In addition, we check for the cookie value to be able to override the maintenance mode. We
do this as follows:

```
!(isset($_COOKIE['secret']) && $_COOKIE['secret']=="password")
```

There's more...

In order to learn more about how to catch all requests in a Yii application and check the production ready solution for maintenance, refer to the following URLs:

- ▶ `http://www.yiiframework.com/doc/api/`
  `CWebApplication/#catchAllRequest-detail`
- ▶ `https://github.com/karagodin/MaintenanceMode`

See also

- ▶ The recipe named *Moving configuration parts into separate files* in this chapter
- ▶ The recipe named *Using multiple configurations to simplify the deployment* in this chapter

Index

Thank you for buying
Yii 1.1 Application Development Cookbook

About Packt Publishing

Packt, pronounced 'packed', published its first book "*Mastering phpMyAdmin for Effective MySQL Management*" in April 2004 and subsequently continued to specialize in publishing highly focused books on specific technologies and solutions.

Our books and publications share the experiences of your fellow IT professionals in adapting and customizing today's systems, applications, and frameworks. Our solution based books give you the knowledge and power to customize the software and technologies you're using to get the job done. Packt books are more specific and less general than the IT books you have seen in the past. Our unique business model allows us to bring you more focused information, giving you more of what you need to know, and less of what you don't.

Packt is a modern, yet unique publishing company, which focuses on producing quality, cutting-edge books for communities of developers, administrators, and newbies alike. For more information, please visit our website: www.packtpub.com.

About Packt Open Source

In 2010, Packt launched two new brands, Packt Open Source and Packt Enterprise, in order to continue its focus on specialization. This book is part of the Packt Open Source brand, home to books published on software built around Open Source licences, and offering information to anybody from advanced developers to budding web designers. The Open Source brand also runs Packt's Open Source Royalty Scheme, by which Packt gives a royalty to each Open Source project about whose software a book is sold.

Writing for Packt

We welcome all inquiries from people who are interested in authoring. Book proposals should be sent to author@packtpub.com. If your book idea is still at an early stage and you would like to discuss it first before writing a formal book proposal, contact us; one of our commissioning editors will get in touch with you.

We're not just looking for published authors; if you have strong technical skills but no writing experience, our experienced editors can help you develop a writing career, or simply get some additional reward for your expertise.

Agile Web Application Development with Yii1.1 and PHP5

ISBN: 978-1-847199-58-4   Paperback: 368 pages

Fast-track your Web application development by harnessing the power of the Yii PHP framework

1. A step-by-step guide to creating a modern, sophisticated web application using an incremental and iterative approach to software development

2. Build a real-world, user-based, database-driven project task management application using the Yii development framework

3. Take a test-driven design (TDD) approach to software development utilizing the Yii testing framework

CMS Design Using PHP and jQuery

ISBN: 978-1-84951-252-7   Paperback: 340 pages

Build and improve your in-house PHP CMS by enhancing it with jQuery

1. Create a completely functional and a professional looking CMS

2. Add a modular architecture to your CMS and create template-driven web designs

3. Use jQuery plugins to enhance the "feel" of your CMS

Please check **www.PacktPub.com** for information on our titles

www.ingramcontent.com/pod-product-compliance
Lightning Source LLC
Chambersburg PA
CBHW080148060326
40689CB00018B/3889